The Theory of Monopoly Capitalism

The Theory of Monopoly Capitalism

An Elaboration of Marxian Political Economy

John Bellamy Foster

Monthly Review Press
New York

Library of Congress Cataloging in Publication Data

Foster, John Bellamy.
The theory of monopoly capitalism.

Includes index.
1. Capitalism. 2. Marxian economics. I. Title.
HB501.F66 1986 330.12′2 85-32097
ISBN 0-85345-688-7
ISBN 0-85345-689-5 (pbk.)

Monthly Review Press
155 West 23rd Street
New York, N.Y. 10011

Manufactured in the United States of America

10 9 8 7 6 5 4 3 2 1

For Kara

Contents

Preface

This book is a revised and expanded version of my doctoral dissertation, defended at York University in Toronto in October 1984. Although its main concern is with the work of Paul Baran and Paul Sweezy, this is mainly a vehicle for examining an entire tradition of thought, loosely associated with the magazine *Monthly Review,* to which numerous theorists—some of no less importance—have contributed. In this respect, Baran and Sweezy belong to what might be referred to—after Gramsci, though not precisely in his way—as a "collective intellectual."

I would like to thank Gabriel Kolko, Paul Sweezy, Harry Magdoff, Henryk Flakierski, Robert Albritton, Leo Panitch, and Susan Lowes for help related to the writing of this study. I have also benefited from correspondence on issues discussed here with Henryk Szlajfer, Jacob Morris, Howard Sherman, Lynn Turgeon, Victor Lippit, and Michael Lebowitz. Bob McChesney and Len McComb provided the initial inspiration for this line of research. Cathy Gage, Griff Cunningham, David Lumsden, Brigitte Maheux, and Laura Tamkin helped provide the necessary motivation. Lastly, I would like to indicate my debt over the years to Kara Baxter, for her forbearance and much else besides.

Eugene, Oregon
January 1986

Preface

1

Introduction

The Economic Crisis Controversy

With the turn for the worse in the U.S. and world economy in the early 1970s, a majority of mainstream economists turned their backs on reality and the Keynesian "revolution" and reverted to the supply-side perspective that had always been the preferred liberal response to crisis. Thus when Paul Samuelson told his readers in 1983 that Keynes's "prescription in its most simple form self-destructed, as the obligation to run a full-employment humanitarian state caused modern economies to succumb to the new disease of stagflation—high inflation along with joblessness and excess capacity," he was simply giving further evidence of the general "about-face" of received economics, which had endeavored to blame the new period of severe economic distress on the overindulgent attitude toward the poor and unemployed that had supposedly characterized the earlier, Keynesian era.[1] The only way out of the present crisis, according to this viewpoint, was through a direct assault on employment and wages, the granting of additional tax concessions to corporations and the wealthy, and massive cutbacks in state welfare spending.

That mainstream economists should "reverse themselves" in this way, in response to the return of stagnation, was of course to be expected. More surprising was the fact that many economists on the left turned around at about the same time and began to argue that the chief constraints of the system were to be found on the supply side, with high costs at the point of production squeezing profitability.

Among radicals, this shift in perspective frequently took the form of criticism of *Monopoly Capital: An Essay on the American Economic and Social Order* (1966) by Paul Baran and Paul Sweezy, which in the years immediately following its publication had received widespread recognition as the leading attempt to bring

Marx's *Capital* up to date, describing those laws of motion that constituted the *differentia specifica* of advanced accumulation.[2] In Baran and Sweezy's conception, the concentration on lowering costs and maximizing profits, under the reign of giant corporations with significant monopoly power, had contributed to the "widening gap, at any given level of production, between output and socially necessary costs of production. This gap we call surplus."[3] The main problem of accumulation under monopoly capitalism was therefore to find ways in which this increasing surplus could be absorbed. Capitalist consumption—which constituted one possible outlet for the surplus—tended to account for a decreasing share of capitalist demand as income grew, while investment itself was held down by the fact that it took the form of new productive capacity, which could not be expanded for long periods of time independently of final, wage-based demand. Thus the system became increasingly dependent on the promotion of economic waste, both through the private channel of the "sales effort" and the public channel of military spending (which accounted for the greater bulk of federal expenditures on goods and services). Even then, the surplus was not entirely absorbed, with the unrealized or unabsorbed portion leaving its "statistical trace" in actual unemployment and excess capacity. Hence what could be called the "relative overexploitation" of labor power under monopoly capitalism manifested itself in a realization crisis, or—in Keynesian terms—a shortage of effective demand.

Monopoly Capital had pointed to a strong tendency toward secular stagnation under advanced capitalism, reflected in a widening underemployment gap. But with the reemergence of stagnation only three or four years later this type of analysis increasingly lost ground to two forms of radical supply-side theory: (1) the classical Marxian "law of the tendency of the rate of profit to fall," and (2) the underexploitation theory of the "neo-Ricardian" profit-squeeze school. For those who turned to the former—which gained numerous adherents following the publication of Paul Mattick's *Marx and Keynes* (1969) and David Yaffe's "The Marxian Theory of Crisis, Capital, and the State" (1973)—the issue had less to do with changing historical conditions or transformations in liberal ideology than with what were viewed as the categorical imperatives of Marxian political economy.[4] Since Marx himself had devoted three whole chapters of *Capital* to this "tendential law"—according to which any increases in the rate of exploitation of labor power, as accumulation proceeds, will be overshadowed by a rising organic composition of capital (capital-labor ratio), thereby decreasing labor's production of new value (and hence profits) per unit of constant (material) capital—and had advanced demand-side or "underconsumptionist" notions of crisis, like those of Baran and Sweezy, only in a scattered way, the falling rate of profit theory was seen by many to be the most definitively "Marxist" approach to the question of crisis. Moreover, while Baran and Sweezy had referred to the "tendency of the surplus to rise" as a new law of monopoly capitalism, replacing the classical law of the tendency of the rate of profit to fall, the growing turbulence surrounding profits in the 1970s gave the impression—to those with only a superficial understanding of their theory—that they had spoken too soon.[5] Finally, the more traditionalist Marxists were inclined to view the substitution of the surplus category for the concept of surplus value in *Monopoly Capital,* along with the emphasis on monopoly and the location of economic contradictions within the exchange process (i.e., on the demand side), as indications of fundamental departures from Marxism. Similar reservations were to be raised with respect to the dependency theory of imperialism, which Baran had helped to introduce into the Marxian discussion on the basis of the same analytical framework.

Nevertheless, as the debate lingered on it became increasingly apparent that there was absolutely no empirical evidence whatsoever to indicate that a rising organic composition of capital (capital-labor ratio) was a major factor contributing to crisis tendencies in the twentieth century. Theorists continuing to stress the direct importance of the law of the falling tendency of the rate of profit therefore either contended that it was simply a "tendential law" that never had to materialize, or resorted to ever more eclectic formulations in which the falling rate of profit theory played a secondary, and highly ambiguous, role.[6] Hence, discussions of crisis within this tradition seldom if ever got beyond the mere repetition of Marx's original ideas of a century before.

The falling rate of profit theory had argued that the shift in the organic composition of capital away from variable capital (or wage labor) and toward constant (or material) capital was endangering profits at the point of production, thereby causing a capital shortage. The logic of the crisis, from the standpoint of the system, therefore demanded a supply-side strategy that would intensify the exploitation of labor and redistribute income from the poor to the rich. But since (1) the rising capital intensiveness of production (in value terms) was presumed to be an inherant feature of technological progress under capitalism; (2) the rate of exploitation was constantly rising as well (although at a slower pace); and (3) a revolutionary response could sooner or later be expected from the working class, such a strategy was bound to fail in the medium and long run in the eyes of most fundamentalist Marxists.[7] In contrast, the profit-squeeze interpretation of contemporary economic distress that emerged within the "neo-Ricardian" left in the 1970s and 1980s—in such works as *Capitalism in Crisis* (1972) by Andrew Glyn and Bob Sutcliffe, and *Beyond the Wasteland* (1983) by Samuel Bowles, David Gordon, and Thomas Weisskopf—saw the problem as one of a rising wage share in national income and a decline in the rate of growth of labor productivity.[8] Since the cause of the crisis, in this case, was presumed to be a relative underexploitation of labor power, resulting from the growing strength of labor during the long post-World War II boom, the type of policy solutions adopted by President Reagan in the United States and Prime Minister Thatcher in Great Britain were thought to improve the underlying conditions of accumulation—though such policies were to be resisted on the left, and countered by either revolutionary strategy (Glyn and Sutcliffe), or radical industrial policy initiatives, including the reorganization of class relations within the labor process (Bowles, Gordon, and Weisskopf).[9]

Within the United States, profit-squeeze theorists argued against the "stagnation theory" of neo-Marxian, underconsumptionist thinkers like Michael Kalecki, Josef Steindl, Paul Baran and Paul Sweezy by pointing to what appeared to be an increasing share of wages in national income during the Vietnam war period (1965–73).[10] However, for theorists within the neo-Marxian tradition (as well as for many of those in the fundamentalist, falling rate of profit school) this simply confused the wage and profit shares in national income accounts with the rate of exploitation at the level of production. Thus for Baran and Sweezy the rate of exploitation could be rising rapidly within production *even if* the wage share was increasing in national income accounts, as long as the potential surplus had its statistical trace in various forms of waste production, as well as unemployment and excess capacity. As Baran said in his reply to the same argument when utilized by Nicholas Kaldor to attack Marxian theory in the 1950s, "Treating productive and unproductive labor indiscriminately as *labor* and equating profits with surplus obviously obscure this very simple proposition."[11] By 1985 profit-squeeze theorists such as Bowles, Gordon, and Weisskopf were forced to admit that the main economic constraints of the system had, in the United States at any rate, "shifted back" to the demand side (a fact that they attributed to the effectiveness of the Reagonomic strategy), and therefore had to supplement their original analysis with the heroic observation that "There can be little doubt that the familiar supply-side contradictions of the 1970s will reemerge in the 1980s, unless the Reagan administration chooses instead to put the economy through the wringer once again."[12]

As can be seen from the foregoing discussion, the profit-squeeze argument was related to the modern, neo-Ricardian rejection of the labor theory of value, and thus of any theory of the rate of exploitation along strict Marxian lines. Hence Bowles and Gintis were to declare that, "The labor theory of value, once the centerpiece of Marxist thought, has become its embarrassment"—in a 1985 essay *abandoning* the proposition that "Labor values, or more technically, the socially necessary abstract labor time embodied in commodities, is the foundation of the Marxian theory of exploitation and accumulation."[13] Baran and Sweezy's "law of the tendency of the surplus to rise," in sharp contrast, had been based on a radical extension of the surplus value category, emphasizing such elements as (1) the "upkeep of the state apparatus," (2) the "incomes of unproductive workers," and (3) the "expenses of circulation" (those expenses that, in Marx's words, "arise only from changes of form" and thus "do not add any value to the commodities" themselves)—elements that Marx had considered secondary under freely competitive capitalism but that had come to play an important part in what Sweezy called the "protective reaction of the system" under monopoly capitalism.[14]

The present study is concerned with demonstrating that the basic analytical approach adopted in *Monopoly Capital*—which was also utilized by Baran to investigate imperialism and by Sweezy to investigate actually existing socialism—was rooted in a deep appreciation of Marxian methodology, one that leads to conclusions that are radically opposed not only to modern supply-side theories of capitalist crisis in the advanced states but also to "vicious circle of poverty" explanations of underdevelopment in the periphery and to economistic explanations of the "laws" governing postrevolutionary social formations. Since the purpose of what follows is to elaborate upon a particular *Marxian* methodology, the main focus is on various methodological criticisms raised by the more traditionalist Marxists—although the relation to neo-Ricardian and neoclassical perspectives is always implicit and occasionally explicit. The areas of contention can thus be grouped into six categories: (1) the value status of the surplus concept; (2) the issue of competition and monopoly; (3) the theory of accumulation and crisis; (4) the theory of the state; (5) the problem of imperialism; and (6) the meaning of actually existing socialism.

Economic Surplus and Surplus Value

What is at issue with respect to the economic surplus concept employed by Baran and Sweezy is best elucidated by referring to one of the most frequently quoted passages in *Monopoly Capital.* Pointing out that "in a highly developed monopoly capitalist society, the surplus [or "the difference between total social output and the socially necessary costs of producing it"] assumes many forms and disguises," they added in a footnote that:

> It is for this reason that we prefer the concept of "surplus" to the traditional Marxian "surplus value," since the latter is probably identified in the minds of most people familiar with Marxian economic theory as equal to the sum of profits + interest + rent. It is true that Marx demonstrates—in scattered passages of *Capital* and *Theories of Surplus Value*—that surplus value also comprises other items such as the revenues of state and church, the expenses of transforming commodities into money, and the wages of unproductive workers. In general, however, he treated these as secondary factors and excluded them from his basic theoretical schema. It is our contention that under monopoly capitalism this procedure is no longer justified, and we hope that a change in terminology will help to effect the needed shift in theoretical position.[15]

This passage makes it clear that for Baran and Sweezy the use of the surplus concept, rather than surplus value as such, had to do with the necessity of dealing with the various forms of economic waste—namely, realization costs and unproductive labor—that are central to the entire accumulation process under monopoly capitalism. Yet they also imply that an inquiry of this sort could be conducted in terms of surplus value itself, although presumably with greater difficulty. Thus the reasoning behind their preference for the surplus value concept over Marx's key category remains obscure and difficult to grasp when viewed solely from the vantage point of their own explanation.

However, the whole question is radically transformed once one realizes that Baran and Sweezy's use of the surplus concept is tied to theoretical considerations which suggest that much more than a mere "change in terminology" is actually at stake. This can be understood through the critical assessment of a comment by the fundamentalist Marxist economist Mario Cogoy. Writing of the passage from *Monopoly Capital* quoted above, Cogoy states:

> In complete contrast to this, all those who are familiar with Marxian economic theory know that for Marx ". . . the best points in my book are . . . the treatment of *surplus value independently of its particular forms* as profit, interest, ground rent, etc. . . . The treatment of the particular forms by classical political economy, which always mixes them up with the general form, is a regular hash." *Monopoly Capital* was therefore, likewise, a "regular hash" and it remains difficult to understand the reasons for the "needed shift" in theoretical position.[16]

The present study will argue that the reasons for this "needed shift in theoretical position" had to do with the very methodological point that Cogoy has raised. In a monopoly capitalist economy, according to Baran and Sweezy's framework, produced *and realized* surplus value increasingly becomes a *particular form* of the social accumulation fund potentially available for expanded reproduction. This is not only due to the problem of a chronic effective demand gap, but also relates to the fact that specifically capitalist use values, of a socially irrational character, are integrated into the structure of production as "essential costs." Thus the economic surplus category becomes a means of extending the analysis of the social accumulation fund so as to encompass its most *general form.* This outlook, basic to Baran and Sweezy's entire theory (though not adequately or consistently explained therein) has been refined in the recent work of the Polish economist Henryk Szlajfer (to be examined in Chapters 2 and 4), which, along with important insights on the role of unproductive labor in both Marx and Baran and Sweezy that can be found in the work of Ian Gough, provides the essential basis for a reinterpretation of *Monopoly Capital* as a whole.[17] At this point, suffice it to say that Szlajfer's argument demonstrates "that the concept of economic surplus, as introduced by Paul Baran and Paul Sweezy, forms an absolutely necessary complement to 'the traditional calculus of surplus value' under conditions of monopoly capitalism."[18] In this context, Sweezy's insistence—in response to one of the most persistent criticisms of *Monopoly Capitalism,* evoked by such theorists as Cogoy, Paul Mattick, Ernest Mandel, Ph. Herzog, and David Yaffe—that he and Baran never even considered the possibility of rejecting the labor theory of value takes on added meaning.[19]

Competition and Monopoly

For Baran and Sweezy, the rise of the giant firm is responsible for important changes in the *modus operandi* of the system in the twentieth century, requiring modifications in the theory of accumulation if it is to stay abreast of historical reality. This interpretation has been challenged ever more frequently of late by radical political economists on both theoretical and empirical grounds. The theoretical argument—developed by James A. Clifton, Willi Semmler, John Weeks, James Becker, Paul Mattick, and others—contends that Baran and Sweezy took their conception of monopoly from the "imperfect competition" theory of neoclassical economics, in opposition to the classical and Marxian theory of competition. Semmler has called into question not only the analysis of competition in the theory of monopoly capitalism, but also the empirical basis of monopoly profits.[20] And Weeks has gone so far as to state that:

> The monopolies that stalk the pages of the writings of Baran and Sweezy have no existence beyond the work of these authors. For these monopolies, which at will set prices, control and suppress innovation, and the like, are idealistic resurrections of "feudal monopolies before competition."[21]

These strictures, related to century-old issues within the Marxian paradigm, have been contested, in one way or another, in recent works by Sweezy, the present author, Michael Lebowitz, and Howard Sherman. These, along with brief considerations of Marx's own position (and that of Engels), the relevant views of Rudolf Hilferding and Lenin, the early contributions of Sweezy, and a recent examination of the empirical literature by Joseph Bowring, will form the basis for the interpretation of competition and monopoly capital provided in Chapter 3. This will lead to a reaffirmation of the conclusion, long taken for granted within Marxian thought, that the modern corporate monopolies with their surplus profits, far from being "idealistic resurrections of feudal monopolies" or the abstract by-product of the "methodology of bourgeois economic theory,"[22] are instead the main manifestations of the process of concentration and centralization of capital that Marx was the first to describe. This line of thought will be accompanied by the theoretical observation, arising out of Braverman's analysis in *Labor and Monopoly Capital* (and Sweezy's incorporation of it within the larger analysis of competition and monopoly), that the changes in the system's laws of motion during the monopoly stage are of a secondary order, relating mainly to the *utilization* of potential surplus product.[23]

Overaccumulation and Modes of Surplus Absorption

In Baran and Sweezy's theory (like that of Kalecki and Steindl), the growing intensity of monopoly in the economy as a whole is reflected in the widening profit margins of the giant firms. They therefore argue that the "classical Marxian law of the falling rate of profit" must give way, in a highly developed monopoly capitalist system, to the "law of the rising surplus" and the problem of surplus absorption. The majority of methodological objections to this theorem on the left—put forward by critics like Michael Bleaney, Anwar Shaikh, David Yaffe, Ben Fine, Laurence Harris, and Anthony Brewer—have focused on the underconsumptionist elements in Baran and Sweezy's thought.[24] Hence fundamentalist Marxists commonly stress the scattered attacks on "crude underconsumptionism" to be found in the work of Marx, Engels, and Lenin as an authoritative basis for rejecting any approach along these lines whatsoever. This criticism loses much of its persuasive power, however, once one becomes cognizant of the fact that theoretical strictures of an identical kind can be found in the work of Rosa Luxemburg, Sweezy, Baran, and Harry Magdoff.[25] Chapter 4 will therefore suggest that the applicability of this type of criticism, even in relation to Sweezy's early study, *The Theory of Capitalist Development,* is highly dubious. Still, it will be emphasized that Sweezy's original underconsumptionist approach, although not wrong in the sense of presenting a "crude underconsumptionist" perspective, was much weaker than it could have been since it constituted little more than a logical proof of a basic contradiction in the accumulation process. Attention will be given to the important critiques of Sweezy's early theory developed by Evsey Domar and Josef Steindl.[26]

The core of Chapter 4 will then be devoted to demonstrating how a more sophisticated theory of advanced accumulation emerged out of the fusion of the underconsumptionist strand in crisis theory with the analysis of monopoly capitalism. Thus Baran and Sweezy's joint sketch of contemporary economic reproduction will be viewed in three stages: (1) the basic conception of realization crisis and monopolistic accumulation arising out of classical Marxism and the contributions of Kalecki and Steindl; (2) the incorporation of the "secondary determinants" of accumulation, associated with the category of unproductive labor, within the central framework of economic analysis (taking into consideration Szlajfer's refinement of Baran and Sweezy's model); and (3) the complex interconnection between the tendency toward overaccumulation under monopoly capitalism and the larger historical dilemma of capitalist maturity. The pivotal point in the modern, neo-Marxian theory of crisis, it will be stressed, is the notion that investment itself, under monopoly capitalism, becomes a function of the large-scale enterprise's careful regulation of present and prospective output.[27]

In line with this interpretation, I will argue that the theory of accumulation under monopoly capitalism revolves around the issue of surplus productive capacity. This is so for two reasons. First, excess capacity is one of the chief indicators of the realization (or effective demand) gap, and thus of the shortfall of actual surplus (or final, realized, aggregate profits) from potential economic surplus. Second, the degree of capacity utilization is perhaps the most important factor determining investment in the short run.[28] Hence Chapter 5 will review some of the data in this area, and the methodologies upon which they rest, based partly on a study by Ron Stanfield.[29] The main purpose will be to clarify certain broad theoretical and historical questions. No attempt will be made to "prove" the empirical validity of the theory, but merely to suggest that it is based on a relatively plausible interpretation of the facts, and thus to reinforce the analytical framework at hand at a more concrete historical level.

"The Crisis of the Tax State"

Baran and Sweezy argued that, given the existence of vast amounts of idle productive capacity, it was possible for state spending to play a major role as a bulwark to the imperiled economic system. Hence under modern capitalist conditions there was no reason to suppose—in line with classical and neoclassical theories of public finance prior to the Keynesian revolution—"that anything government might take from total output of society would necessarily be at the expense of some or all of its members," with the main burden falling on the "surplus-receiving classes."[30] Instead, increases in state spending could be expected to narrow the gap in demand left by insufficient consumption and investment. It was at the level of the state, therefore, that the question of the "protective reaction of the system" came entirely to the fore.

The most influential radical work on the state in the United States is James O'Connor's important book, *The Fiscal Crisis of the State* (1973). O'Connor presents the thesis that there is a "structural gap" in state finance, based on a faster increase in state outlays (on public investment and public consumption) than in state tax receipts. The weaknesses of O'Connor's argument, as Hugh Mosley points out, are: (1) a failure to connect the theory of fiscal crisis in a systematic way to the more general theory of accumulation under monopoly capitalism; and (2) an inadequate analysis of the revenue side of the fiscal crisis.[31] The main part of Chapter 6 is therefore devoted to providing an elaboration of the very different theory of the "crisis of the tax state," one that concentrates on the problem of state revenue, that is embedded in the analysis of Kalecki, Steindl, Baran, Sweezy, Magdoff, Paolo Sylos-Labini, and Craig Medlen.[32]

The discussion of state spending in *Monopoly Capital* was not so much concerned with the "fiscal crisis of the state" as with the actual composition of government spending. In the United States, government purchases had increasingly taken the form of military spending, and of projects primarily of benefit to capital. But was this necessarily the case? Could not the state just as well devote the bulk of its revenue to welfare and housing for the poor, and to public investment designed to meet the needs of society as a whole? And could not the state also introduce a massive program of income redistribution designed to smooth over the contradictions emanating from what Schumpeter called the "civilization of inequality and of family fortune"?[33] In the wake of the Keynesian revolution some theorists on the left answered the last two questions in the affirmative.[34] For Baran and Sweezy, in contrast, the possibility of effecting major reforms of this kind within capitalist boundaries was largely precluded by the class structure of society and the ultimate subordination of the state to the imperatives of capital accumulation. Constructing their argument in concrete historical terms, they proceeded to deal with this general problem in three ways: (1) the issue of formal versus substantive political power in the highly structured class environment of the capitalist state; (2) the forces opposed to significant increases in civilian government spending; and (3) the economic and social contradictions of "capitalist state planning."[35] This will form the subject matter in a further section of Chapter 6.

The Underdeveloped World

At the core of most objections to dependency theory as a mode of understanding imperialism is the argument, perhaps best expressed by John Weeks and Elizabeth Dore, that the "surplus extraction thesis" of theorists like Baran and Samir Amin is divorced from all notions of class-based accumulation at the level of production, and thus falls prey to many of the same illusions as liberal thought.[36] After a brief consideration of these charges, Chapter 7 provides a careful reading of the relevant chapters in *The Political Economy of Growth* (1957) by Baran, as well as a fairly detailed discussion of Amin's theory of unequal exchange. This eventually leads to a point-by-point rejection of the criticisms most commonly leveled at their analysis, and to a reaffirmation of the liberating aspects of this tradition.

Although sharing much of the same understanding of accumulation and crisis in advanced capitalism as Baran, Sweezy, and Magdoff, Albert Szymanski nevertheless argued against the analysis of imperialism that they had provided on the grounds that (1) it failed to demonstrate the "necessity of imperialism"; and (2) it was contradicted by empirical evidence, since the net transfer of value in the 1970s (according to Szymanski) was from center to periphery rather than the other way around.[37] An additional part of Chapter 7 is therefore devoted to these questions, and to Magdoff's closely connected discussion of the "reverse flow process" affecting loans to third world nations.

Actually Existing Socialism

"The political economy of growth," as understood by Baran, obtained its full meaning only in the context of the discussion of economic planning in postrevolutionary societies, provided in a tightly compressed argument at the very end of his book. The first part of Chapter 8 is concerned with extracting the main outlines of his argument in this respect. This is followed by a discussion of the further application of Baran's methodology in work on socialist construction in postrevolutionary countries of the third world by Victor Lippit and Clive Thomas.[38]

From here the argument turns to the problems posed for Marxist theory by postrevolutionary societies of the Soviet type. A short sketch of four possible positions is followed by an elaboration of Sweezy's argument (developed as a critical response to interpretations advanced by Charles Bettelheim) that these states constitute an altogether new social formation, neither capitalist nor socialist in character.[39]

In the end, the enduring contribution of Baran and Sweezy (along with others in the same tradition) is their ability to employ a common critical method, emphasizing the production and *utilization* of potential surplus product, to uncover the interlocking imperatives that govern the advanced capitalist, dependent capitalist, and postrevolutionary societies that make up the modern world system. It is only through this kind of unified understanding of contemporary social struggles, as a reflection of a shared history, that there is any real hope of transcending the growing threat to humankind that increasingly overshadows our age.

2

The Economic Surplus Concept and Marxian Value Theory

Common Criticisms

Paul Mattick, representing the traditionalist Marxist perspective, has suggested that Baran and Sweezy's substitution of the concept of economic surplus (defined as the "difference between total social output and the socially necessary costs of producing it") for surplus value in *Monopoly Capital* merely reflected the fact that they had "switched from Marxian to bourgeois economic analysis, which does not operate with class terms such as value and surplus-value but with the amalgam national income, the concept of 'effective demand,' and Keynesian remedies for capital stagnation."[1] Ph. Herzog has likewise remarked that Baran and Sweezy "remain prisoners of the bourgeois problematics of surplus,"[2] while Ernest Mandel has argued that "By jettisoning the field of value production for the field of monetary aggregate demand, Baran and Sweezy obscure . . . simple basic relationships."[3]

On the other hand, as Henryk Szlajfer has pointed out, orthodox economists, while also assuming that Baran and Sweezy abandoned the labor theory of value, were almost universally opposed to the concept of surplus, which they saw as a direct threat to their own methodology.[4] This is clearly revealed in a statement by Raymond Lubitz:

> Baran and Sweezy link the large corporation to the central theme of their work, the "generation and absorption of surplus under conditions of monopoly capitalism." . . . The use of the term "surplus" is one of major ethical significance. If you want to argue that an economic system is based on "exploitation" then merely pointing to an unequal distribution of income or wealth is not enough. It is always possible that these inequalities might be shown, in some sense, to have been "earned." If certain incomes can be defined as "surplus," those who get the surplus can establish no *economic* right to it.[5]

Neoclassical economics had arisen out of an attempt to demonstrate that all incomes were "earned," in this sense, and Lubitz's remarks only highlight the fact that Baran and Sweezy's surplus category was derived from classical rather than neoclassical theory. This means that *if* Baran and Sweezy's category can be legitimately characterized as "bourgeois," in line with the argument of Mattick, Herzog, and others, it has to be traced to the classical political economists other than Marx: Adam Smith, Thomas Malthus, David Ricardo, and John Stuart Mill. Thus Anthony Brewer, also representing the fundamentalist Marxist view, has asserted that in utilizing the surplus category in *The Political Economy of Growth* (1957), and later with Sweezy in *Monopoly Capital,* "Baran reverts, essentially, to the classical, i.e., the pre-Marxist, definition [of surplus product] and this for very much the same purpose as those of the classical economists: he wishes to discuss the 'nature and causes of the wealth of nations.'"[6]

In the labor theory of value of classical economics, the surplus was a residual above both wages, and material (constant) capital carried over into the value of the product. Actual prices of production, or "natural prices," were determined through a percentage mark-up on cost price (or constant plus variable capital), so as to obtain the socially average rate of profit.[7] In neoclassical economics, which has no concept of capital independent of the prevailing price structure, each factor of production (land, labor, and capital) is said to receive (or "earn") an income equal to its marginal productivity. According to this framework, the concept of surplus in the classical sense is virtually meaningless, since interest and rent are both classified as necessary costs of production equivalent in theoretical importance to wages in determining the rate of profit.[8]

The characterization of Baran and Sweezy's use of the surplus concept as "bourgeois" is therefore at best misleading. Today's liberal economists almost invariably adhere to neoclassical theory, and the classical argument (whether in terms of Ricardo or Marx) is largely confined to theorists on the left. Moreover, Baran and Sweezy themselves make it clear that their approach is derived not from classical economics in general but from Marx.[9] In the preface to the second printing of the Greek translation of *Monopoly Capital* (published in English under the title, "Monopoly Capital and the Theory of Value"), Sweezy explained that he and Baran had made an error of omission in not emphasizing the relationship of their theory of monopoly capitalism to Marxian value analysis, which they had taken for granted. Given the importance of this admission, it is well worth quoting the relevant paragraph in its entirety:

> Many of our Marxist critics have stated, as though it were a self-evident fact, that Baran and Sweezy reject the Marxist theory of value (hence also, by implication, the theory of surplus value). This is not so. At no time in our long period of association and collaboration did it ever even occur to us to reject the Marxist theory of value. Our procedure in *Monopoly Capital* was to take the labor theory of value for granted and go on from there. I can now see that this was an error. We should have begun our analysis with an exposition of the theory of value as it is presented in Volume I of *Capital.* We should then have proceeded to show that in capitalist reality, values as determined by socially necessary labor time are subject to two main kinds of modification: first, values are transformed into prices of production, as Marx recognized in Volume 3; and second, values (or prices of production) are transformed into monopoly prices in the monopoly stage of capitalism, a subject which Marx barely mentioned, for the obvious reason that *Capital* was written well before the onset of the monopoly capitalist period. At no time did Baran and I explicitly or implicitly reject the theories of value and surplus value but sought only to analyze the modifications which became necessary as the result of the concentration and centralization of capital. If we had pursued this course, I believe many misunderstandings could have been avoided. This is not to argue, of course, that our analysis of the modifications made necessary by monopoly is necessarily complete or even correct. That is for the critics to judge. But I insist that they cannot form a useful or valid judgment unless they first have a clear understanding of what we are trying to do. To the extent that lack of such understanding is the fault of the authors, I am truly sorry and offer sincere if belated apologies.[10]

In utilizing the surplus concept Baran and Sweezy therefore had no intention of rejecting Marxian value theory by reverting to pre-Marxist classical political economy, as Brewer, Mattick, Herzog, Mandel, and numerous others have suggested. But although Sweezy has made essentially the same point on several occasions, neither in the above passage nor in any of these other attempts to clarify the issue does he explain, in so many words, why he and Baran believed that the change in terminology would "help effect the needed shift in theoretical position" associated with the changeover from freely competitive to monopoly capitalism.[11] One may agree that the analysis provided in *Monopoly Capital* is compatible with the main thrust of classical Marxism, while nevertheless failing to perceive any substantive reason for the change in terminology.[12] Until this question is answered, the criticism of Baran and Sweezy's surplus concept, as a source of unnecessary analytical confusion, retains considerable force. Hence the remainder of this chapter will be devoted to demonstrating that Baran and Sweezy's terminological innovation was a necessary part of their larger endeavor to extend the scope of Marxian political economy in order to deal with those problems that distinguished the monopoly stage of capitalism.

Economic Surplus and *The Political Economy of Growth*

The beginnings of an answer as to why a change in terminology seemed appropriate to Baran and Sweezy can be provided by looking at Baran's earlier use of the surplus concept in *The Political Economy of Growth.* As Szlajfer has pointed out, Baran's employment of the surplus category (rather than surplus value) in this work was greeted with enthusiasm by nearly all Marxist economists.[13] Since the main influence of the book derived from its second half, which dealt with the causes of underdevelopment in the third world, this response to the reintroduction of the surplus category is understandable. To utilize the surplus value concept in relation to societies where the capitalist system is poorly developed, and where the law of value has never been fully operative, would go against the basic principles of Marxian political economy.[14] Moreover, some of those acquainted with Marx's thought were no doubt aware that he himself had employed the surplus category (also in preference to surplus value) when dealing with the Indian social formation of his day.[15] Only Anthony Brewer appears to have been critical of Baran's methodology in this respect, apparently believing that the mere use of the surplus concept, even in a third world context, was an unfortunate reversion to pre-Marxian thought.[16]

In other words, Baran's methodology, insofar as it pertained to the third world, seemed to be predicated on a recognition of the fact that the notion of economic surplus (or surplus product) was a more general category than surplus value—which, in Marx's theory, was specific to a capitalist mode of production, where the law of value had the upper hand. The surplus concept allowed Baran to focus directly on the problem of the "social accumulation fund" in the third world, while preserving the historical (and theoretical) integrity of Marx's most important concept.[17] But the use of the surplus concept also had more positive theoretical implications. As a more general concept than surplus value it provided the basis for a comparison between alternative social orders. Thus, in relation to *The Political Economy of Growth,* Michael Kalecki wrote that the "most important and original contribution of the book is certainly the characterization of various economic systems by the way in which the economic surplus is generated and utilized."[18] To accomplish this Baran defined three forms of the surplus: "actual," "potential," and "planned." *Actual* economic surplus was equal to current savings, consisting of "difference between society's *actual* current output and its *actual* current consumption." Potential economic surplus was the "difference between the output that *could* be produced in a given natural and technological environment with the help of employable productive resources, and what might be regarded as essential consumption." *Planned* economic surplus, which related to socialism, was defined as the "difference between society's 'optimum' output attainable under conditions of planned 'optimal' utilization of all available productive resources, and some chosen 'optimal' volume of consumption."[19] The method, as he pointed out, was one of "comparative statics," which ignored the "paths of transition from one economic situation to another," considering "these situations, as it were, *ex post.*"[20]

While the concept of actual economic surplus presents no difficulties of interpretation, this is not the case for the potential and planned economic surpluses.[21] Potential economic surplus, Baran wrote,

> refers to a different quantity of output than what would represent surplus value in Marx's sense. On the one hand, it *excludes* such elements of surplus value as what was called above *essential* consumption of capitalists, what could be considered *essential* outlays on government administration and the like; on the other hand, it comprises what is not covered by the concept of surplus value—the output lost in view of underemployment or misemployment of resources.[22]

Baran's "revision" of Marx's surplus value calculus with respect to socially necessary consumption—incorporating *essential* outlays on capitalist consumption and government administration, in addition to wages themselves—seems to have had the object of determining more precisely the size of the investment fund realistically available to a given society under conditions of rational employment. His "revision" in terms of output takes into consideration both the existence of structural unemployment (the quantitative employment problem) and the systematic promotion of nonproductive expenditures (the qualitative employment problem).

Baran endeavored to make this framework still more explicit by pointing to "four headings" under which the potential surplus currently appeared, when judged from the critical standpoint of "a more or less drastic reorganization of the production and distribution of social output," implying "far-reaching changes in the structure of society": (1) "society's excess consumption"; (2) the "output lost" through unproductive labor; (3) the "output lost because of the irrational and wasteful organization of the existing productive apparatus"; and (4) the "output foregone" due to systemic underemployment.[23] Victor Lippit has noted that in formulating this more precise notion of the potential surplus Baran considered only waste, leaving existing investment out of his calculation and thus made a "major oversight."[24] However, since Baran did not make this mistake elsewhere, and since his main purpose was to highlight the surplus available for investment, this in fact creates no difficulties of interpretation. A more important criticism is that there is considerable overlap between Baran's four criteria for adducing wasted surplus. In fact, the first, second, and third categories refer to much the same thing viewed from slightly different perspectives.[25] Therefore, these categories represented differences in emphasis with regard to qualitative factors, rather than strict quantitative distinctions. Finally, it is crucial to recognize, as Szlajfer has stressed, that in devising the concept of potential economic surplus Baran introduced the external criterion of socialist rationality, making it difficult to discern the dividing line between that concept and planned economic surplus.

Planned economic surplus, for Baran, reflected the "considered judgment of a socialist community guided by reason and science" rather than the profit-making "considerations of individual firms" or the "income distribution, tastes, and social pressures of a capitalist order." This implied a "far-reaching rationalization of society's productive apparatus." Moreover, the "optimum" level of consumption and economic growth pursued in such a society would be determined by rational considerations of human welfare, leaving open the possibility that the planned surplus would be smaller than the potential surplus under capitalism if preference was given to current as opposed to future consumption.[26]

Despite this quantitative distinction with respect to the planned and potential surpluses, however, the lines of demarcation between these two forms of surplus remain difficult to discern qualitatively, since both are formulated in terms of the external criterion of socialist rationality. While there is no difficulty with the category of planned surplus, according to Szlajfer, the concept of potential surplus is "methodologically imprecise."[27] He therefore contends that the range of the potential surplus concept should be restricted so as to sharpen the critical force of Baran's entire analytical framework. The basis for distinguishing between the three types of surplus then becomes the three standpoints of "individual capital," "global capital," and "society as a whole."[28] From the perspective of individual capital it is impossible to perceive advertising expenditure, to take just one example, as a form of waste as long as it enhances surplus value for the individual firm. But from the standpoint of global capital (reflected in the concept of potential surplus) it is quite apparent that this constitutes a form of unproductive consumption in a very broad sense.

We can determine more precisely what is meant by the perspective of "global capital" by looking at two general historical situations. The ideal of the capitalist economic order from the standpoint of the capitalist class as a whole (mirrored in mainstream economic theory) is that of a system in which Say's so-called "law" that supply calls forth its own demand formally applies, with the constraints of the system lying entirely on the supply side. This means that there is full utilization of productive capacity (full employment by capitalist standards), a seller's market, a shortage of savings in relation to investment opportunities, and a basic need to minimize luxury consumption. Generally speaking, these conditions pertained during the nineteenth century era of free competition and early industrialization. Hence, in neo-Marxian theory the competitive stage of capitalism is often taken as a gauge of capitalism in its most rational form—adequate to its own concept and adhering to the standards of global capital. The advent of monopoly capitalism is therefore viewed as a departure from capitalism's own standards of rationality.[29]

The other way in which the outlook of global capital can be concretely ascertained is in terms of a capitalist war economy, where the "interests of the individual capitalists are subordinated to the interests of the capitalist class as a whole."[30] Under these circumstances it becomes necessary to maximize overall output and to minimize luxury expenditures (other than those required for the war effort). Herein lies the critical potential implicit in Keynesian economics, which emerged historically as the economics of depression, on the one hand, and the economics of war, on the other.

Still, it need hardly be said that the critical outlook obtainable from the vantage point of the capitalist class as a whole—in both of these historical situations—remains strictly limited and does not permit a thoroughgoing scrutiny of the structure of production itself.

Hence in Szlajfer's reformulation of Baran's theory all questions involving the external criterion of socialist rationality are confined to the concept of planned surplus. The significance of this change in formulation will become more apparent in relation to *Monopoly Capital* itself. For the moment, it is enough to point out that by restricting the range of potential surplus to the standpoint of global capital, Szlajfer has tried to make it equivalent to "potential surplus value," while planned surplus—which involves far-reaching changes in the structure of production, eliminating waste built into the use-value structure of a monopoly capitalist economy—goes far beyond the "traditional calculus of surplus value."[31] Thus insofar as the question of planned (and not simply potential) surplus is involved, it is necessary, in conformity with the method generally employed in Sweezy's later writings, to refer to "potential surplus product" rather than "potential surplus value."[32] Although differing with Baran's definitional framework, Szlajfer's approach seems more closely attuned to the logical requirements of Baran's theory as a whole, and thus can be treated as a refinement of the core analysis. Unless otherwise indicated, therefore, the terms "potential and planned surplus" will be employed in Szlajfer's sense in the following pages.

The evaluation of the economic surplus concept according to the external criterion of socialist rationality (in addition to the critical perspective of global capital) has its counterpart in Baran's conception of unproductive labor, which has continued to be the most controversial feature of *The Political Economy of Growth* within the left. Unproductive labor is defined by Baran, in terms reminiscent of Rudolf Hilferding, as "all labor resulting in the output of goods and services the demand for which is attributable to the specific relationships of the capitalist system, and which would be absent in a rationally ordered society."[33] It would appear at first glance that this is radically opposed to Marx's own notion of unproductive labor, the most famous definition of which is that labor which is exchanged against revenue rather than capital. Matters, however, are neither so simple nor so entirely adverse to Baran's model when judged in terms of Marxian orthodoxy.

In the most systematic discussion of Marx's theory of productive and unproductive labor to date, Ian Gough has argued that Marx approached the question from two standpoints. The first was whether the labor was exchanged against capital (rather than revenue) and directly enhanced surplus value. The second had to do with whether the labor was technically necessary with respect to the production of a given use value. In the latter case an external criterion of rationality was applied, according to which certain economic forms could be adduced as deriving entirely from antagonistic class relations and from conditions of production that were specifically capitalist in nature.[34] As Marx wrote, it is only the "apologetic endeavors of the vulgar economist" that perceives

> commercial capital and money-dealing capital as forms arising necessarily from the process of production as such, whereas they are due to the specific forms of the capitalist mode of production, which above all presupposes the circulation of commodities, and hence money, as its basis.[35]

This referred merely to circulation, but Marx also used the same approach in relation to supervisory workers:

> One part of the labour of superintendence merely arises from the antagonistic contradiction between capital and labour, and from the antagonistic character of capitalist production, and belongs to the incidental expenses of production in the same way as nine-tenths of the "labour" occasioned by the circulation process.[36]

Hence it was Marx's view that certain "incidental expenses" that were to some extent built into the very cost structure of capitalist production and constituted an inescapable feature of generalized commodity production could be considered irrational from the critical standpoint of society as a whole. For Marx, writing in the middle of the nineteenth century, this problem of technically useless circulation costs and supervisory personnel was a relatively minor matter, to be noted merely in passing. However, in the age of scientific management, advanced marketing, and financial control, this type of distortion of the cost structure of the system is no longer "incidental."[37] And although Marx, as Gough explains, did not carry this external, historical criterion for determining the "labor necessary to produce a given use value" (and hence whether the labor so utilized was productive or not) to the point that he actually questioned the productive worth of use values themselves, it seems completely in accord with his general method—given the historical reality of a monopoly capitalist economy—to follow Baran and Sweezy in doing exactly that.[38]

This can be accomplished in a fairly rigorous manner by recognizing that the three perspectives of individual and global capital and society as a whole (introduced by Szlajfer) are equally applicable to the issues of economic surplus and economic waste (which, of course, represent two sides of the same problem).[39] With this as a clue, it is possible to retain the essential features of Marx's notion of unproductive labor while extending its critical range, by distinguishing between unproductive, unreproductive, and socially useless expenditures (corresponding to the three perspectives of individual and global capital and society as a whole). Thus unproductive labor proper is labor that is not organized under the direct domination of capital (the law of value) and does not produce surplus value for the capitalist.[40] The concept of unreproductive labor (and consumption) brings the further element of luxury production (department 3 in the Marxian reproduction schemes) within the category of waste (as visible to global capital),[41] whereas useless labor incorporates still another form of waste, discernible only from the external vantage point of socialistically defined use values and technical necessities.[42] Although the second category of waste expenditure (plus actual unemployment) falls within the critical range of potential economic surplus, as delimited by Szlajfer, the last category of waste can be seen only from the standpoint of planned surplus. What should be apparent by now, in any case, is that this general approach, associated most notably with Baran, Sweezy, and Szlajfer, represents a critique of present-day capitalist reality, not only in terms of the system's internal logic, but also in terms of the higher, external logic of a rationally planned society.

Economic Surplus and *Monopoly Capital*

In *Monopoly Capital* Baran and Sweezy approached the question of the economic surplus in a somewhat different way than

Baran had in *The Political Economy of Growth*. As we have seen, Baran utilized a method of "comparative statics" in his earlier book, with each of the main concepts being directed at determining the social accumulation fund "actually," "potentially," or "optimally" available for productive investment. In *Monopoly Capital*, in contrast, Baran and Sweezy employed a method of successive approximations, starting from a position in which the economic surplus was simply equal to aggregate profits (property income), with the implicit assumption of full capacity utilization, and gradually moving to a developed notion of economic surplus, which was supposed to be equal to (but actually went beyond) total surplus value.[43] The intended relationship to surplus value was indicated much later by Sweezy himself, in an article on the Japanese economy, where he pointed out that the fully developed version of the surplus in *Monopoly Capital* was conceived as being an equivalent (or near equivalent) to total surplus value, deviating from the "textbook version" of the latter as aggregate profits (profits + interest + rent).[44] Hence in beginning with a notion of aggregate profits—or the "difference between sales revenue and costs of production"—as a "first approximation to a fully developed concept of economic surplus," Baran and Sweezy were simply starting with what had become the conventional textbook version of surplus value as a first step toward determining the potential social accumulation fund, which under monopoly capitalism increasingly takes on the labyrinthine character of economic waste of various kinds.[45]

Before following out the logic of their analysis further, it should be mentioned, parenthetically, that in the dozen or so years prior to Szlajfer's initial contribution on the subject, none of the critics of *Monopoly Capital* seem to have fully appreciated the fact that the method adopted in the book was one of successive approximations. While some of the critics appeared to take the "first approximation" of the concept of economic surplus as *the* definition in the book, others, such as Otto Nathan, Michael Lebowitz, and M. Salvati, complained about the "multiplicity of definitions."[46] Needless to say, this widespread failure to comprehend the method employed in *Monopoly Capital* (the responsibility for which no doubt lies partly with Baran and Sweezy themselves), generated a great deal of added confusion and prevented radicals and nonradicals alike from perceiving some of the more subtle implications of Baran and Sweezy's approach to political economy.

In the first three chapters of the book, Baran and Sweezy generally based their argument on the category of aggregate profits in national income, as a first approximation to the concept of economic surplus, while *"tacitly assuming" the full utilization of productive capacity.*[47] Nevertheless, where necessary for their argument they introduced variations in the level of employment as a factor determining the actual quantity of gross profits (or total property income). This is particularly evident in their response to an argument by Nicholas Kaldor, attacking the Marxian theory of exploitation, and therefore calling into question the tendency for the surplus to rise, on statistical grounds. In a famous essay entitled "A Model of Economic Growth," Kaldor had argued that

> all statistical indications suggest that the share of profits in income in leading capitalist countries such as the United States have shown a falling rather than a rising trend over recent decades, and is appreciably below the level of the nineteenth century; despite the extraordinary severity and duration of the depression of the 1930's, the problem of "realizing surplus value" appears no more chronic to-day than it was in Marx's day.[48]

In reply, Baran and Sweezy pointed out that the actual "share of profits"—or the surplus, as they had generally referred to it up to this point, while abstracting from the problem of unused productive resources—was in fact only part of the total surplus, since existing unemployment and excess capacity constituted a sizable component of the surplus, potentially available. Thus it is in the actual figures on unemployed workers and idle plant and equipment that much of the profit-making potential of the economy leaves its "statistical trace" rather than in final income accounts.[49]

In the fourth chapter, on the role of the capitalists' consumption and investment as a means of absorbing the surplus, Baran and Sweezy drop their tacit assumption of full utilization of productive capacity.[50] This can be seen in their discussion of profitability schedules for monopolistic enterprises. Using data on the U.S. Steel Corporation compiled by John Blair, they showed (by means of a scatter diagram) that the profitability schedule (the relationship between profits and operating rate) for U.S. Steel shifted dramatically in an upward direction after 1955, with higher rates of return on stockholders' investment at every given level of capacity utilization, and a lower rate of capacity utilization at every given level of profit. They argued that this upward shift in profitability schedules for monopolistic firms provided additional support for their contention that not only would the potential surplus tend to rise, but that its "investment-seeking" portion would rise even faster (partly as a consequence of this very tendency to produce greater profits with a given operating rate). As Sweezy was to write later, "At anything approaching full employment, the surplus accruing to the propertied classes is far more than they can profitably invest."[51]

In any case, Baran and Sweezy managed to reconfirm the fact, central to Keynesian (and Kaleckian) theory, that the profits of firms are dependent in the short run on the level of capacity utilization and employment. But in doing so they switched rather abruptly from an approach that implicitly assumed near full employment to one that operated in the real world of unemployment, underemployment, and excess capacity. It is scarcely surprising that this bewildered some of their readers.[52] Nevertheless, there was nothing illogical or even haphazard about their mode of procedure in these pages, since it made perfectly good sense to move from a concept of aggregate profits in national income accounts, with the simplifying assumption of full capacity utilization, to the historically concrete observation that the existence of unemployment meant that part of these aggregate profits were merely *potential.* By dropping the assumption of full capacity utilization, they did not alter their assessment of the size of the surplus up to this point, but merely uncovered one of its "many forms and disguises."[53]

Only in the fifth chapter, on the "sales effort," did they introduce the second approximation to a full developed concept of the surplus—now defining it as the "difference between total social output and the socially necessary costs of producing it"—but without indicating that this was indeed a second approximation.[54] It is significant that when forced to provide a single, succinct definition of the surplus in their "Early Introduction" to the 1962 drafts of chapters 2 and 10, they had defined it—basically in line with this second approximation in the final version of their book—as the "steadily widening gap, at any given level of production, between output and socially necessary costs of production."[55] It is clear, however, that in contrast to this 1962 definition the second approximation, like the first, is formulated at the outset with the tacit assumption of full capacity utilization. What served to distinguish the second approximation, then, was the fact that the more developed definition incorporated a critical assessment of the cost structure of a capitalist economy. Thus their conception of "socially necessary costs," as Szlajfer has stressed, deducted "interest, ground rent, excessive depreciation, selling costs, and wages of nonproductive workers."[56] Given this outlook, Baran and Sweezy were also able to rephrase the second approximation as the "difference between the aggregate net output and the aggregate real wages of productive workers."[57]

It would seem that the more developed definition of economic surplus is very close to that of Marx's surplus value, which undoubtedly was Baran and Sweezy's intention. But it is in the chapter on selling costs that they actually depart from what Szlajfer has called the "traditional calculus of surplus value." As Sweezy was later to acknowledge, it was at this point that elements of the planned surplus (or the external criterion of socialism) enter into their definition.[58] This is important in two respects: (1) it underlines the difference between their conception of surplus and Marx's concept of surplus value; and (2) it provides us with the additional critical perspective on monopoly capitalism, one from outside the system.

Baran and Sweezy began their discussion in this chapter by pointing out that Marx had clearly recognized that there were "other modes of utilization" of society's economic surplus besides that of the "capitalist's consumption and investment" (which had been discussed in the previous chapter).[59] In this context they list the expenditures of state and church, the wages of unproductive workers, and what Marx called the "expenses of circulation." In relation to this last factor they quote from Marx himself:

> *The general law is that all expenses of circulation, which arise only from changes in form, do not add any value to the commodities.* They are merely expenses required for the realization of value, or for its conversion from one form into another. The capital invested in those expenses (including the labor employed in it) belongs to the dead expenses of capitalist production. They must be made up out of surplus product and are, from the point of view of the entire capitalist class, a deduction from the surplus value or surplus product.[60]

As Sweezy was to say of this same quote five years later, in his 1971 Marshall lecture at Cambridge University, "It seemed to Baran and me—and still seems to me—that this provides the needed conceptual framework to bring the whole problem of selling costs within the framework of Marxian theory."[61] The difficulty that they were to face in attempting to do so, however, derived from the fact that, while following Marx in assuming that expenses of circulation could be criticized "from the point of view of the entire capitalist class," they also believed, along with Veblen, that under monopoly capitalism the "sales and production efforts interpenetrate to such an extent as to become virtually indistinguishable."[62] Hence the very logic of their argument carried Baran and Sweezy beyond the traditional confines of the surplus value calculus by calling into question the system of needs incorporated within the cost structure of production itself. Insofar as the sales effort and the production effort have become inseparable under monopoly capitalism, the problem of selling costs is no longer amenable, as was the case in Marx's day, to full-fledged critical treatment from the standpoint of the capitalist class as a whole. It is therefore necessary to rely ever more directly on the principle that capitalism is a transitory historical formation.

The "sales effort," in Baran and Sweezy's terminology, was "conceptually . . . identical to Marx's expenses of circulation."[63] They did not, however, investigate all aspects of this broad phenomenon but mainly confined their discussion to two of its manifestations: (1) advertising expenses and (2) spurious selling costs built into the product mix of a monopoly capitalist economy. It is of course in relation to the latter, and not the former, that problems arise for the theory of surplus value. Baran and Sweezy approached the fundamental dilemma by concisely summing up the way in which socially necessary costs were conceived in the classical model of free competition:

> In the competitive model . . . only the minimum costs of production . . . combined with the minimum costs of packaging, transportation, and distribution . . . could be recognized by the market—and by economic theory—as socially necessary costs of purveying a product to its buyer. The product itself, although under capitalism not produced with a view to its use value but as a commodity with a view to its exchange value, could be legitimately considered an object of utility satisfying a genuine human need. To be sure, even during capitalism's competitive phase, to which this model approximately applies, socially necessary costs exceeded what they would have been in a less anarchic system of production, but there was no real problem of selling costs and certainly no interpenetration of the production and sales efforts. Socially necessary costs could be unambiguously defined, and at least

> in principle measured, as those outlays indispensable to the production and delivery of a given output. . . . And once costs had been defined, the social surplus was easily identifiable as the difference between total output and costs.[64]

But if it could be reasonably assumed under freely competitive capitalism that the structure of production—despite the exchange value basis of a commodity economy—had socially useful labor and serviceable use values as its real content, this is not true to the same extent under monopoly capitalism, where the very output mix of the economy is increasingly subject to the irrational exigencies of the system. Here it is important to follow Szlajfer in noting that Marx had, in effect, employed the concept of a "specifically capitalist use value"—lacking any intrinsic worth from the standpoint of production in general—in relation to gold.[65] With this as a methodological clue, Szlajfer goes on to argue that in the monopoly stage of capitalism the giant corporations strive to promote purely "formal use values" of all shapes and sizes, for the sole purpose of absorbing the potential economic surplus. To this we need only add that such spurious labor and commodities (as in the case of planned obsolescence and armaments production) often have the peculiar use value *for capital alone* (in the context of an overcapacity to produce) of being completely useless with respect to social reproduction.[66]

Obviously, all of this enormously complicates the problem of determining what constitutes essential labor and socially necessary costs. The issue is not difficult, in principle, where nonreproductive luxury commodities are concerned (department 3 in the reproduction schemes), since this form of waste is easily discernible from the perspective of global capital.[67] However, it is no easy matter to determine the extent to which "expenses of circulation" penetrate into the consumption basket of workers (department 2), or even into capital goods production (department 1). As Baran and Sweezy put it:

> The question is: what are socially necessary costs when, in Veblen's words, the distinction between workmanship and salesmanship has been blurred? This question does not arise from the mere existence of selling costs. As long as the selling "industry" and the sales departments of producing enterprises are separate and do not impinge upon the production departments, everything is plain sailing. In that case, selling costs, like rent and interest, can be readily recognized as a form

> of surplus to be subtracted from aggregate costs in order to arrive at the true socially necessary costs of production. But how should we proceed when selling costs are literally indistinguishable from production costs, as is the case, for example, in the automobile industry? . . . How can the productive workers be distinguished from the unproductive? How can selling costs and production costs be separated?[68]

It would be difficult to avoid the conclusion that such questions are not easily asked, much less answered, within the classical Marxian framework of surplus value analysis: to raise the issue of the productiveness or nonproductiveness of labor within the deep structure of industrial output itself is to transcend the entire *immanent* critique of the capitalist mode of production. Yet in an irrationally constituted system, where planned obsolescence is built into key commodities like the omnipresent automobile, it is scarcely possible to avoid asking these questions if part of one's purpose is to ascertain the manner in which the social accumulation fund potentially available for the satisfaction of human needs is wasted, and thus to gain a rough indication of the degree to which monopoly capitalism obstructs social progress. What is more, it is well worth underlining the fact that even though these contradictions are only clearly visible from outside the system, as it were, it is nevertheless true that they have a direct bearing on the entire disarticulation of the capitalist mode of production in our time.

According to Baran and Sweezy, then, the only meaningful way of analyzing the distortion of costs at the level of production is to compare the "actual product mix" for a commodity such as the automobile to a "hypothetical product mix" that excludes all nonessential expenses of circulation. A similar approach, they pointed out, had been employed—in very broad theoretical terms—by the classical political economists, who had confronted prevailing reality with the reason and science of a nascent social order when they criticized the "hybrid feudal-mercantilist-capitalist system against which they fought their ideological and political battles."[69]

Thus with respect to the automobile, Baran and Sweezy argued—based on findings by economists Franklin M. Fisher, Zvi Grilliches, and Carl Kaysen—that more than 25 percent of the purchase price in the 1950-1956 period was accounted for by unnecessary model changes, and a further $968 million per year over the period by the added gas consumption that went hand in hand with these innovations in "car design and construction." The point is driven home once one realizes that none of this included the economic costs associated with the well-known "accelerated obsolescence" of particular repair parts and of the vehicle as a unit.[70]

What was true of automobiles, Baran and Sweezy suggested, was also true, albeit in a less dramatic sense, in other areas of basic industry where waste had invaded the production process—taking the form of sumptuous packaging, unnecessary changes in product design, an excess of supervisory personnel, etc. Given the universality of the phenomenon, and the sheer guesswork involved in determining a "hypothetical product mix" conforming to the dictates of science and reason in the context of the present social order, Baran and Sweezy argued that "a full-scale computation" of useless labor integrated into the production of actual use values in the economy was virtually impossible at that time. Still, there was no doubt about the key conclusion:

> What is certain is the negative statement which, notwithstanding its negativity, constitutes one of the most important insights to be gained from political economy: an output the volume and composition of which are determined by the profit maximization policies of oligopolistic corporations neither corresponds to human needs nor costs the minimum possible amount of human toil and human suffering. The concrete structure of a rational social output can only be established in the fullness of time—by a process of groping, of trial and error—in a socialist society where economic activity is no longer dominated by profits and sales but instead is directed to the creation of the abundance which is indispensable to the welfare and all-round development of man.[71]

Hence if the *quantitative* impact of the penetration of the sales effort into production itself could not be measured in any comprehensive way, there could be no doubt about the *qualitative* issues involved. It was no longer valid to believe that production consisted entirely of socially necessary labor, when judged from the perspective of a rational socioeconomic order.[72]

Analytically, the general method employed in the chapter on selling costs seems similar to the one Marx himself used when briefly considering the expenses of supervisory labor, at least part of which can be viewed alternatively as socially *necessary* costs in the determinate historical environment of a capitalist economy with an antagonistic class structure, and as socially *unnecessary* costs from the standpoint of society as a whole (the viewpoint of socialism).

Faced with this contradiction, Marx adopted the latter point of view, while treating it as a minor qualification to the theory of a purely capitalist economy, based on the concrete historical conditions of his day. By merely raising the same general issue a century later, however, Baran and Sweezy were inexorably driven to the conclusion that Marxian political economy had to be extended beyond an *immanent* critique of the system if it was to retain any direct historical relevance. Under monopoly capitalism a growing proportion of workers employed within production itself are, to borrow an appropriate phrase from Marx, "useful and necessary only because of the faulty social relations—they owe their existence to social evils."[73] Needless to say, this cannot be entirely understood within the narrow historical confines of capitalist reasoning, even in its most generalized (or "global capitalist") form.

The chapter on the "sales effort" as a mode of surplus absorption, in which the second approximation to the concept of economic surplus was introduced, was followed by a chapter on "civilian government" as still another form of surplus absorption. From this point on, the tacit assumption of full capacity utilization, adopted initially with respect to the first approximation and then subsequently relaxed, only to be renewed in introducing the second approximation, was finally rejected altogether. Since the traditional, pre-Keynesian criticism of government spending had been based on the assumption, in accordance with Say's purported law, that the capitalist system tended to draft to the full its available productive capacity, Baran and Sweezy began their discussion of state spending by stressing the everyday reality of excess capacity, as a fundamental characteristic of accumulation under monopoly capitalism (except in times of war or preparation for war).[74] Government expenditures in a modern economy, according to this outlook, were to be understood as part of the protective reaction of a system that was no longer self-sustaining in the strict economic sense. Hence the remaining chapters of *Monopoly Capital* were concerned with the real world of unused productive resources, compensatory state spending, and *potential* economic surplus. While the second approximation represented the fully developed concept of economic surplus in a quantitative sense, it is only with the explicit recognition of the fact that in reality much of this surplus finds it "statistical trace" in unemployment and excess capacity that the concept is fully developed in a qualitative sense as well.

The various components of Baran and Sweezy's final version of the economic surplus concept were summarized by Joseph D. Phillips in the statistical appendix to *Monopoly Capital:*

> The totals of these three major categories of economic surplus—property income, waste in the business process, and government expenditure—were . . . added together to obtain our grand totals. It should be noted, however, that these totals still do not include all elements of surplus. Some could not be estimated on a year-by-year basis because of inadequate data. One of these elements is the penetration of the productive process by the sales effort, but some data for recent years have been assembled to indicate its order of magnitude. Another element which might reasonably be incorporated in the surplus, but is omitted here, is the output foregone owing to the existence of unemployment.[75]

It will be noticed that of the five components of the economic surplus mentioned here, the first, property income, is basically equivalent to the first approximation, or the "difference between what a society produces and the costs of producing it," while the next three components—waste in the business process (the outlay on sales), government expenditure, and the penetration of the sales effort into the production process—form the additional elements making up the second approximation, or the "difference between total social output and the socially necessary costs of producing it."[76] The fifth component, as previously noted, is initially abstracted from in both the first and second approximations, which, for the sake of simplicity, tacitly assume full employment by ideal capitalist standards (full utilization of existing plant and equipment). Here it bears repeating that the category of economic surplus can be considered fully developed in a qualitative sense only insofar as it explicitly recognizes the harsh reality of underemployment, and the didactic device of assuming near full employment must obviously be abandoned in any statistical endeavor to measure potential surplus product.

In grouping these five components of the economic surplus into three distinct sets, in the statement quoted above, Phillips was no doubt expressing more than a mere problem of measurement.[77] As Szlajfer has noted, in relation to the first of these sets, "the sum total of . . . income from property, waste in business, and state spending" is equivalent "to the notion of *produced and realized surplus value*."[78] In contrast, both the penetration of the sales effort into the production process and output lost through unemployment, when considered as elements of surplus product, go beyond the traditional surplus value calculus. This should be clear enough by now in the case of the former. But it is also true that it is rather awkward from the standpoint of the traditional calculus to include, as part of total surplus value, the *potential* surplus product lost through unemployment. Moreover, although the waste associated with idle capacity (and the associated unemployment) is visible from a global capitalist perspective, which has no difficulty with the idea of a "full employment surplus," this is not the case with respect to "Marxian unemployment"—that is, the industrial reserve army that invariably remains when all plant and equipment is fully employed—since this also extends beyond the historically limited perspective of global capital (and the surplus value calculus) to that of society as a whole (planned surplus). In all of these various ways, Baran and Sweezy's approach to political economy seems to be predicated on an intellectual standpoint external to the system itself.

The figures provided by Phillips indicated that the total surplus for 1963 equaled 56.1 percent of GNP.[79] Some critics have contended that there was a certain amount of double counting in the determination of these results,[80] and, since the figures were compiled by taking certain elements from both the income and expenditure sides of the national product accounts, it is easy to see how this could have occurred. Thus it seems undeniable that a certain portion of government expenditures are counted as well in property income.[81] Much of this has to do with the intrinsic difficulty of ascertaining the relevant Marxian categories and quantities in national income accounts designed for quite a different purpose. In any case, there can be little doubt about the sheer magnitude of the surplus, or about its tendency to rise in relation to income as a whole, as Ron Standfield and Edward Wolff have demonstrated with somewhat different methods of measurement.[82] Moreover, it is absolutely essential to recognize that the Phillips estimates were conservative in several crucial respects. Although Phillips did attempt to develop rough estimates for the penetration of the sales effort into the production process, which amounted, in rough order of magnitude, to something like 10 percent of GNP, he was unable to compute year by year estimates and therefore left this component out of the grand totals of the economic surplus.[83] In addition, the further element of output lost through official unemployment, amounting during the years 1953–1960 to some $252 billion (in 1959 dollars), was also excluded.[84] In other words, the total surplus as estimated in the Phillips tables was only meant to represent produced and realized surplus value, and did not include those additional elements of the potential surplus product that represented the *differentia specifica* of Baran and Sweezy's analytical framework when compared to the classical surplus value approach.

History and Theory

The foregoing analysis of Baran and Sweezy's concept of economic surplus should make it clear that their intention was to modify and extend the Marxian cognitive perspective in accordance with what they perceived as important historical changes, rather than to abandon the core components of value theory. It would appear that the economic surplus concept was introduced, at least in part, to deal with phenomena that could not be incorporated through a mere "mechanical broadening of the surplus value notion."[85] In this sense they were, at the same time, defending the theoretical integrity of the Marxian perspective by conforming to what Karl Korsch had called the "principle of historical specification."[86] The notion of surplus value, like nearly all of the key categories in *Capital,* was conceived by Marx as being specific to the capitalist mode of production and could not be applied to phenomena that lay outside of the purview of capital in general.[87] The concept of economic surplus therefore became a necessary complementary category for comparing alternative social orders (whether actual or merely potential).

Ironically, what was undoubtedly the most pointed attempt to refute Baran and Sweezy's methodology ended up asserting the very methodological principle that lay at the core of their study. As we have seen, Baran and Sweezy had argued that certain secondary determinants of accumulation, "such as the revenues of state and church, the expenses of transforming commodities into money, and the wages of unproductive workers," had been considered by

Marx but were largely excluded from his core theoretical schema.[88] Under monopoly capitalism, they argued, this procedure was no longer satisfactory, and these factors had to be brought into the very center of politico-economic analysis. For this purpose, the broad notion of economic surplus, rather than the more historically concrete and theoretically delimited concept of surplus value as such, was thought to be most appropriate. In direct response to this, Paul Mattick, anticipating an argument later to be employed by Mario Cogoy, wrote:

> Because for Marx "the relation between wage-labour and capital determines the entire character of the capitalist mode of production," his capital analysis is in terms of value and surplus-value. Even the division of surplus-value into profit, interest, and rent disappears in his value analysis. The best points in *Capital,* Marx wrote to Engels, "are (1) the twofold character of labour, according to whether it is expressed in use-value or exchange-value (all understanding of the facts depends on this) and (2) the treatment of surplus-value independently of its particular form of profit, interest, ground rent, etc." . . . If there is no point in considering interest and rent in the value analysis of capitalist development, there is even less in considering the additional items enumerated by Baran and Sweezy into which surplus-value is divided in capitalist society.[89]

It would be difficult to gainsay the fact that a fundamental misunderstanding of Baran and Sweezy's analysis is revealed in Mattick's argument. The only reason for developing a framework that explicitly accounts for the "additional items" of unproductive labor, expenses of circulation, underemployment, unused capacity, and the distortion of the use-value structure of the economy is to obtain a more complete notion of the social accumulation fund potentially available for economic expansion. Thus Baran and Sweezy were not interested in these secondary determinants of accumulation in themselves, but were simply attempting to obtain a notion of the potential surplus product as a whole. If they departed from Marx, it was only in their belief that under the increasingly deranged system of monopoly capitalism, produced and realized surplus value no longer encompassed the entire potentially available social accumulation fund and thus had to be supplemented—if the historical limitations of the system were to be understood—by the more general category of economic surplus.

Another objection of a more serious kind was leveled by

William Barclay and Mitchell Stengel, who charged that in appealing to an abstract concept of socialism when formulating the category of economic surplus Baran and Sweezy adopted a "position outside of history."[90] David Yaffe has put forward a similar criticism, suggesting that Baran and Sweezy relied on the sort of abstract recourse to "reason" characteristic of the Frankfurt School, rather than on classical Marxian notions of historical necessity.[91]

The trouble with all such criticisms, particularly when made by those on the left, is that they are self-defeating. What distinguishes the Marxian outlook is the perception of capitalism as a transitory historical system. This demands an intellectual standpoint that is in some respects outside of capitalist history, with respect both to the known precapitalist past and the still largely unknown postcapitalist future. In relation to the latter, it is not all "utopian" (using the word in the original, negative, Marxist sense) to conceive of a more rational order in the broadest possible terms, as one in which many of the class-based contradictions of the profit system have been negated.[92] Such a perspective would of course be ahistorical and crudely utopian if thought of as a definite description of the future as history. It is anything but ahistorical, however, insofar as it allows us to perceive the historical limitations, and unfolding contradictions, of the present social order. "To the Marxist," as Sweezy wrote in *The Theory of Capitalist Development,* "the specific historical (i.e., transitory) character of capitalism is a major premise. It is by virtue of this fact that the Marxist is able, so to speak, to stand outside the system and criticize it as a whole."[93]

The "fundamental principle" of historical materialism, Baran argued, was the "continuous, systematic, and comprehensive *confrontation of reality with reason.*" But this was not to be understood in an idealistic sense:

> To Marxism the meaning of reason and the nature of reality are closely interwoven, inseparable aspects of historical development. In terms of the *long run,* of the entire historical process, the content and the injunctions of reason are relative. They change with the changing forces of production, they enrich themselves with the expansion of our knowledge.[94]

Marxism, Baran contended, must remain realistic through a thoroughgoing scrutiny of existing historical conditions, but it must also retain the "courage to be utopian," setting "its sights on the not yet realized but already visible potentialities of the future."[95] "The confrontation of reality with reason," he wrote,

> is by no means an abstract, intellectual undertaking. In every society that is split into classes, i.e., based on the exploitation of man by man, the exploiting class is vitally interested in the preservation of the existing pattern of social relations; and in administering the affairs of society it will seek to admit of only such change as will not endanger this pattern. The point is therefore unavoidably reached when the progress of reason and the expansion of our knowledge of reality are impeded, when existing and maturing possibilities for society's further advancement, for further growth and development of all its members, are sacrificed in favor of the interest of the dominant class in the continuation of the established social order—when, in other words, the particular interests of society come into conflict with the interests of society as a whole. At such historical junctures the confrontation of reality with reason reveals the irrationality of the existing social order, turns—in the words of Marx—into "ruthless criticism of everything that exists, ruthless in the sense that the criticism will not shrink either from its own conclusions or from conflict with the powers that be," and becomes the intellectual expression of the practical, existential needs of the entire society, and in particular of its overwhelming majority, the oppressed and exploited classes.[96]

To deny any aspect of what would be rational from the standpoint of society as a whole—even if this can only be intellectually ascertained from a position, as it were, outside of the capitalist system, and thus by going beyond the categories appropriate to the analysis of that system in and for itself—to deny any part of this human potentiality, is to shy away from a "ruthless criticism of everything that exists" and to restrict the range of the "confrontation of reality with reason" to that which is defined by the status quo. For Baran, it is the very refusal to cooperate with establishment ideology by artificially limiting the scope of social inquiry in this manner that constitutes the most essential characteristic of the Marxian outlook.

From this vantage point, it can be argued that Baran and Sweezy's approach to political economy— and much of what has all too often been condemned as mere "critical theory" as well—belongs to the classical tradition of historical materialism, placing its emphasis on history as a creative process. Although there is—to take just one example—little room for criticism of the use-value structure of the economy in terms of the internal logic of capital itself, it seems entirely appropriate to rely on the perspective of society as a whole (embodied in the historical potential of the working class) to carry out this all-too-necessary task of revolutionary reason.[97]

Yet if Baran and Sweezy's approach to political economy can be defended as being consistent with the leading principles of historical materialism, one is nonetheless forced to acknowledge that their attempt at a reformulation of Marxian economics for the era of monopoly capitalism tends to leave radical political economy in a state of conscious disarray. Thus it is impossible to avoid the conclusion that the day-to-day workings of the law of value—quite apart from the issue of monopoly profits in themselves—are far less clear cut in the society of monopoly capital, as pictured by Baran and Sweezy, than in the atomistically competitive system of Marx's time.

According to Sweezy, what Marx called the "law of value"

> summarizes those forces at work in a commodity-producing society which regulate (a) the exchange ratios among commodities, (b) the quantity of each produced, and (c) the allocation of the labor force to the various branches of production. The basic condition for the existence of a law of value is a society of private producers who satisfy their needs by mutual exchange. The forces at work include, on the one hand, the productivity of labor in the various branches of production and the pattern of social needs as modified by the distribution of income; and, on the other hand, the equilibriating market forces of competitive supply and demand. To use a modern expression, the law of value is essentially a theory of general equilibrium developed in the first instance with reference to simple commodity production and later on adapted to capitalism.[98]

More generally, the law of value, as Thomas Sekine has written, "simply states that the value of a commodity is equal to the quantity of socially necessary labor directly or indirectly spent for the production per unit of that commodity."[99] The "law of value," then, is a kind of shorthand expression for the central gravitational tendency of a purely capitalist economy (modeled after the era of free competition), through which conditions of market equilibrium and technical efficiency are established on the basis of labor values.

The penetration of the sales effort into the production process and the promotion of what Szlajfer has called "formal use values"—or use values that have social utility only for capital itself—obviously destroys much of the logical coherence of the law of value insofar as it pertains to concrete capitalist conditions. Thus it is much more difficult to assume, on anything like realistic grounds, that there is a developmental tendency for socially necessary labor alone to be incorporated into the structure of output.[100] And this means that much of the potential surplus product may be concealed through waste built into the cost structure of variable capital itself.

When added to better known distortions in the operation of the system under monopoly capitalism, such as the modifications in transformed values (or prices of production) induced by monopolistic mark-ups and the increasing degree of control that individual giant firms are able to exercise over the technological traits of the system, it is only realistic to conclude that the law of value no longer works in an orderly fashion. But does this mean that value theory should be abandoned? This is a question that Baran and Sweezy did not answer directly. Nevertheless, if they had done so, as Sweezy has since made clear, their answer would have been an emphatic "No." As Szlajfer has stated, it is just at this point that Marxian value theory "proves to be absolutely supreme over any other theory of profit and distribution."[101]

In the first place, the very principles that allow us to perceive the distortions at the level of production provide us, at the same time, with the basis for a further synthesis. Thus it is possible to activate the secondary determinants of accumulation in the Marxian scheme, involving the question of unproductive labor in the widest possible sense (including the issue of specifically capitalist use values), as a conceptual bridge between the theory of a comparatively rational order, based on nineteenth-century conditions, and its comparatively irrational successor in the twentieth century.

In the second place, it is possible to make sense of the present as history by looking forward from the past and "backward from the future." The relatively irrational world of monopoly capitalism, in which the law of value asserts itself only in the most general terms, need not be viewed solely by looking forward from the era of free competition, but can also be discerned by "looking backward" from a rationally ordered socialist society. And in this way one is better able to perceive the extent to which surplus value is becoming an ever more antagonistic form of the surplus product.

3

Free Competition and Monopoly Capital

Competition

Much of the "stagnation of Marxian social science," Baran and Sweezy contended in the opening pages of their book, could be attributed to the fact that, notwithstanding the contributions of Hilferding and Lenin, "the Marxian analysis of capitalism still rests in the final analysis on the assumption of a competitive economy."[1] And thus real history could be expected to diverge to an ever greater extent from the world of Marx's *Capital* within the crucial realm of competition itself:

> We must recognize that competition, which was the predominant form of market relations in nineteenth-century Britain, has ceased to occupy that position, not only in Britain but everywhere in the capitalist world. Today the typical economic unit in the capitalist world is not the small firm producing a negligible amount of a homogeneous output for an anonymous market but a large-scale enterprise producing a significant share of the output of an industry, or even several industries, and able to control its prices, the volume of its production, and the types and amounts of its investments. The typical economic unit, in other words, has the attributes which were once thought to be possessed only by monopolies. It is therefore impermissable to ignore monopoly in constructing our model of the economy and to go on treating competition as the general case. In an attempt to understand capitalism in its monopoly stage, we cannot abstract from monopoly or introduce it as a mere modifying factor; we must put it at the very center of the analytical effort.[2]

All of this was very persuasive since it accorded with the dictates of common sense and drew on a long-established tradition in Marxian economics. But from a radical standpoint the realm of appearance, to which competition belongs, can be deceiving. To many of their critics Baran and Sweezy gave the impression of having derived their entire analysis of modern capitalism from the forms of competition, while ignoring the innermost essence of the capitalist system.[3] Thus a long debate on the status of competition and monopoly within the classical-Marxian framework was to emerge, the full dimensions of which have only become apparent in the last few years.

For Marx and the classical economists in general, competition did not create the basic laws of accumulation. Nor, however, was competition a phenomenon to be regarded lightly. In the first place, it was only through this means that the law of value was enforced. As Marx put it in the *Grundrisse,* "Competition executes the inner laws of capital; makes them into compulsory laws toward the individual capital, but it does not invent them. It realizes them."[4] In the second place, it was through competition that prices of production, as transformed labor values and "centers of gravity" for market prices, were introduced.

"Unlimited competition," to quote from another passage in the *Grundrisse,*

> is . . . not the presupposition for the truth of the economic laws, but rather the consequence—the form of appearance in which their necessity realizes itself. . . . Competition therefore does not *explain* these laws; rather it lets them be *seen,* but it does not produce them.[5]

Hence Marxian theory, focused on the inner logic of capital, abstracting from those aspects of the competitive process that related to the diversity of phenomena. And as long as it could be reasonably assumed that free competition between capitals would become in every way more intense as the system evolved, there was no particular reason to give a great deal of attention to the actual functioning of competition as the enforcer of value relations—a role that could be taken for granted.

It is important to understand just how much this approach differed from the neoclassical theory that was to follow. Since the new liberal orthodoxy denied the very existence of labor values as such—the inner essence of the capitalist system in the Marxian outlook—it ended up relying on a very rigid, and mathematically "stylized," notion of competition as an external assumption from which everything else followed.[6] John Elliott has summarized the conditions of "perfect and pure competition" as they evolved in neoclassical theory as follows:

> The conditions of *pure* competition essentially are two: (1) a large number of small households and firms, none of which is large enough relative to the others and/or to the market as a whole to exert significant control over the quantity and, thus, the price of any good or resource: (2) homogeneity within groupings or categories so that no buyer or seller has control over prices through differentiating what he has to buy or sell in the sellers' or buyers' minds. . . .
>
> For pure competition to be characterized by conditions of *market perfection,* two additional qualities are required: (1) perfect knowledge of market conditions (specifically prices and price differences); and (2) mobility and freedom in the movement of households and firms from purchase, production, or sale of one good and/or resource to another.[7]

Obviously, such degrees of purity and perfection are not to be met with in reality. Thus Elliott adds in a footnote:

> It is doubtful that the intellectual giants of economic individualism—men like Adam Smith, David Ricardo, John Stuart Mill, and Alfred Marshall—had very precise concepts of competition and monopoly in mind in their theories of capitalism. Nor is it clear that capitalism's philosophical rationale requires complete *purity* or *perfection* of competition. However, the institutional basis for economic coordination and control in capitalism is some form of competition among economic units, and if competition is to be "workable," it must involve: (1) a relatively large number of buyers and sellers; (2) a high degree of substitutability among products, services, and productive services; (3) a reasonable amount of knowledge among buyers and sellers; and (4) reasonable freedom or mobility in the movement of resources.[8]

If this is the case, then why do orthodox economists insist so strenously on the importance of absolutely *perfect* and *pure* competition in their base level analysis? The theory of "imperfect competition," after all, has never been more than a minor qualification. The answer seems to be that general equilibrium theory, and thus the notion that all factors of production receive an income equal to their marginal product, is entirely dependent on perfect and pure competition as an a priori assumption. Thus no less an authority than John Hicks has remarked that

> it has to be recognized that a general abandonment of the assumption of perfect competition, a universal adoption of monopoly, must have very destructive consequences for economic theory. Under monopoly

> the stability conditions become indeterminate; and the basis on which the economic laws can be constructed is therefore shorn away. Not only is falling average cost consistent with monopoly; falling marginal cost is consistent with monopoly too. There must indeed be something to stop the indefinite expansion of the firm; but it can just as well be stopped by the limitations of the market as by rising marginal costs.[9]

The "destructive consequences for economic theory" that Hicks sees are, however, specific to the neoclassical paradigm. The whole idea of the "productivity of capital" is dependent on the axiom of rising marginal costs, but once the assumption of perfect (and pure) competition is generally abandoned this axiom is called into question.[10] This is not a problem for neo-Marian theory, which argues that marginal costs are fairly constant, and even decreasing, over the relevant range of output, and in a manner consistent with the underlying valorization process,[11] but for neoclassical theory there is no easy way out, as Hicks goes on to explain:

> It is, I believe, only possible to save anything from this wreck—and it must be remembered that the threatened wreckage is that of the greater part of general equilibrium theory—if we can assume that the markets confronting most of the firms with which we shall be dealing do not differ very greatly from perfectly competitive markets. If we can suppose that the percentages by which prices exceed marginal costs are neither very large nor very variable, and if we can suppose (what is largely a consequence of the first assumption) that *marginal* costs do generally increase with output at the point of equilibrium (diminishing marginal costs being rare), then the laws of an economic system working under perfect competition will not be appreciably varied in a system which contains widespread elements of monopoly. At least, this get-away seems well worth trying. We must be aware, however, that we are taking a dangerous step, and probably limiting to a serious extent the problems with which our subsequent analysis will be fitted to deal. Personally, however, I doubt if most of the problems we shall have to exclude for this reason are capable of much useful analysis by the methods of economic theory.[12]

In other words, the choice is a stark one: between dealing seriously with the problem of monopoly as a growing factor in the modern economy and thus undermining neoclassical theory, or denying the essential reality of monopoly and therefore preserving the theory. Quite in keeping with their primary role as apologists, establishment theorists have generally followed Hicks in choosing the latter course.

Unworldly assumptions about competition are therefore particularly characteristic of neoclassical theory. But one should not underestimate the extent to which economists in general are constantly driven toward the postulate of unbridled competition. As John Stuart Mill remarked, it is "only through the principle of competition that political economy has any pretension to the character of a science."[13] Thus the recent revival of classical economic theory in certain quarters has gone hand in hand with an attempt to redefine and reestablish the centrality of free competition, resulting in attacks on both the neoclassical theory of perfect/imperfect competition and neo-Marxian monopoly capital theory (Baran and Sweezy).

Working primarily within the neo-Ricardian paradigm, theorists like James Clifton, John Eatwell, and Philip Williams have tried to distinguish the range of characteristics associated with competition in the classical and neoclassical views. Somewhat paradoxically, this has led to the conclusion that the conception of competition employed by the former was narrower in certain crucial respects than is presently the case for the former. Thus it is argued that the classical theory of competition included notions of the high mobility of capital and widespread access to information, but did not include the idea that competition would be more severe where firms were small and numerous or that the "anonymity" of the individual enterprise was an essential condition.[14] Not surprisingly, the weak point in the argument arises where Marx is concerned. The fundamental contention is that Marx did not go substantially beyond Ricardo's *Principles* with respect to competition, in spite of his analysis of the concentration and centralization of capital. Thus it is argued that for Marx as well, firm size and numbers had little to do with competition.[15] Moreover, Marx's theory of concentration and centralization of capital, we are told, did not relate to competition within particular industries (the issue of market concentration), but was directed simply at aggregate concentration.[16]

These arguments seem to be sufficiently contradicted by Marx himself, who wrote:

> The battle of competition is fought by the cheapening of commodities. The cheapness of commodities depends, *ceteris paribus,* on the productiveness of labor, and this again on the scale of production. Therefore, the larger capitals beat the smaller. It will further be remembered

> that, with the development of the capitalist mode of production, there is an increase in the minimum amount of individual capital necessary to carry on a business under normal conditions. The smaller capitals, therefore, crowd into spheres of production which Modern Industry has only sporadically or incompletely got hold of. Here competition rages in direct proportion to the number and in inverse proportion to the magnitudes, of the antagonistic capitals. It always ends up in the ruin of many small capitalists, whose capitals partly pass into the hands of their conquerors, partly vanish.[17]

Marx not only argued that the "number" and "magnitudes" of capitals within an industry were important factors conditioning the level of competition, but was also the first (apart from Engels) to suggest that economies of scale in production would give large capitals an advantage over smaller ones, accelerating the concentration and centralization of capital both in the economy as a whole and within individual industries (or "spheres of production"). Thus, as he wrote in his *Economic and Philosophical Manuscripts* of 1844, "competition is only possible if capitals multiply and are held in many hands" while "large capital accumulates more rapidly, in proportion to its size, than does small capital, quite apart from deliberate competition."[18]

Theorists like Clifton, Eatwell, and Williams are not unaware of these and other similar passages in Marx, but find various ways of downplaying their importance. Clifton, for instance, writes that, "The concept of competition used by the classical economists and Marx did not require the atomism of individual agents—the essential 'perfection' of perfect competition."[19] But to make this contention acceptable, in the face of statements by Marx like the ones just quoted, he finds it necessary to argue that there is an inconsistency in Marx's argument. In the first volume of *Capital,* Clifton admits, Marx had pointed to the importance of numbers and size as a limitation on the process of competition in its pure sense (associated with the concentration of capital). But in the third volume, Clifton argues, Marx had suggested that

> Competition like all other economic laws—has been assumed by us for the sake of theoretical simplification. . . .in theory it is assumed that the laws of capitalist production operate in their pure form. In reality there exits only approximation; but this approximation is the greater,

the more developed the capitalist mode of production and the less it is adulterated and amalgamated with survivals of former economic conditions.[20]

In the face of this supposed theoretical inconsistency, Clifton claims that "the clear-cut implication" is that the second view has priority—the presumption apparently being that the third volume necessarily represents a more developed theoretical view than the first.[21] However, Marx's position is better understood if we recognize that in presenting the argument on economies of scales, and indeed on centralization itself, in the first volume, he carefully prefaced his remarks by stating that the "laws of this centralization of capitals, or of the attraction of capital by capital, cannot be developed here. A brief hint at a few facts must suffice."[22] This seems to be in conformity with Marx's general methodological approach in which he almost invariably argued from the standpoint of the *strengths* of the capitalist system—in the present context, by assuming that competition operated in its pure form. One might reasonably conclude, then, that the problem of the concentration and centralization of capital, though it originated within the essence of the capitalist system and thus appeared within the first volume, was nonetheless left to be considered in its entirety at a later stage of Marx's unfinished theoretical system. Be that as it may, one cannot simply get around the issue by implying, as Clifton does, that the third volume is, in some sense, Marx's last word—and that the centralization process was therefore entirely compatible with unlimited competition—since the third volume was written before the published version of the first, and represented a lower lever of abstraction (further removed from the essence of the system).[23]

In effect, Clifton adopts George Stigler's contention that "the Marxian theory of the increasing concentration of capital was a minor and inconsistent dissent from the main position in the classical theory of competition."[24] Eatwell merely continues Clifton's argument in this respect, and suggests that the centralization of capital leading to the foundation of joint-stock companies, in Marx's analysis, simply pointed to the greater mobility of capital and thus to a purer concept of competition. Thus we are told that the analysis of competition provided by Marx is "essentially unchanged from the formulation of Smith" and Ricardo.[25]

Perhaps the most cogent argument along this general line is provided by Williams. After referring to Marx's thesis that "larger capitals beat the smaller," and that "competition rages in direct proportion to the magnitudes of the antagonistic capitals," Williams cautions us against thinking that this means what it seems to mean, since there is no indication that Marx had "read Cournot's book"—hence there is no real reason to believe that Marx's views extended to the problem of concentration in particular industries.[26] "It is much more plausible to interpret Marx's writing on monopoly and competition," Williams tells us, "as being in the tradition of English classical economists. Such an interpretation suggests that Marx's notion of the concentration of capital has very little a great deal to do with his understanding of competition."[27] But then how are Marx's comments on the number and size of capitals to be explained? Williams argues that Marx used the term "number of capitals" as "a proxy for the extent to which funds are committed to the market."[28] This is rather specious reasoning, to say the least. On the surface, it would seem much more plausible to conclude that Marx's notion of the concentration (and centralization) of capital has a great deal to do with his overall understanding of competition.

Given this background, it is ironic that certain fundamentalist Marxists have used the ideas of Clifton, in particular, to launch an attack on Baran and Sweezy.[29] After describing the neoclassical approach as the "quantity theory of competition," because of its emphasis on the number and size of firms, John Weeks declares:

> To suggest, as Sweezy and Baran do, that competition is the existence of many competitors, and the absence of monopolized and centralized production, is to use bourgeois ideology as theory. . . .Numbers are not the key, nor is the size of the competitors; the key is the social relations that determine the interaction of producers.[30]

It is true that Baran and Sweezy in *Monopoly Capital*—as distinguished from Sweezy's earlier work, *The Theory of Capitalist Development*—left themselves open to the criticism that their notion of competition was a superficial one since they did not relate it directly to a value theory basis, and thus to the immanent development of the system. However, it is quite a different matter to disparage their approach for its emphasis on the number and size of firms as a central factor conditioning competition in capitalism. As we have seen, Marx had a much wider (as well as deeper) conception of competition than his classical predecessors.[31] For Marx, the magnitude and quantity of individual capitals was a key factor in the competitive struggle—although not by any means the only, or even the most important, one. It is therefore reasonable to suppose that any historical alteration along these lines would also alter the historical conditions of competition in a material way, modifying the accumulation process at a secondary theoretical level.

Monopoly

The foregoing considerations with respect to the theory of competition can only be understood if we turn our attention to the other side of the coin: the issue of monopoly at its highest level of abstraction. In neoclassical theory any departure from the four interrelated conditions of perfect (and pure) competition—an indefinitely large number of small enterprises, homogeneity of products, perfect information, and perfect mobility of capital—involves market imperfections, and—what amounts to the same thing—elements of monopoly.[32] In the newly fashionable approach to competition associated with the current revival of classical economics, it is frequently asserted that only the last two factors properly belong to a general theory of competition, and that product differentiation and the rise of highly concentrated capital do not in themselves imply an increase in monopoly power.[33] It is in this rather convoluted context that Weeks can write, with Baran and Sweezy especially in mind, that "it seems to be the view, among Marxists and non-Marxists alike, that while Marx broke new ground in other areas, his treatment of competition was the same as that of the bourgeois theorists."[34] Since Weeks himself defines the bourgeois approach as the "quantity theory of competition," in line with the work of Clifton and others, he finds it incomprehensible that this element might have entered into Marx's theory as well—even though recent discussions of classical theory have, somewhat inadvertently, added credence to the view that this is one of the ways in which Marx did in fact break new ground. To put the matter differently, it would seem that Weeks is quite right in suspecting that where the *specific* issue of the relative importance of firm size and numbers is concerned, Baran and Sweezy's perspective on competition and monopoly is much closer to the neoclassical approach than it is to the currently popular neo-Ricardian, and fundamentalist Marxist, view. But the same could be said of Marx, Engels, and Hilferding. What serves, first and foremost, to distinguish the neo-Marxian outlook from that of the neoclassical economists is that the former are able to acknowledge the monopoly element as a factor modifying the law of value at a secondary theoretical level, without abandoning any core assumptions.[35] In contrast, neoclassical economists, who derive virtually their entire analysis of capitalism from perfect competition as an external assumption, are faced—because of the indeterminacy of the fundamental cost curves where a substantial monopoly element is concerned—by what Hicks has described as the "threatened wreckage . . . of the greater part of general equilibrium theory," encouraging them to downplay the importance of market imperfections to an absurd degree.

Despite all the recent attempts to conflate the classical-liberal and classical-Marxian theories (to the obvious detriment of the latter), it is difficult to avoid the conclusion that the notion of monopoly capital develops quite naturally out of Marx's theory of accumulation. Capital, by its very nature, is self-expanding value. The individual capitalist experiences the compulsion to enlarge "his" capital as both an objective and a subjective necessity. In the cutthroat world of the capitalist order, both survival and success are largely a function of the rate of accumulation of individual capitals. Moreover, the logic of this process is synonymous with the monopolization of productive resources by an ever diminishing number of capitalists. Capital accumulation presupposes both a growth in the size of individual capitals (concentration) and the fusion together of many capitals into "a huge mass in a single hand" (centralization). The latter process occurs primarily through economies of scale in production and the growth of the credit system (including so-called primary securities or share capital). The competitive struggle therefore results in the destruction of many small capitals and their centralization into a few giant capitalist concerns controlled by a small number of corporate owners and managers. It was on the basis of this analysis that Marx and Engels—in sharp contrast to all of their forerunners and contemporaries—were able to shift quickly and easily to the concrete analysis of joint-stock companies as the rising element in the accumulation process during the latter half of the nineteenth century.[36]

In *Capital,* Marx does not consider whatever modifications in the competitive process might be brought about by the concentration and centralization of capital. Nevertheless, this does not mean that we have to conclude, as many of the traditionalist Marxists have, that Marx believed that this dual process simply increased competition and did not generate monopoly power. Instead it seems more plausible to argue that Marx generally abstracted from any possible effects of the uneven development of the capitalist firm in his analysis of a purely capitalist economy. And in this way the supposed "inconsistency" between Marx's analysis of concentration and centralization (explicitly taking into account the number and size of firms), on the one hand, and his basic assumption that competition would develop in a purer and more unbridled form, on the other, which theorists like Clifton and Williams have pointed to, simply disappears—without denying any single part of his general theory.

All of this is indicative of the fact that Marx's political economy cannot be critically interpreted from the same standpoint as is appropriate in the case of the other classical theorists. Marx's system, in its very conception, was historically specific and was thus consciously modeled after conditions pertaining to the freely competitive stage of capitalism. It was therefore entirely consistent with his overall method to perceive secondary historical tendencies that logically pointed beyond the system (or its existing phase), while initially abstracting from such secondary contradictions and tendencies in order to get closer to the system's own internal logic (adequate to its own concept) and current historical forms. Moreover, it was certainly realistic in the mid-nineteenth century, when Marx was preparing *Capital,* to presume, for the sake of analysis, that capitalism was evolving in the *direction* of a full realization of the bourgeois ideal of free competition. The first definite signs of the emerging order of monopoly capitalism, clearly complicating the competitive process, only appeared in the last quarter of the nineteenth century. Apparently believing, as Baran and Sweezy put it, that the "overthrow of capitalism" would occur "well within the system's competitive phase," Marx tended to view the new, large-scale, corporate enterprise as a manifestation of the socialization of production within the very womb of capitalist society.[37] Hence, while "Marx's vision of the future of capitalism," as Baran and Sweezy also remarked, "certainly included new and purely capitalist forms of monopoly," he provided little systematic analysis of this phenomenon.[38]

Still, Marx does tell us, in a quite different context, how the general problem of monopoly price and its relation to value (and price of production) is to be solved. In a chapter entitled "Illusions Created by Competition" near the end of the third volume of *Capital,* he examines this issue in terms of two possibilities:

> If equalization of surplus-value into average profit meets with obstacles in the various spheres of production in the form of artificial or natural monopolies, and particularly monopoly in landed property, so that a monopoly price becomes possible, which rises above the price of production and above the value of commodities affected by such a monopoly, then the limits imposed by the value of commodities would not thereby be removed. The monopoly price of certain commodities would merely transfer a portion of the profit of the other commodity-producers to the commodities having the monopoly price. A local disturbance in the distribution of the surplus-value among the various spheres of production would indirectly take place, but it would leave the limit of this surplus-value itself unaltered. Should the commodity having the monopoly price enter into the necessary consumption of the labourer, it would increase the wage and thereby reduce the surplus-value, assuming the labourer receives the value of his labour-power as before. It could depress wages below the value of labour-power, but only to the extent that the former exceed the limit of their physical minimum. In this case the monopoly price would be paid by a deduction from real wages (i.e., the quantity of use-values received by the labourer for the same quantity of labour) and from the profit of the other capitalists.[39]

Since the introduction of monopoly price would leave the limits imposed by the value of commodities and by surplus value itself unaltered, it is clear that its effect lies mainly in the area of distribution: with the additional monopoly profits representing either a transfer of surplus value from other capitalists to those enjoying the monopoly position, or from wage labor to the monopolists through a general reduction in the level of real wages. These two possibilities obviously do not preclude each other and as far as commodities consumed by workers are concerned, both types of redistribution are likely to be involved. A deeper understanding of Marx's argument here, however, is dependent on the recognition of three additional facts: (1) Marx has in mind merely a "local disturbance in the distribution of the surplus value" and not a more generalized phenomenon of monopolistic pricing; [40] (2) the argument is an *ex post* one, in the sense that the amount of surplus value is already determined (or, in other words, represents a given static situation);[41] (3) it is assumed that any redistribution from wages would take the form of a *reduction* in real wages (below the value of labor power) rather than a decrease in labor's relative share of income.[42] It is therefore necessary to reinterpret Marx's argument in wider and more dynamic terms.

This has been done by Paul Sweezy:

> The reasoning can be extended to encompass a more generalized spread of monopoly, i.e., of industries able to charge prices above the price of production or value, whichever is higher, and a continuing process of concentration and centralization. In addition to a redistribution of surplus value from more competitive to less competitive sectors, there could take place an increase in total surplus value at the expense of real wages (implying a rise in the rate of surplus value), if workers are unable to protect themselves against monopoly prices for wage goods. To this it might be objected that monopoly prices cannot raise the rate of surplus value except through depressing wages below the value of labor power, and that this would be essentially an unstable and temporary effect. This objection, however, fails to see monopolization as a process that must be viewed historically and as an ongoing part of the accumulation process. While at any particular time the value of labor power can be treated as a given, over a period of time it tends to rise (because of increasing costs of producing labor power and workers' struggles to improve their standard of living). In this context, growing monopolization must be seen not as depressing wages below the value of labor power, but as slowing down the rise in the value of labor power. To this extent, it favors capital against labor by raising the rate of surplus value above what it would otherwise have been.[43]

In this way—as reformulated by Sweezy—the general nature of the link between monopoly price and value in a modern capitalist context becomes clear. But what determines monopoly price in the first place? To this question there is no simple and straightforward answer. As Sweezy has put it:

> There are no general rules for relating monopoly prices to prices of production as there were for relating prices of production to values. About all we can say is that monopoly prices in various industries tend to be higher than prices of production in proportion to the difficulties new capitals have in entering those industries. And of course a corre-

sponding hierarchy of profit rates will emerge, highest in the industries most difficult to enter, lowest in those where entry is free (as is assumed to be the case under competitive capitalism).[44]

The indeterminacy of the solution is connected to the fact that the law of value does not operate in an unobstructed fashion under monopoly capitalism. At the same time, this does not require a repudiation of the labor theory of value: the source of value is not disturbed, only its equilibrium solution. No doubt this is somewhat incomprehensible from a neoclassical economic standpoint, which generally reasons in a huge circle, beginning and ending with the concept of general equilibrium (the circular flow).[45] From the perspective of historical materialism, however, this is less of a problem since it is possible to perceive economic reality as increasingly irrational (even when judged by the standards of capital itself).

The Monopoly Stage

This notion of increasing irrationality has of course been at the core of monopoly theory from the beginning. And since the whole idea of a monopoly stage of capitalism—particularly as conceived by Baran and Sweezy—has been called into question of late in the work of many of the more traditionally minded Marxian theorists, partly on the basis of recent neo-Ricardian conclusions about the theory of competition, it is important to reconsider some of the major tenets of this train of thought.

A great sea change in the history of capitalism occurred during the last two decades of the nineteenth century and the first decade of the twentieth. Hitherto industry had consisted of numerous small family enterprises. But with the sudden emergence of the giant multidivisional corporation near the turn of the century the entire world economy underwent a massive transformation. It has been estimated that between a quarter and a third of *all* U.S. capital stock in manufacturing was directly affected by mergers taking place between 1898 and 1902 alone. The formation of U.S. Steel in 1901 fused 165 separate companies to create a monopolistic corporation controlling approximately 60 percent of the total steel industry.[46] The horizontal integration that occurred in the mergers of this period was to be followed, in successive waves of mergers extending up to the present day, by vertical integration, conglomeration, and multinational corporate development.[47] Needless to say, the new order of business meant that powerful corporate enterprises were now capable of evading, to a considerable extent, the competitive discipline of the market. In short, the transition from freely competitive to monopoly capitalism had taken place.[48]

Although Marx and Engels had noted the appearance of the joint-stock company as a by-product of the concentration and centralization of capital, they had generally viewed this as a harbinger of socialism rather that as the beginnings of a new stage of capitalism. Nevertheless, during the last few months before his death in 1895 Engels was working on a two-part supplement to Marx's *Capital.* The first part was completed, but the second, which concerns us here, remained in outline form. This outline, entitled "The Stock Exchange," starts with observations on the emergence of the industrial securities market, connects this to the fact that "in no industrial country, least of all England, could the expansion of production keep up with accumulation, or the accumulation of the individual capitalist be completely utilized in the enlargement of his business," and views this as the basis for the *founding* of giant capital and the speeding up of the outward impulse toward world colonization.[49]

Although the first major theorist of monopoly capitalism was Thorstein Veblen, a rebel economist of the left who had been influenced by Marx but was not himself a Marxist, it was in the Marxist paradigm that a continuing tradition of monopoly capital theory was to emerge. Thus Rudolf Hilferding's *Finance Capital: A Study of the Latest Phase of Capitalist Development* was published in 1910, and was soon followed by Nikolai Bukharin's *Imperialism and World Economy,* written in 1915, and Lenin's *Imperialism, the Newest Stage of Capitalism,* written in 1916.[50] However, despite "all of his emphasis on monopoly," Baran and Sweezy wrote, "Hilferding did not treat it as a qualitatively new element in the capitalist economy; rather he saw it as effecting essentially quantitative modifications in the basic Marxian laws of capitalism."[51] And while Bukharin and Lenin had extended Hilferding's analysis to construct a theory of imperialism as the monopoly stage of capitalism, the matter was not pursued "into the fundamentals of Marxian economic theory. There, paradoxically enough, in what might have been thought the area most immediately involved, the growth of monopoly made the least impression."[52] Hence Baran and Sweezy declared in the opening pages of their study that:

> We believe that the time has come to remedy this situation and to do so in an explicit and indeed radical fashion. If we are to follow the example set by Marx and make full use of his powerful analytical method, we cannot be content with patching up and amending the competitive model which underlies his economic theory.[53]

Paul Sweezy had already made a major attempt to analyze the laws of motion of monopoly capitalism in his early work, *The Theory of Capitalist Development.* His argument there had focused on interindustry capital flows. Under monopoly capitalism "the equal profit rates of competitive capitalism are turned into a hierarchy of profit rates, highest in the most completely monopolized industries, lowest in the most competitive."[54] In concentrated industries with high profits and high barriers to entry (due to economies of scale, product differentiation, accesss to finance, etc.), investment decisions for the monopolist are "guided by the marginal profit rate in his own industry," inhibiting the actual level of investment. Capital therefore tends, somewhat paradoxically, to flow in reverse: from high to low profit sectors. But as capital flows into the remaining competitive sectors, and—what amounts to the same thing—as competition between giant firms in these areas increases, the average rate of profit, which determines investment in these areas, is driven down. In a nutshell:

> Investment in monopolized industries is choked off; capital crowds into the more competitive areas. The rate of profit which is relevant to investment decisions is therefore lowered. This is a factor causing depressions independent of both the general falling tendency of the rate of profit and the tendency to underconsumption.[55]

Strangely, this argument, which appears to be an indispensable part of any general theory of the laws of motion of monopoly capitalism and which recurs in Sweezy's later writings, does not explicitly appear in *Monopoly Capital* itself.[56] In their joint work Baran and Sweezy did not gear their core argument to an industry-level analysis at all, although the broad phenomenon of barriers to entry and hierarchies of profit rates between industries was always assumed, either explicitly or implicitly. Instead, their analysis was primarily concerned with the Kaleckian observation that the "degree of monopoly" (gross profit margins as a share of total output) would tend to widen in the economy as a whole. Or, in other words, that surplus value would tend to rise at the expense of wages, and would become increasingly concentrated within the realm of large-scale capital.[57] Thus *Monopoly Capital* itself was mainly concerned with the utilization of the potential social accumulation fund, "the problem of surplus absorption."

From the start Baran and Sweezy had made it clear that their analysis was far from being complete, if only because they had neglected the critical issue of the labor process under modern capitalism. The better part of a decade later, Harry Braverman was to fill the gap with his important work, *Labor and Monopoly Capital: The Degradation of Work in the Twentieth Century* (1974). Braverman described the critical impact of Taylorism, or scientific management, on the cost side of advanced industry. This proved to be the real basis for the prodigious profitability of monopoly capital.[58] He verified the fact that Marx's "general law of accumulation" retained all of its validity (aside from the penetration of production by the sales effort) within the labor process itself. Thus it became apparent that the qualitative changes brought about by the rise of monopoly capitalism were chiefly confined to the secondary, but nonetheless fundamental, area of the realization of potential surplus product.[59]

Braverman saw his analysis of the contemporary labor process as belonging to the same internally consistent theoretical framework as *The Political Economy of Growth* and *Monopoly Capital,* and with the addition of his contribution, the neo-Marxian analysis of monopoly capitalism became, in a sense, a complete sketch of the advanced accumulation process.[60] Nevertheless, it became fairly common practice in more traditionalist Marxist circles to suggest that Braverman had been wrong in thinking that his approach was consistent with that of Baran and Sweezy, since the latter, it was frequently alleged, had abandoned Marxian value theory.[61]

Recently the whole idea of a monopoly stage theory, particularly in the form advanced by Baran and Sweezy, has come under attack within the left. John Weeks has argued that Baran and Sweezy's giant corporations, with considerable control over price, output, innovation, and investment, were simply "idealistic resurrections of 'feudal monopolies before competition'"; that the authors of *Monopoly Capital* had asserted that the contemporary economy was "noncompetitive"; that they had, in effect, adopted the views of Proudhon that Marx had rejected; and that their perspective was derived from the perfect/imperfect competition theory of liberal economics.[62] Willi Semmler has written that "recent discussion about the classical and Marxian theories has raised doubt" with regard to both "the correctness of this description of the two stages in the development of capitalism" and "the underlying theory of competition in theory of monopoly capitalism."[63] According to Semmler, there were two separate strands of thought on this question in the work of the early "post-Marxian" theorists. One, represented by Hilferding, had considered Marx's theory of competition as "obsolete," replaced by the organized system of finance capital; while, the other, represented by Lenin, "posited that competition is not abolished by concentration but renewed on a higher level."[64] Thus "Lenin speaks not only of increased monopoly, but also of *monopolistic competition*."[65] In Semmler's view, "Later economists, such as Dobb, Kalecki, Lange, Sweezy, Steindl, and Sherman pick up only one tradition in Marxian literature [that of Hilferding] by concluding that concentration leads to the emergence of a persistent hierarchy of profit rates."[66] Following Clifton and Weeks, Semmler adds that the neo-Marxian perspective is largely derived from neoclassical theory, which can be characterized as a "quantity theory of competition," with its emphasis on the issue of market concentration.[67] And he goes on to argue at length that the empirical evidence purporting to show a significant hierarchy of profit rates based on monopoly power is highly "ambiguous."[68] Anthony Brewer, adopting a similar perspective, has indicated that Baran and Sweezy had advanced a "*static* argument" for "an essentially *dynamic* problem" by claiming that monopolistic firms would restrain output, and had thus abandoned the approach to competition characteristic of classical Marxists like Bukharin and Lenin, who supposedly rejected the idea that corporations might adopt a "live and let live" policy in their overall "rejection of 'ultraimperialism.'"[69] Steve Zeluck, in like-minded fashion, tells us that "Marx never advanced a monopoly stage theory"; that monopoly capital theory is "incompatible" with Marxian value theory; that "empirical proof of this stage cannot be found in contemporary capitalism"; and that "it is hard to resist the temptation to liberal politics if one starts with 'monopoly theory.'"[70] Nor are the arguments of Weeks, Semmler, Brewer, and

Zeluck simply isolated criticisms; rather, they reflect what has become an article of faith among many fundamentalist Marxists. Hence, similar perspectives on monopoly capital theory have been advanced of late by James Becker, Paul Mattick, Paul Walton, Andrew Gamble, and others.[71]

More recent defenses of monopoly capital theory by Sweezy, Howard Sherman, Michael Lebowitz, and myself have made it clear that most of the foregoing criticisms are based on fundamental misunderstandings of the theoretical framework in question. It is true that Marx had no monopoly stage theory (as Baran and Sweezy themselves pointed out, and as Sweezy has indicated on numerous occasions since), but this is scarcely surprising if one considers the historical facts: (1) there was no monopoly capitalism in Marx's day, and (2) Marx was, as it turns out, overly optimistic about the immediate prospects for socialism.[72] Matters were somewhat different for Lenin, who actually popularized the idea that capitalism had evolved from its "freely competitive" to its "monopoly stage."[73] Tracing its ancestry to both Hilferding *and Lenin,* neo-Marxian monopoly capital theory, as Sherman and I have argued, does not assume that the present economy is "noncompetitive," but merely that the nature of competition is radically transformed, with price competition, in particular, playing a much smaller role. Under conditions of oligopolistic rivalry, competition is, to use Schumpeter's term, "corespective," each firm carefully taking into account the price, output, and investment strategies of its major oligopolistic (or monopolistic) competitors. This leads to a situation, in highly concentrated markets, which is roughly analogous to that of a single firm monopoly. At the most fundamental level, it means that monopolistic firms are not simply compelled to invest by the force of competition alone.[74] Whereas there is nothing wrong with the designation "monopolistic competition" (which Semmler has attributed to Lenin), from the standpoint of neo-Marxian theory it is seldom actually used, for the simple reason that it has a very special, technical meaning in the quite different conceptual framework of neoclassical imperfect competition theory.[75]

In fact, none of the modern monopoly capital theorists depart from Marx's analysis of competition per se; instead they interpret it quite differently than Clifton, Eatwell, Williams, Weeks, and Semmler, believing, like Hilferding and perhaps even Lenin, that market concentration (arising out of horizontal integration) and the number and size of firms were important aspects of Marx's theory of competition (and concentration and centralization of capital). As Michael Lebowitz has convincingly demonstrated through close textual examination, the logical "tendency of capital to become One" takes the form, in Marx's writings, of three distinct processes, which can be described in contemporary terminology as horizontal integration, vertical integration, and conglomerate integration (all of which are reflected in aggregate concentration).[76] In this sense it can be said that the classical Marxian approach was equal in scope to that of present-day neoclassical theory, and somewhat wider than that of classical theorists like Smith and Ricardo. Hence it would seem to be self-defeating for radicals to argue that Marx did not go beyond the views of the other classical theorists. Still, one should be careful, at the same time, not to confuse Marxian theory in this respect with the rigid, static models of competition characteristic of neoclassical thought.

Indeed, Sweezy himself has clearly warned against the danger of straightjacketing neo-Marxian monopoly capital theory, after the fashion of more orthodox models:

> One should be careful not to freeze monopoly capitalist theory into the kind of rigid static models that are the hallmark of neoclassical economics. When we say that the average rate of profit is superseded by a hierarchy of profit rates, there is no implication that the industries (or firms) at various levels of the hierarchy must always be the same. There is constant movement within the hierarchy in reponse to both internal and external factors.[77]

But it is precisely this general tendency "to freeze monopoly capitalist theory into . . . rigid static models" that is most evident in the various attempts by radical theorists to disprove the reality of monopoly power and monopoly profits. Semmler's argument that the existence of substantial monopoly profits is presently in question is based on an insufficiently critical approach to the current liberal antitrust debate and the orthodox foundations on which it is erected. For a long time it has been recognized by the more discerning theorists that market concentration, or the percentage of sales accounted for by the four (or eight) largest firms in a single industry, is a poorer and poorer basis on which to measure monopoly power. The reasons for this—as Baran and Sweezy noted, somewhat in advance of the general literature—is that horizontal integration has been succeeded by vertical intregration, and especially conglomeration, as the main forms in which merger activity takes place.[78] Few if any of the giant firms are now confined to a single industry, and the entire system of "industrial classification" has lost much of its former meaning. Conservative, pro-trust theorists, like Harold Demsetz, Yale Brozen, and Stanley Ornstein, have taken advantage of this situation to argue, against the more progressive antitrust theorists, that monopoly power (as measured in terms of market concentration) is either stable or weakening. But to make such arguments stick they have also had to supplement their basic findings by suggesting that the considerable differentials in profits that remain reflect temporary monopoly positions (the Schumpeterian argument), greater efficiency, economies of scale, etc., and not entrenched market power in and of itself. Having once assumed, incorrectly, that the neo-Marxian position on monopoly profit rates is the same as that of the liberal theorists, traditionalist Marxists like Semmler and Zeluck are able to use the arguments of the so-called conservative realists to attack the conclusions of Baran, Sweezy, Dobb, Sherman, Steindl, etc.[79]

In the meantime neo-Marxian theorists, who are not particularly endeared to either side of the liberal antitrust debate, have been working out wider historical conceptions of monopoly power. Thus economists like Richard Edwards, Joseph Bowring (basing part of his analysis on Sweezy's contribution in *The Theory of Capitalist Development*), and Howard Sherman have been shifting from an industry-based to a firm-based analysis, in which a distinction is made (in the formulations of Edwards and Bowring) between "core" and "periphery" firms, defined in terms of *both* size and market share, in order to capture the larger phenomenon of monopoly power on an interindustry level (in the face of widespread conglomeration). Utilizing this approach, it has been possible for Edwards to show that "core firms" in U.S. manufacturing—those holding at least $100 million in assets and located in industries with a four-firm concentration level of 40 percent or more—had profit rates that exceeded those of all other U.S. manufacturing firms by approximately 30 percent in the 1958–71 period. In 1963 (a year in which adequate data is available) such core firms accounted for about half of all income in U.S. manufacturing. This in itself explains why the share of total U.S. manufacturing assets owned by the largest 100 manufacturing firms rose from 35.1 percent in 1925 to 48.5 percent in 1970.[80] Using the core/periphery framework, which as Sherman pointed out in his criticism of Semmler's argument, is merely a broad conception of monopolistic versus competitive firms, Bowring has provided a systematic critique of the question-begging techniques of Demsetz, Brozen, and other conservative theorists in the antitrust debate—the very theorists that Semmler had relied on in the empirical part of his argument.[81] Thus it can still be said that there is an important body of literature pointing to a hierarchy of profit rates related to degrees of monopoly power.[82]

These various disputes within the left about the validity of monopoly stage theory as a general mode of analysis can be traced, in the end, to two basic issues. First, the law of value operates in its fullest sense—establishing an orderly relationship between production and exchange—only as long as competition between capitals serves to enforce the innermost relations of the system in a straightforward way. Recognizing this, Hilferding had written that "the realization of Marx's theory of concentration, of monopolistic merger, seems to result in the invalidation of Marx's value theory."[83] There can be little doubt, in light of the foregoing analysis, that Hilferding overstated the case. What is actually undermined to some extent is not value theory per se, but the Marxian theory of relative prices, i.e., a determinant model of long-run equilibrium prices at the level of exchange.[84] For many radical economists this seems to threaten the very possibility of a scientific approach to capitalist production; and, what is worse, to challenge the direct relevance of Marx's *Capital.* Hence, the more traditionally minded theorists are strongly motivated to search for ways of downplaying the role of monopoly. In fact, this is the case for economists in general, applying to the neoclassical and neo-Ricardian schools as well—and for reasons that are not altogether dissimilar.

For neo-Marxian economists, in contrast, the principle of historical materialism always has priority over the law of value.[85] Since capitalism is becoming increasingly irrational from the standpoint of its own logic, it is necessary to recognize that the theory of a purely capitalist economy, where the law of value operates virtually unhindered, is no longer an adequate guide to the present as history; which means that it is necessary (even at the risk of abandoning pure economic logic) to find ways of adapting the theory to take account of modifications in the laws of motion of the system.[86]

It is at this point that Marxian value theory, given the link made between the quantitative and *qualitative* aspects of value relations, proves itself to be far superior to all other economic paradigms, enabling it to incorporate the monopoly factor into the core of its analysis.[87] It should be remembered that in Marxian theory, as Samir Amin has emphasized, the concept of relative prices—the central problem of most orthodox economic theory—is a relatively minor issue, overshadowed by more fundamental relations of production and distribution.[88]

Second, many of the more fundamentalist Marxists believe that the criticism of monopolies serves—as is definitely the case for the liberal antitrust tradition—as a means of avoiding root and branch criticisms of capitalism itself. Thus Zeluck has argued that Baran and Sweezy lean toward reformism: namely, the notion that by eliminating monopolies and their effects it is possible to create a better, more rational capitalist system.[89] In fact, the neo-Marxist view has nothing in common with liberal theory in this respect. The problem of the monopoly stage, as generally perceived by neo-Marxian theorists, was succinctly expressed by Joseph Gillman:

> To "curb monopoly" would mean to curb capitalism as it has developed into the twentieth century. It is naive to think otherwise. The "fight" against monopoly cannot be to reform it—to transform its private power into public power. That is, the fight has meaning only as a means of transforming capitalism into socialism.[90]

Be that as it may, the existence or nonexistence of the monopoly stage of capitalism must be judged in historical terms, not in terms of whether or not it promotes reformist politics. Historical analysis has to precede revolutionary praxis; their order cannot be reversed.

4

Accumulation and Crisis

The Problem of Capital Accumulation

The modern, neo-Marxian theory of accumulation, of which Baran and Sweezy's *Monopoly Capital* is the best-known example, arose out of the fusion of two distinct strands in Marx's thought: (1) the underconsumptionist approach to the crisis phenomenon, and (2) the analysis of concentration and centralization (leading to the notion of monopoly capital). Since it is only under monopoly capitalism that underconsumptionist tendencies come to the fore, the second strand, with its emphasis on the stagnation of investment, came to characterize the theoretical synthesis as a whole in the eyes of its main proponents.[1]

Most critics of *Monopoly Capital,* however, have continued to single out the underconsumptionist element alone, failing to comprehend the central role of monopolistic accumulation as envisioned in the larger, more complex, synthesis. This seems partly to account for Erik Olin Wright's declaration, made less than a decade ago, that:

> The most serious weakness in the underconsumptionist position is that it lacks any theory of the determinants of the actual rate of accumulation. . . . I have not yet seen an elaborated theory of investment and the rate of accumulation by a Marxist underconsumptionist theorist, and thus for the time being the theory remains incomplete.[2]

Although somewhat misguided—particularly when viewed from the standpoint of the works of Kalecki, Steindl, Baran, Sweezy, and Magdoff as a whole—Wright's statement was not entirely devoid of truth and raised important theoretical issues which we will consider in detail at the end of this chapter.[3] For the moment, it should suffice to point out that the theory of accumulation—at all times the major focus of neo-Marxian political economy—was only presented in skeletal form in *Monopoly Capital* itself.

Hence it would seem that a certain amount of elaboration is needed. In order to accomplish this, it is useful to begin with the earlier analysis of underconsumption presented by Sweezy in *The Theory of Capitalist Development.* Against this backdrop, it should be possible to develop a clearer understanding of the subsequent theory of accumulation under monopoly capitalism provided in such works as Steindl's *Maturity and Stagnation in American Capitalism,* Baran's *The Political Economy of Growth,* and Baran and Sweezy's *Monopoly Capital.*

Underconsumption

Criticisms of the underconsumptionist strand in Marxian crisis theory, while quite common, have generally remained at a fairly low level of sophistication, seldom taking the form of an immanent critique. One of the most widespread procedures—adopted by such major fundamentalist theorists as David Yaffe—is to quote various passages from Marx, Engels, and Lenin criticizing what is variously referred to as "crude," "naive," or "vulgar" underconsumptionism, as seemingly incontestable proof that this general approach to crisis theory is beyond the pale.[4] The problem with this is that not only did Marx, Engels, and Lenin present what can be considered underconsumptionist arguments—i.e., arguments emphasizing the social disproportionality between investment and consumption, the contradiction between the appropriation of surplus product and its ultimate realization—in their own writings, but it is also true that all of the leading realization crisis theorists (including Luxemburg, Sweezy, Baran, Magdoff, and Sherman) have criticized exactly the same "crude," "naive," and "vulgar" approaches to the general problem of underconsumption in what appears to be an identical fashion, and on frequent occasions.[5] It is true that a classic underconsumptionist fallacy existed in Marx's day in the works of Sismondi and Rodbertus, based on the idea that workers cannot buy back the full value of their product. And there have also been crude variants of underconsumptionism (like that of the Russian Narodniks), which claim that a domestic market is inherently insufficient, or other versions, like those of Malthus and Hobson, which assume that oversavings automatically lead to overinvestment and overproduction. However, none of these errors have any place whatsoever in the works of those writers whose names have become synonymous with modern Marxian underconsumptionism, which belong to what Joseph Schumpeter called "the non-spending type" of underconsumptionist analysis.[6]

In his 1942 study *The Theory of Capitalist Development,* Paul Sweezy provided extensive evidence that the contradiction associated with the underconsumption of the masses was an important, though not fully developed, stream of Marx's thinking on the subject of crisis. In order to make a comprehensive theory out of this approach to crisis, Sweezy believed that it was necessary to elucidate it in a more systematic way, demonstrating that it was an obstacle that inhered in the very nature of capital accumulation. "The real task of underconsumption theory," he explained,

> is to demonstrate that capitalism has an inherent *tendency* to expand the capacity to produce consumption goods more rapidly than the demand for consumption goods. To put the point another way, it must be shown that there is a tendency to utilize resources in such a way as to distort the relation between the potential supply and potential demand for consumption goods.[7]

To be sure, as Sweezy had noted previously, one could object to this line of thinking by arguing, in the manner of the early Russian Marxist Tugan-Baranovski, that capitalism was an "antagonistic" system, and hence there was no a priori reason to assume that the expansion of means of production was tied to actual consumption. After all, Marx himself had warned that "it is never to be forgotten that in the case of capitalist production it is not directly a question of use value, but of exchange value, and more particularly of the expansion of surplus value."[8]

Tugan-Baranovski went so far as to insist that capitalism could expand smoothly over the long run with a steady reduction in the share (and even the volume) of consumption, provided that investment picked up the slack (and that the proper proportions in the exchange between departments were maintained).[9] In a not altogether dissimilar fashion the orthodox economist J. B. Clark asserted, in his criticism of Rodbertus, that there was no clear reason why capitalists could not simply "build more mills that should make more mills for ever."[10]

In countering this kind of argument Sweezy provided what was to be the pivotal notion in his early attempt to elucidate the logical foundations of Marxian underconsumptionism. It is important to recognize, he insisted,

> that a contradiction between the ends of production regarded as a natural-technical process of creating use values, and the ends of capitalism as a historical system of expanding exchange value does exist. Not only does it exist; it constitutes the fundamental contradiction of capitalist society from which all other contradictions are ultimately derived.
>
> Traditional political economy tries to slur over or deny this contradiction by the device of assuming that the subjective aim of capitalist production is identical with the objective aim of production in general, namely, the augmentation of utility. Tugan, on the other hand, adopted the opposite method of assuming that the indefinite expansion of exchange value is compatible with the ends of production in general. Marxian political economy, in contrast to both, not only recognizes the contradiction but proclaims it to the skies and rests on this foundation its proof that capitalism is no more permanent than the various social systems which have preceded it.[11]

What served to distinguish Sweezy's early approach to the question of the realization crisis was the idea that this "natural-technical" limitation on capitalist accumulation, imposed by the use-value structure of the system, could be specified in a concrete way. The procedure that he adopted in his attempt to construct a logical proof of a basic underconsumptionist tendency was to begin by assuming full capacity utilization, and then to show that, in the absence of countervailing factors, this would lead to a logical contradiction, one that could be resolved only through "a violation of the original assumption." On the one hand, the characteristic behavior of capitalists ensured that surplus value would rise as a proportion of national income, that accumulation (expansion of capital goods and wage goods) would rise "as a proportion of surplus value," and that investment (expansion of capital goods) would rise "as a proportion of accumulation."[12] This meant that the ratio of the rate of growth of consumption to the rate of growth of means of production would experience a "steady decline." And yet, on the other hand, according to Sweezy, it could be shown that there was a "natural-technical" limitation governing the ratio of the rate of growth in output of consumption goods to the rate of growth of means of production, such that a constant ratio (or "approximate stability") was maintained. As empirical support for this last hypothesis, Sweezy cited a statistical study by Carl Snyder in the *American Economic Review* that had indicated that there was a fairly stable relationship, over the long run, between increases in investment and growth in the value of the product. Taken together, these conditions pointed to the fact that, if national income was increasing at a constant (or declining) rate, potential supply would, in the absence of countervailing variables, exceed potential demand for consumption goods. But since this contradicted the original assumption of full capacity utilization, Sweezy's proof was now complete. In brief, by viewing supply partly as "a natural technical process of creating use values," it was possible to demonstrate that there was a strong tendency toward overproduction in the consumption goods sector, and, by extension, in industry as a whole.[13]

For Sweezy, this tendency toward underconsumption could "manifest itself in one of two ways": (1) actual overproduction of commodities, or (2) a failure to utilize productive capacity fully, and the subsequent atrophy of investment once it was "realized that the additional capacity would be redundant relative to the demand for the commodities it could produce."[14] The first case involved a definite economic decline, or *crisis;* the second case pointed to a longer period of slow growth and rising unemployment, or *stagnation.* In his proof of underconsumption as a contradictory tendency intrinsic to the very nature of capital accumulation, Sweezy did not immediately explore these historical outcomes, but left that problem until two chapters later, to be considered along with "forces counteracting the tendency to underconsumption."

Since, according to Sweezy, a powerful tendency toward underconsumption lay at the very heart of the capitalist system, why had this not generated a state of almost continual crisis, instead of the prodigious upward advance that characterized much of the first four centuries of capitalist history? The answer, he suggested, lay in the larger history of the system where certain counteracting forces could be located. The underlying tendency toward underconsumption did "not in itself constitute a bar to indefinite capitalist expansion," but if it could be demonstrated that the countervailing influences were weakening in extent or intensity, there would be reason to suppose that crises and stagnations were becoming the norm rather than the exception.[15] Five counteracting factors of this type were considered in his analysis: (1) new industries, (2) faulty investment, (3) population growth, (4) unproductive consumption, and (5) state expenditures.

Of these five factors, the first, fourth, and fifth were most crucial to Sweezy's argument. New industries, based on major innovations, might easily spur investment without an equivalent effect, in the short run, on the "output of the finished product." As an example, Sweezy pointed to the railroads, which had been characterized by a period of initial construction (the laying of a vast quantity of track, etc.), before the final demand for the actual transportation service began to assert itself as the overriding influence in this sphere of production. Generalizing on this process with an eye to the economy as a whole, it was possible to argue that all economies went through a period of *industrialization* in which the basic means of production were built up virtually from scratch. After this *maturing process* had run its course, however—that is, after the means of rapidly increasing final output in nearly all spheres of production had been created—the effect of any further new industries, and new innovations, could be expected to diminish "relative to total production," reducing the impact of the kind of relatively self-sustaining investment that had characterized the eighteenth and nineteenth centuries. In this way Sweezy was able to contend that the effect of such spontaneous—or non-income-induced—investment outlets had diminished in importance as a means of countering the tendency to underconsumption during the twentieth century.[16]

Unproductive consumption could be seen as still another means whereby the system compensated for the tendency to underconsumption. The growing magnitude of this phenomenon, Sweezy noted, was closely connected to the "growth of monopoly and the rise of a so-called 'new middle class.'" Economic waste of this kind had the effect of increasing total consumption while absorbing a large part of the social accumulation fund potentially available for investment. It could therefore play a major role in staving off any tendency toward stagnation caused by underconsumption.[17]

State expenditure, most of which actually fell under the category of unproductive consumption, was nevertheless treated by Sweezy as a special case. In terms of social reproduction, he argued, there were three basic types of state spending: (1) state capital outlays, (2) state transfers, and (3) state consumption. State capital outlays, as the first and quantitatively least important of the three, involved the state assuming the role of a capitalist, and thus would probably not modify the basic tendency toward underconsumption in any material way. State transfer payments could only play a counteracting role if the tax system, taken as a whole, became progressive in structure and if transfer payments substantially increased consumption by shifting income from the rich to the poor. While "transfer payments had been evolving in the direction to offset the tendency to underconsumption," this was unlikely to go far enough to play much of a counteracting role. Matters were somewhat different in the case of state consumption. To the extent that this was financed from surplus value itself, it could become a major prop for the imperiled economic system.[18]

Yet in the end Sweezy decided that the tendency to underconsumption outweighed these various countervailing influences in a modern capitalist environment—since the single most important element, the creation of new industries as additional outlets for investment, had been waning in relative importance. In general agreement with the position adopted by Karl Kautsky in 1902 during the great "breakdown controversy," Sweezy argued that objective conditions seemed to foreshadow a persistent tendency toward "chronic depression"—or a trend-line of stagnation around which cyclical ups and downs would still occur—rather than any ultimate "economic breakdown."[19]

If there was a controversial point in Sweezy's overall argument on underconsumption, thus understood, it was to be found in the hypothesis that there was a fixed technical relation between the rate of growth in the output of consumption goods, on the one hand, and the rate of growth of the means of production on the other. Indeed, some critics pointed out that Snyder's data, which had related capital spending to total output rather than to the output of consumption goods directly, provided no definite empirical support for Sweezy's argument.[20] Still, assuming that the sum of investment in means of production and the output of consumption goods are roughly equal to total output, it would appear that any data indicating that (1) the rate of growth in investment over the long run is proportionate to the rate of increase in total output, would, since (2) the rate of growth in investment is clearly proportionate to itself, suggest that (3) the ratio of the rate of growth of the means of production to the rate of growth in output of consumption goods is fairly constant as well.[21] In fact, many economists, including a majority of economists on the left, would probably agree that there are natural-technical forces that ensure, by means of periodic crises of overproduction or overcapacity, that the investment and consumption sectors of the economy expand roughly in tandem *over the long run*—and this in spite of the fact that investment demand constantly threatens to outpace the demand for consumption goods.[22] Within established economics itself, this basic connection between consumption (or income) and investment finds its formal expression in the well-known accelerator principle.[23]

But it would be entirely unacceptable to leave the matter here. Generalizing on the empirical evidence, Sweezy had formulated a theoretical law that there was a fairly stable relationship between the growth in capital stock and increases in the output of consumption goods (or of total output). Yet this, as one of his Japanese critics, Y. Yoshida, pointed out, appeared to contradict a more fundamental Marxian axiom: the rising organic composition of capital. In response to Yoshida's criticism, Sweezy acknowledged that he had overstated the case *theoretically:*

> Professor Yoshida is correct that the constant ratio between stock of means of production and output of consumption goods (or output of all kinds) cannot be theoretically defended. Given a rising organic composition of capital, this ratio must also rise. But I do not think this is very important from the point of view of the problem of underconsumption. The growth of constant relative to variable capital is a gradual, long-term, technically conditioned trend which certainly cannot be expected to accommodate itself to the manner in which fresh surplus value is capitalized. As a first approximation, therefore, it may be quite legitimate to postulate a constant ratio between capital and output.[24]

The significance of this statement is best understood if we recognize that Sweezy—although he may not have been fully cognizant of it yet—was in effect denying any major historical role for Marx's tendential law of the falling rate of profit under modern capitalist conditions, while still recognizing its validity at a purely *theoretical* level (and with reference to the nineteenth century).[25] The tendency to underconsumption, as elaborated by Sweezy, relied on the proposition that "the growth of constant relative to variable capital" (i.e., the rising organic composition of capital) was "a gradual, long-term, technically conditioned trend," which had little immediate bearing on the actual course of events—allowing the adoption of the postulate of "a constant ratio between capital and output" (or between capital and the output of consumption goods) "as a first approximation." Since it was also assumed, in Sweezy's model, that the rate of surplus value was rising at a rapid pace, it was clear, as Sydney Coontz was to point out, that the tendency to underconsumption was actually equivalent to the notion that "the theoretical rate of profit" (the value rate of profit at the level of production) was *rising*.[26] In brief, the tendency to underconsumption constituted almost a complete inversion of the classical-Marxian law of the falling rate of profit.

It is not altogether surprising, then, that when the tendential law of the falling rate of profit gained in popularity, during the fashionable "back to Marx movement" of the 1960s and 1970s, underconsumptionist theory was often treated as the main enemy. Nor is there much occasion for surprise in the fact that the resulting polemics often did more to obscure the real issues than otherwise. Thus in his very influential review of crisis theories Anwar Shaikh wrote:

> The fundamental error in Sweezy's analysis is the traditional underconsumptionist one of reducing Department I to the role of an "input" into Department II. Once this assumption is made, it necessarily follows that an increase in production of producer goods must expand the capacity of *consumer* goods. But this is false: producer goods may be used to make producer goods also, and as we noted in the critique of Luxemburg, expanded reproduction *requires* that they so be used. Contrary to Sweezy's reasoning, it is perfectly possible to have a rising ratio of machines and materials per worker and proportional growth of both Departments, *while still having expanded reproduction.*[27]

The trouble with this interpretation is that not only did Sweezy *not* advance the "fundamental error" alluded to here, but Shaikh's method was simply to set up a "straw man" version of the general underconsumptionist approach, to be knocked down with the arguments of Tugan-Baranovski. Given the fact, noted above, that Sweezy constructed his entire theory of underconsumption with an eye to Tugan's views, it is not difficult to provide an answer to this type of criticism. Thus while it is quite true that (1) Department I (the investment goods sector) cannot be entirely reduced to an "input" into Department II (the consumption goods sector); (2) producer goods may be used to make producer goods; and (3) "it is perfectly possible to have a rising ratio of machines and materials per worker and a proportional growth of both Departments, while still having expanded reproduction," all of this merely indicates that the smooth expansion of capitalism is *always possible on paper* (where the realization problem is concerned). It is quite another matter—as Luxemburg, Lenin, Bukharin, Sweezy, Kalecki, Coontz, and others have argued—to presume that this *formal possibility* becomes a *material reality.*[28] Although mills can be built to produce more mills, it would be wrong to conclude from this, as Tugan did, that there are no natural, technical, or social limitations to this process. Sooner or later investment is brought up short by the fact that it must satisfy final demand, and hence it cannot be expected to expand for long periods of time independently from consumption. In Sweezy's theory, the specific goal of capitalist production, namely, the expansion of *exchange value* for its own sake, and the closely connected tendency for the investment-seeking surplus (in the language of *Monopoly Capital*) to grow at the expense of consumption, eventually comes up against the barrier imposed by *production in general,* requiring the creation of definite *use values.* Herein lies the fundamental contradiction of capitalist production, from which all others are ultimately derived.

Overaccumulation

Nevertheless, it need hardly be mentioned that what requires further elaboration in the foregoing analysis of the accumulation process is the specific pattern of investment demand. Unless it can be shown to encompass the reality of both underconsumption *and* underinvestment, the general underconsumptionist, or realization crisis, perspective necessarily falls short of theoretical closure.

Some of the larger implications of Sweezy's analysis, with respect to the theory of investment, were taken up by Evsey Domar in an article entitled "The Problem of Capital Accumulation," which appeared in the *American Economic Review* in December 1948.[29] Domar, one of the originators, along with Roy Harrod, of Keynesian growth theory, introduced his discussion of Sweezy's model by stating:

> The problem of capital accumulation has been fairly popular among economists, particularly among those with underconsumptionist leanings, such as Marxists and Keynesians. In recent literature, the most interesting and explicit formulation belongs to Paul M. Sweezy, to whom the main part of the present section will be devoted. A good

theoretical exposition belongs to R. F. Harrod, in a paper published in 1939. Similar views can be found also, in one form or another, in the writings of Hansen, Kaldor, Kalecki, and others.[30]

The crucial assumption in all of these theories, Domar argued—whether it was explicit, as in Sweezy, or merely implicit, as in Hansen—was the notion that the capital-output ratio was fairly stable (increasing only very slowly). Thus a rising proportion of savings *(ex ante)* in total output could not be easily absorbed by a simple process of capital deepening. Adopting Sweezy's premises—although substituting the more general capital-output ratio for Sweezy's capital-consumption goods output ratio—Domar argued that Sweezy had in certain respects *understated* the contradiction intrinsic to the capital accumulation process. According to Domar, Sweezy had made a "logical error" in contending (in the algebraic appendix to his argument) that if an increasing fraction of an expanding national income is to be invested without a crisis ensuing, national income itself would have to grow at an *increasing absolute rate.* On the contrary, Domar argued, if the percentage ratio of investment to income is increasing it is necessary for national income to grow *at an increasing relative rate* in order for full employment to be maintained. But according to Sweezy's overall analysis it was highly unlikely that even an increasing absolute rate of growth could be maintained for any length of time in a mature capitalist economy. Thus the tendency toward a widening underemployment gap seemed all the more probable. By actually implying that an increasing absolute rate of growth might provide a possible way out of the dilemma, Sweezy had weakened his own theory unnecessarily.[31]

Commenting on Domar's article two years later in his "Reply to Critics," Sweezy stated:

> *From the point of view of aggregative analysis* [as opposed to the use of the Marxian reproduction schemes], Professor Domar's criticisms seem to me to be on the whole well taken. If one looks at aggregates, there is no justification for postulating a special relation between stock of capital and output of consumption goods . . . and Professor Domar is right to substitute the relation between stock of capital and total output. Moreover, by making this change, and by a few further emendations, he shows that it is possible to obtain stronger results than I obtained in the book. There is, however, this important difference: since consumption has been merged into total output, the results

> obtained by Professor Domar's method can no longer be said to have any relation to the problem of underconsumption. That problem simply diasppears, and what emerges from his reasoning—or it might be more accurate to say, what could be derived from his reasoning—can perhaps be called a theory of a tendency to overaccumulation.[32]

Yet, as we shall see, it was Domar's explanation of the difficulties inherent in maintaining a rate of investment that was an increasing proportion of national income, rather than Sweezy's earlier purely underconsumptionist approach, that was to be utilized to demonstrate the absurdity of a "Tugan-Baranovsky path" of self-sustaining investment within *Monopoly Capital* itself.

A far more important elaboration of Sweezy's underconsumptionist argument was to be provided by Josef Steindl in *Maturity and Stagnation in American Capitalism* (1952). In a discussion of underconsumption theory at the end of his book, Steindl agreed entirely with the substance of Sweezy's proof.[33] But he went on to state that, "As the theory stands, there is, however, a snag in it. It presupposes a secular increase in the ratio of investment to consumption."[34] It will be recalled that Sweezy's attempt to construct a logical proof of a tendency to underconsumption had initially assumed full utilization of capacity and thus the automatic investment of the social accumulation fund. The proof had then consisted in showing that given Sweezy's theoretical premises, a logical contradiction emerged, pointing to the reality of excess capacity and the wasting away of a considerable part of the investment-seeking surplus. Rather than emphasizing crises of overproduction, his analysis had suggested that the most likely result was slow growth and rising unemployment, or secular stagnation, rooted in the stagnation of investment itself. Yet Sweezy did not actually extend his analysis to the point that he systematically examined the concrete aspects of the contradiction in the context of a real world economy in which the rate of investment, the rate of growth, and final realized profit rates were all stagnant (or in decline).[35] For Steindl it was not enough to demonstrate that a tendency to underconsumption was deeply rooted in the mode of capitalist development; it was also necessary to provide a theory of the specific determinants of the actual rate of accumulation.

Steindl then proceeded to explain that the theory of "maturity and stagnation" that he had developed in his book, on the basis of Kalecki's earlier analysis of accumulation under monopoly capitalism, contained all of the elements necessary to complete the Marxian underconsumptionist framework. Describing the main contours of his theory with the utmost brevity, he wrote:

> To take account of the realities of the situation the under-consumption theory needs a different re-interpretation. If we think of it, the tendency for the capitalists' share of the product to increase does, after all, exist *potentially*. It is a consequence of the growth of oligopoly. The expression of this tendency can only be an *increase in the gross profit margins*. That means that the actual share of *net* incomes of capitalists need not increase at all. The increased gross profit margins may be compensated by a reduced degree of utilisation, so that there is not a shift of actual income from wages to profits, but a shift of potential income of workers to wastage in excess capacity.
>
> This could be very easily represented in Marxian terms. We should have to say that as a consequence of the rise of oligopoly, the rate of *surplus value produced* tends to increase: the rate of exploitation rises. But as Marx explained, producing surplus value does not necessarily mean realising it, and the realisation depends on the existence of a sufficient market. We should now say that surplus value can be realised only to the extent to which there is a corresponding amount of investment and capitalists' consumption. If this amount does not increase, then the rise in the rate of surplus value *produced* will not lead to any increase in surplus value *realised* but only to excess capacity.[36]

By indicating the need for "a different reinterpretation," Steindl seemed to be saying that Sweezy's own attempt to extend Marx's underconsumptionist argument, while logically consistent, could be largely supplanted by the wider ranging, and more historically applicable, reinterpretation made possible by Kalecki's theory of the modern accumulation process. The latter approach arose out of a synthesis of the notion of the class composition of social output implicit in Marx's reproduction schemes, on the one hand, and the theory of concentration and centralization of capital, on the other.[37] And by placing its emphasis squarely on the second of these two strands in Marx's argument—i.e., the analysis of concentration and centralization, and the theory of monopoly capital to which it naturally led—the Kalecki-Steindl theory was able to solve not only the problem of the specific determinants of investment demand, which must form an integral part of any fully elaborated underconsumptionist argument, but was also able to provide a precise explanation as to why this contradiction suddenly came to the fore in the twentieth century and not before.

As Steindl went on to remark, the "gross profit margin," or the mark-up on cost price in Kaleckian theory, might be "tentatively" identified with "surplus value produced" (although it would certainly be more correct to identify it with the "value rate of profit" in the Marxian scheme, which is the surplus over cost price).[38] The theory then states that although the rate of surplus value, and the value rate of profit at the level of production, are increasing, net realized profit rates may actually be stagnant (or even in decline, along with investment), as reflected in rising amount of excess capacity. Moreover, the logic of the argument is such that it is precisely because monopoly capital seeks to maintain its high gross margins (and excessive rates of surplus value), in the face of downturns in demand, by reducing its utilization rate (rather than its prices), that a chronic condition of secular stagnation emerges, since the degree of capacity utilization is itself the main determinant of investment demand. At one and the same time monopoly capital promotes excess capacity in order to maintain its gross profit margins ("degree of monopoly"), and demonstrates an enormous "fear" of additional excess capacity—causing it to cut back on the level of investment whenever the operating rate falls beyond a certain point.[39] According to Steindl,

> this theory can be organically developed out of the underconsumptionist approach of Marx. It requires a few additional concepts and hypotheses, especially the effect of excess capacity on accumulation, but basically it rests on the idea of a production of surplus value which is not realised, and this happens to be the way in which Marx literally formulated the underconsumptionist approach.[40]

With the general stagnation of investment and the emergence of an endemic realization problem, the degree to which the effective demand gap actually materializes comes to depend, as Kalecki metaphorically expressed it after the fashion of Rosa Luxemburg, on the existence of so-called external markets, such as government spending on armaments.[41] Thus, the Kalecki-Steindl theory (in a manner not unlike Sweezy's early analysis) brought the issue of economic waste into the very center of economic analysis.

Steindl had attempted to formulate a purely "endogenous" theory of long-run (in addition to short-run) investment—going beyond Kalecki to some extent in this regard—based on the laws of motion of monopoly capital. It was possible to offer an explanation of the entire problem of maturity and stagnation, he believed, without being forced (like Hansen and Schumpeter) to take "the explanation . . . back to certain events like technological change which remain unexplained."[42] However, Sweezy openly dissented from this part of Steindl's argument. Reviewing Steindl's book, Sweezy wrote that there were "many factors that escaped his analytical net" as a consequence of his endeavor to exclude (or subordinate) many of the so-called exogenous factors. The most significant of these missing elements, in Sweezy's opinion, was the relative impact of "new industries as outlets for accumulation," as the system moved from one phase to another. For Sweezy, the object was to view "the logic of the economic system" in a way that would include all of the vital historical forces "shaping the trend of accumulation."[43]

In *The Political Economy of Growth* (1957), Paul Baran advanced a theory of accumulation under monopoly capitalism along the lines worked out by Kalecki and Steindl. But while Baran relied heavily on Steindl's conception of the part played by excess capacity in limiting investment, he stopped somewhat short of a systematic discussion of the problem.[44] And although Baran came out strongly in favor of Steindl's attempt to construct an endogenous theory of long-run investment, in which "technological progress and innovation" were "a function of investment rather than *vice versa*" (even going so far as to criticize the views of Kalecki and Sweezy in this respect), he was later to acknowledge that he had "devoted insufficient space to the undeniable dialectical interaction of the two processes."[45]

Monopoly Capital, in contrast, provided a fairly complete, if somewhat skeletal, theory of investment. Basing their argument on their central law of "the tendency of the surplus to rise"—derived from the Kaleckian notion of widening profit margins (or an increasing "degree of monopoly" in the economy as a whole)—Baran and Sweezy went on to focus their analysis on "the problem of surplus absorption," or the demand side of the accumulation process.[46]

Yet since this involved a definite change in emphasis from the more traditional underconsumptionist argument, placing its stress not on the tendency for the share of *consumption* in total product to decline but on the other end of the disproportionality between the underlying consumption base and the social accumulation fund—

i.e., on the problem of realizing the entire surplus product potentially available for productive *investment*—Sweezy was eventually to relabel this more advanced approach as "overaccumulation theory."[47] Although the root contradiction was still one of underconsumption, the neo-Marxian theory of accumulation under monopoly capitalism was directed at solving the much more difficult problem of the various modes of utilization of potential surplus product.

"In general," Baran and Sweezy wrote, "surplus can be absorbed in the following ways: (1) it can be consumed, (2) it can be invested, and (3) it can be wasted."[48] Since capitalist consumption as such tended to decrease in relative importance with the growth of surplus, the question of realizing a rising share of surplus in total income came to rest increasingly on the availability of investment outlets and the spread of economic waste. The bulk of *Monopoly Capital* itself was thus devoted to a consideration of the problem of economic waste. But it was preceded by a very tightly constructed argument on the absence of sufficient investment outlets, which took the form of the following logical steps: (1) the economic absurdity of a "Tugan-Baranovsky path" of accelerating investment; (2) the interdependence between investment and operating rate; and (3) the subordination of "normal" innovations to the capital accumulation process.[49]

In criticizing the exteme case put forward "by Tugan-Baranovsky in his well-known attempt to refute all underconsumption theories of economic crisis,"[50] Baran and Sweezy did not rely directly on Sweezy's original underconsumptionist argument, constructed with an eye to Tugan, but on Domar's reformulation of Sweezy's argument (discussed above):

> The logic of the situation is as follows: if total income grows at an accelerating rate, then a larger and larger share has to be devoted to investment; and, conversely, if a larger and larger share is devoted to investment, total income must grow at an accelerating rate. [Here they cited Domar's essay, discussed above.] What this implies, however, is nonsensical from an economic standpoint. It means that a larger and larger volume of producer goods would have to be turned out for the sole purpose of producing a still larger and larger volume of producer goods in the future. Consumption would be a diminishing proportion of output, and the growth of the capital stock would have no relation to the actual or potential expansion of production.[51]

But if the snowballing growth pattern suggested by Tugan's analysis is thus "ruled out as totally unrealistic," Baran and Sweezy go on to argue,

> one is left with the inescapable conclusion that the actual investment of an amount of surplus which rises relatively to income must mean that the economy's capacity to produce grows more rapidly than its output. Such an investment pattern is not impossible; indeed, it has frequently been observed in the history of capitalism. But what is impossible is that it should persist indefinitely. Sooner or later, excess capacity grows so large that it discourages further investment. When investment declines, so do income and employment and hence also surplus itself.[52]

It will be noticed that the argument at this point resembles Steindl's, in the sense that it is the growth of excess capacity that eventually shuts off investment. But in Steindl's analysis the fear of unplanned excess capacity conditions investment directly through its influence on the profit expectations (and output planning) of capitalists.[53] Baran and Sweezy, in contrast, generally argue more along the lines of a theorist like Hansen in couching even the short-run problem in terms of investment outlets.[54] Thus in their version of the nonlinear investment function, Baran and Sweezy introduced the notion of the "profitability schedule," or the relationship between profit rates and capacity utilization, showing that since the share of overhead in total costs falls steadily as the utilization rate continues to rise above a certain point (the break-even point in which profits and costs are exactly equal), and since, moreover, variable costs per unit of output can be assumed to be fairly stable over the relevant range of output, it follows that aggregate profits will rise rapidly as higher capacity utilization rates are obtained, and fall rapidly as the level of utilization falls.[55] The entire relationship between profit rates and capacity utilization was illustrated empirically, in the form of a positively sloped linear function (with the rate of return on the vertical axis and the operating rate on the horizontal axis), using the case of U.S. Steel.[56] Treating surplus at this point in their argument as basically equal to aggregate profits, Baran and Sweezy could then write:

> As surplus shrinks, the investment-seeking part of it shrinks more than in proportion. On the downswing, in other words, the ratio of consumption to both surplus and total output rises, and this sooner or

> later puts a stop to the contraction. The lower turning point is reached when the amount of surplus seeking investment is exactly absorbed by the available investment outlets. At this point a temporary equilibrium is reached which is characterized by the existence of excess productive capacity and unemployed workers. The reverse side of the coin is that an upswing, however initiated, generates a similar rapid absolute and relative increase of surplus. As soon as the investment-seeking part of the surplus exceeds available investment outlets, the expansion comes to an end. And it should be remembered that this upper turning point may be reached long before full utilization of capacity or full employment of labor is achieved.[57]

This description of the normal investment cycle actually reflects Baran and Sweezy's view that secular stagnation, or a widening underemployment gap, is endemic to the monopoly capitalist economy. Although there is a "temporary equilibrium" at the bottom of the downswing (where the investment-seeking surplus "is exactly absorbed by available investment outlets"), which will be followed sooner or later by another upswing ("however initiated"), it is suggested that the expansion may abort well before full capacity utilization is reached. Here it must be remembered that not only does the surplus rise rapidly in an expansion—and its investment-seeking portion even more so—but the motor force of any expansion is the creation of new productive capacity. Eventually "the investment-seeking surplus exceeds available investment outlets" as a condition of overcapacity in relation to the underlying consumption base emerges, making any further expansion of productive capacity through new investment unprofitable—in the near term for the individual firm.[58] Moreover, the problem is likely—unless certain countervailing factors intervene—to get worse over time. The reason for this is "the law of the rising surplus" itself, which Baran and Sweezy illustrate by an upward shift in the entire (positively sloped) profitability schedule; and which can be translated as lower levels of capacity utilization at every given profit rate, and higher profit rates at every given level of utilization, creating (as the rate of surplus value continues to rise) a constantly compounded problem of realization.[59]

The essence of the stagnation dilemma, then, lies in the fact that as the rate of exploitation rises in the economy as a whole, it is more and more difficult to maintain an upswing, since the economy is constantly faced by a condition of overcapacity in relation to final demand.[60] "The tragedy of investment," Kalecki wrote, "is that it causes crisis because it is useful."[61]

All of this, however, related only to the "endogenous" theory of investment, as Schumpeter and others had framed the problem.[62] In confronting the issue of "exogenous" (non-income-induced) investment associated with the introduction of new technological innovations, Baran and Sweezy argued that where "normal" innovations were concerned—"the kid of new methods and new products . . . which have been forthcoming in a steady stream throughout the capitalist period"—the narrow profit maximization strategies of monopolistic firms were paramount.[63] Thus the large corporations tended to slow down the actual implementation of the more capital-absorbing innovations so as to preserve existing capital values. As Baran and Sweezy themselves put it:

> Whereas in the competitive case no one, not even the innovating firms themselves, can control the rate at which new technologies are generally adopted, this ceases to be true in the monopolistic case. It is clear that the giant corporations will be guided not by the net effect of the new method considered in isolation, but by the net effect of the new method on the overall profitability of the firm. And this means in general that there will be a slower rate of introduction of innovations than under competitive criteria.[64]

Hence Baran and Sweezy came out strongly in support of Steindl's basic conclusion that "under monopoly there is no necessary correlation, as there is in the competitive system, between the rate of technological progress and the volume of investment outlets."[65] Still, this did not mean that monopoly capitalism would not be characterized by rapid increases in productivity. Here they reinforced their argument with two additional points: (1) there was no indication that monopoly capital would actually "suppress new techniques" altogether; and (2) the implementation of those innovations which required little investment in plant and equipment would continue to occur at a steady pace. In this category, they pointed out, belonged those innovations which mainly had the effect of speeding up the rate of production with existing plant and equipment. Indeed, in Kalecki's argument, from which Baran and Sweezy's was partially derived, this had been tied to the fact that the growing emphasis on scientific management of the labor process had reduced the role of heavy investment, thus intensifying the problem of surplus absorption—an observation that was to find its natural complement years later in Harry Braverman's *Labor and Monopoly Capital,* which, as noted earlier, demonstrated the importance of Taylorism, or scientific management, as the real basis on which the whole monopoly capitalist order was erected.[66]

According to Baran and Sweezy, then, the tendency of the investment-seeking surplus to rise as a proportion of total income under monopoly capitalism ran up against those contradictions that formed its natural counterpart. The kind of accelerating investment and income path that would be required to absorb this surplus, through the creation of ever greater shares of capital stock in total output, could scarcely be maintained for any length of time, given the limitations imposed by final consumption. But the failure to absorb all of this investment-seeking surplus—or the inability to realize potential profits—meant the growth of massive quantities of excess capacity which would depress the rate of investment (and final profit rates) still further. The economy would touch bottom when the actual surplus had fallen to the point that it was entirely absorbed, due to the rising share of consumption in total output during the downswing, and this in itself would help create the conditions for a further rise in output. But faced with a chronic condition of overcapacity, the upswings would generally fall short of full capacity utilization and investment would stagnate over the long run, fluctuating around and close to the level of zero net investment.[67] In Kalecki's simplest model, actual, realized surplus is equal to investment plus capitalists' consumption.[68] But neither of these was sufficient, given existing profit margins, to absorb the potential surplus product. Hence, short of any countervailing influences, the analysis pointed, much as Sweezy's original underconsumptionist position had, to the likelihood of secular stagnation.

Surplus Absorption and Economic Waste

In *The Theory of Capitalist Development,* Sweezy had listed unproductive consumption as a major countervailing influence to the general tendency toward stagnation. In the work of Kalecki, the later analysis provided by Baran, Sweezy, and Madgoff, and the recent contributions of Szlajfer, this factor has been incorporated increasingly within the very core of economic analysis.[69] As usual, Kalecki summed up the essence of the problem with the utmost economy of style, pointing out that the so-called external markets allowed "profits to increase above the level determined by private investment and capitalists' consumption."[70] Simplifying this slightly, we can say that a comprehensive theory of accumulation under monopoly capitalism would have to account for the growing significance of unproductive labor by explicitly recognizing that the social accumulation fund potentially available for development is equal to the sum of capitalists' consumption, investment, *and economic waste.*[71]

The issue of economic waste thus formed the pivotal element around which Baran and Sweezy's *Monopoly Capital* was organized. They began their famous chapter on the "sales effort" by noting that although "economic theory has traditionally centered its attention on capitalists' consumption and private investment"—in treating the various ways in which aggregate profits are employed—"other modes of utilization" have not been entirely neglected, particularly in the work of Marx and "a long line of heretical 'underconsumptionists.'"[72] These earlier insights into the problem pointed to the state and church as consumers of surplus product, as well as to the role of unproductive workers, and what Marx had called "expenses of circulation." Yet even though Marx, in particular, had devoted considerable attention to the issue of unproductive expenditures, this "had been treated as a subject of secondary interest" within the overall analysis of capital accumulation.[73]

The reasons for this, according to Baran and Sweezy, were not difficult to discern. In the early nineteenth century, when industrial capitalism was being consolidated—having displaced the earlier mercantilist phase—the role of unproductive expenditures, broadly perceived, seemed to be diminishing in force, with capitalism evolving toward its "pure form." It was, in any case, clear that the new age of "machinofacture" or "Modern Industry," to use Marx's terminology, had reduced the relative role of state and church, of merchant and landlord capital. Moreover, Victorian capitalism was characterized by a dearth of capital, resulting from conditions of early industrialization and atomistic competition, with the falling rate of profit of classical and Marxian economics constituting the proximate cause of secular crisis in the economic system. Under these circumstances, it was reasonable to assume that waste would be kept to a minimum. However, with the advent of the "law of the rising surplus," and the "problem of surplus absorption," in the monopoly stage, the phenomenon of economic waste began to reassert itself. And as waste rose in relation to capitalists' consumption and investment, it increasingly dominated "the composition of social output, the rate of economic growth, and the quality of society itself."[74]

Having established the theoretical basis for their approach in this way, Baran and Sweezy proceeded to analyze the following forms of waste in the actual utilization of potential surplus product: (1) *The sales effort,* consisting of (a) "waste in the business process" (including "advertising, market research, expense account entertaining, the maintenance of excessive numbers of sales outlets, and the salaries and bonuses of salesmen," as well as expenditures on such closely connected "activities as public relations, lobbying, the rental and maintenance of showy office buildings, and business litigation"); and (b) "penetration of the production process by the sales effort" (including "variation in the product's appearance and packaging, planned obsolescence, model changes," etc.); (2) *military spending;* and (3) *diversion of potential surplus into the financial sector* (listed as "finance, insurance, and real estate" in the national accounts).[75]

In the context of a serious realization problem, these expenditures have played an important role in keeping the effective demand gap narrower than it otherwise would have been, and in bolstering the level of employment and realized profits. At a very general level, the way in which this relates to the accumulation process is not difficult to understand. In Marxian theory the social accumulation fund potentially available for net investment is equal to S, or total surplus value potentially produced. On the demand side, in the simplest Kaleckian model, this finds its counterpart in I + L, where I (in this case) equals net investment, and L equals capitalists' consumption.[76] But an increasing rate of surplus value in the economy as a whole means that the share of L (as well as W, or wages) in total product tends to decline, while I is restrained in relation to the investment-seeking surplus, by the tendency to generate an overcapacity to produce in relation to final demand. Hence I + L, or the portion of surplus value realized through "normal channels," tends to be less than S, holding down the actual rate of profit, in relation to its potential, in the economy as a whole.

Here the other main element of demand for potential surplus product in a closed economy enters in. The absorption of economic surplus, according to Baran and Sweezy, is equal to I + L + U, where U equals the demand for unproductive expenditures (beyond capitalists' consumption itself). The actual rate of profit can therefore live up to its potential, to some degree, despite a decline in "the sum of capitalists' consumption and investment, as a ratio of their capital," depending on the extent to which U rises as a proportion of capital stock.[77] Yet the continual existence of idle productive capacity, notwithstanding the vast outpouring of waste, means that an effective demand gap nonetheless remains, so that S is greater than I + L + U. S is also greater than S_r (its realized portion); and $\frac{S}{K}$, where K is the value of total capital stock, is greater than $\frac{I + L + U}{K}$, or the rate of profit as determined by demand. (In this analysis, government spending is simply resolved into its constituent parts of transfer payments, public investment, social consumption, *and waste,* with the last predominating once transfer payments are abstracted from.)[78]

Szlajfer has expressed much the same thing, using a modified version of the Sraffian formula for the rate of profit. Sraffa had written down the rate of profit as a linear function $r = R(1 - w)$, in which r is equal to the average rate of profit in the economy, R equals the maximum theoretical rate of profit with wages equal to zero, and w equals the share of wages in the social product. This meant, in accordance with the dictates of classical economics, that profit was essentially a residual of wages (with a "negative correlation" thus existing "between the rate of profit and wages"). The strict determinacy of this formula (once the level of wages or the value of labor power is given), however, arises out of the fact that it implicitly assumes the full utilization of productive capacity. Thus unproductive labor cannot be anything but a deduction from profits, since it diminishes the capacity to employ productive labor to the same extent.[79] Szlajfer therefore reformulated the Sraffian equation for the rate of profit, to account for accumulation under monopoly capitalism, as $P = \lambda\,[R(1 - w)]$, with λ representing the output-capital ratio. To quote Szlajfer himself:

> This equation indicates that the level of the actual rate of profit depends *certeris paribus* on the rate of surplus value (here the most important role is played by the "degree of monopoly") and the degree of utilization of capital stock. However the factors that affect λ and

allow its maximization are usually at variance with the tendency to increase (1 − w). This variance appears as an absence of effective demand ("markets"). Within monopoly capitalism, a growth of non-productive labor as the method to maximize λ becomes the solution.[80]

In other words, as the relative share of surplus (or aggregate profits) in total product increases, the ratio of output to capacity output (which seems to convey Szlajfer's meaning more precisely than output to capital stock) is held down by the emergence of a gap in effective demand. Under these circumstances the "negative correlation" between the profit rate and unproductive labor disappears, since the latter allows additional profits to be realized up to the point in which full utilization is achieved.

These formulations, including the earlier discussion of investment, would seem to give us a fairly clear conception of the main determinants of the actual rate of accumulation, in a closed economy, under monopoly capitalism. Still, the incorporation of the waste factor within the theory of accumulation in this way, in conformity with Baran and Sweezy's model, runs into the problem of the actual criteria adopted to determine the structure of waste itself.

Kalecki seems to have generally dealt with this in terms of Department III in the Marxian reproduction schemes based on capitalists' consumption, and commonly extended to encompass luxury goods financed out of surplus value.[81] It should be noted that this kind of extension to Department III—particularly in the now classic case of military spending—of Marx's concept of unproductive labor has been fairly controversial in Marxian economics. The dispute was touched off in the late 1950s when Jacob Morris presented an argument along these lines, based on Joseph Gillman's recently published work, *The Falling Rate of Profit* (1958). Morris was criticized by certain theorists for failing to conform strictly to Marx's definition of productive labor, which (in its more restrictive sense) was designated simply as labor which was exchanged against capital rather than revenue, and which served to enhance surplus value.[82]

A more radical extension of the notion of unproductive labor, however, was presented in *The Political Economy of Growth* by Baran and *Monopoly Capital* by Baran and Sweezy. Baran and Sweezy went considerably beyond a Department III approach to the problem of waste, actually applying the concept to the composition of wage goods themselves—thereby raising a thoroughgoing challenge to the traditional Marxian perspective, though on the grounds of orthodox Marxian methodology.[83]

In a major critical reappraisal of Marxian political economy that originated in an examination of Baran and Sweezy's work, Szlajfer introduced two theoretical refinements in the analysis of productive and unproductive labor (and in the comparison of economic surplus and surplus value).[84] First, Marx's historical methodology, Szlajfer pointed out, involved the use of the three critical perspectives associated with (1) individual capital, (2) global capital, and (3) society as a whole (or production in general). Given these three different perspectives, it was possible for Marx to treat the question of unproductive labor in a number of quite distinct but logically compatible ways, depending on the particular critical standpoint adopted at any given moment.

The most common definition of unproductive labor—labor which is exchanged against revenue rather than capital—represents the viewpoint of individual capital, and originated historically with the nascent industrial bourgeoisie's attacks on the usages of merchant and landlord capital, and on the role of state and church as consumers of social product, during the mercantilist era (when feudal remnants were still quite strong).[85] This can be thought of (in accordance with the discussion in Chapter 2) as unproductive labor proper.

Other forms of unproductive labor (in the generic sense), such as capitalists' consumption, expenditures on war and preparation for war, and advertising, are easily recognizable as forms of waste from the standpoint of global capital (but not from the perspective of individual capital), since they do not enter into the socially necessary costs of either capital goods or wage goods.[86] Hence, the purely *formal* conflict that arose with respect to certain of Marx's definitions of unproductive labor (those associated with the perspective of global capital) can be avoided by simply substituting the term "unreproductive," indicating that the criterion adopted is what is socially reproductive, as visible to global capital. This distinction was already present in Marx's writings, and has been extended by Ian Gough, myself (influenced by Szlajfer), and Jacob Morris.[87]

Moreover, it is worthwhile to note in passing that the unproductive character of luxury goods production is one of the major conclusions associated with the most prominent set of solutions to the "transformation problem," growing out of the work of Bortkiewicz.[88] Indeed, it was in this tradition that Sraffa was to write, with the competitive model in mind, that

> the class of "luxury" products which are not used, whether as instruments of production or as articles of subsistence, in the production of others . . . have no part in the determination of the system. Their role is purely passive. If an invention were to reduce by half the quantity of a "luxury" commodity of this type, the commodity itself would be halved in price, but there would be no further consequences; the price-relations of the other products and the rate of profits would remain unaffected. But if such a change occurred in the production of a commodity of the opposite type, which *does* enter the means of production, all prices would be affected and the rate of profits would be changed.[89]

Matters become more complicated when the notion of unproductive labor (in the generic sense) is viewed from the standpoint of society as a whole (or of production in general). This implied, according to Szlajfer, an "external criterion," going beyond capitalist society.[90] It also meant that the key point of reference was no longer surplus value directly, but the wider historical concept of surplus product. It was this large historical perspective that informed Baran and Sweezy's *Monopoly Capital,* and which accounts in large part for their use of the economic surplus concept instead of surplus value. Thus in their treatment of "the penetration of the productive process by the sales effort," Baran and Sweezy were essentially arguing from the external perspective of socialist rationality (or society as a whole), rather than in terms of the internal logic of capitalism itself. We can encompass this form of waste by referring to socially useless expenditures, implying that the criterion adopted is that of production in general.[91]

Sweezy later acknowledged that the viewpoints of potential and planned surplus had been mixed somewhat indiscriminately in the chapter on the sales effort.[92] But the authors of *Monopoly Capital* were only slightly confused in their formulations. Their whole approach indicated an intuitive grasp of the fact that the role of use value in modern capitalism had been transformed to the point that an immanent critique of the system was no longer sufficient and had to be supplemented by a critique from the standpoint of socialist rationality.

Here we arrive at the second theoretical refinement introduced by Szlajfer. Szlajfer demonstrated that Marx had, in principle, recognized the existence of the category of "formal" or "specifically capitalist" use values in the particular case of gold. Taking this as a methodological clue, Szlajfer suggested that monopoly capitalism has in certain cases (such as planned obsolescence) reversed the relationship between use value and exchange value. Thus it is no longer true, in all cases, that a product only has exchange value if it has use value in general; on the contrary, in the context of an endemic realization problem, a product may have the specific use value—for capital alone—of generating exchange value, while remaining completely useless in terms of production in general. This means that it can no longer be assumed—except perhaps as a first approximation for the sake of analysis—that wage goods, in particular, embody only those costs that are socially necessary. Moreover, this calls into question the supremacy of the concept of surplus value itself, which Szlajfer correctly designated as merely "an 'antagonistic form' of the surplus labor time."[93] Unable to confront the problem of accumulation under monopoly capitalism simply in terms of an immanent critique of the system itself, Baran and Sweezy resorted to certain neglected aspects of the "Marxian cognitive perspective," turning to the external criterion of society as a whole (and production in general).[94]

Yet it must be admitted that the quantitative, as opposed to qualitative, aspects of the accumulation process become somewhat blurred once specifically capitalist use values and—what amounts to the same thing—forms of waste that are visible only from the external perspective of socialist rationality enter into the theory. Does this mean that the approach adopted by Baran, Sweezy, and Szlajfer is inferior to other theoretical models which simply ignore (or, more precisely, fail to perceive) the problem of specifically capitalist use values? The answer to this question may well depend on whether the judgment is primarily grounded in "high theory" or historical analysis.

In her famous 1971 lecture to the American Economics Association, entitled "The Second Crisis of Economic Theory," Joan Robinson pointed out that while the "first crisis" of the 1930s was due to the failure to account for the *"level* of employment," what might be termed the second crisis "arises from a theory that cannot account for the *content* of employment."[95] To this it should be added that the inability to account for the composition of social output, which Robinson pointed to, is a *general crisis* of economic theory—not limited only to the works of those authors who have actually attempted to confront the problem. In fact, aside from the work of Luxemburg, Kalecki, Steindl, Baran, Sweezy, Gillman, Morris, Coontz, and Szlajfer (all within the neo-Marxian tradition), no serious probes in this direction have been made at all.[96] Radical theorists can no more afford to ignore the *structure* than the *level* of output. Nonradicals can, of course, afford to ignore both.

The Long Run

Even with the intervention of waste as a countervailing factor, Baran and Sweezy suggested, the realization problem would not go away, not even in the sense of the temporary achievement of full capacity utilization. One reason for this is that the gap is widened even as it is presumably being closed. If unproductive expenditures (backed up by government financing) cause demand to rise to a certain point—a few points above the 80 percent level of capacity utilization as measured by the Federal Reserve—this sets in motion a sharp increase in productive capacity as business hurriedly builds ahead of demand; but the expectations are soon disappointed and a condition of chronic overcapacity reappears, with further injections of unproductive expenditures becoming necessary in consequence.[97] Overall, monopoly capitalism suffers from what Keynes called the "fate of Midas," with capital formation fluctuating around and close to the level of zero net investment, while the level of underemployment (due to increasing productivity) continues to widen.[98]

But the model that Baran and Sweezy presented, like that of Kalecki (and Keynes), remained "somewhat open at the long-term end."[99] Steindl, it will be recalled, had tried to construct a closed model of the economic process based on the theory of monopolistic accumulation. Turning the Schumpeterian argument upside down, Steindl had suggested that "Technological innovations accompany the process of investment like a shadow, they do not act on it as a propelling force."[100] Although Baran had argued strongly in favor of Steindl's point of view in the original edition of *The Political Economy of Growth,* he was to qualify his position in the preface to the second printing of the book. In *Monopoly Capital* Baran and

Sweezy divided the issue into two parts. With respect to "normal" innovations, as we have seen, they argued that monopoly capital's tendency to place restrictions on the implementation of new methods and new products so as to protect existing capital values was the predominant factor. Those innovations that were introduced at a steady pace tended to be of the type—relating primarily to the scientific organization of the labor process—that required relatively little in the way of additional capital inputs.

This was obviously not the case, however, with what Baran and Sweezy referred to as "epoch-making innovations," or "those innovations which shake up the entire pattern of the economy and hence create vast investment outlets in addition to the capital which they directly absorb."[101] In this class they listed the steam engine, the railroad, and the automobile. The industrial revolution of the late eighteenth and early nineteenth centuries, they pointed out, would have been inconceivable without the steam engine. The railroad had directly accounted for between 40 and 50 percent of *all* capital formation in the United States during the last two decades of the nineteenth century. The growth of the automobile industry also led to vast upsurges in the steel, glass, and rubber industries, and provided the basis for the construction of roads and highways across the nation. Like the railroad, it radically altered the economic geography of the entire system, thus creating enormous new outlets for surplus absorption.[102] Even a major innovation like electricity was dwarfed in comparison to epoch-making innovations of this sort.[103] The general implication was that although the emergence of new epoch-making innovations was always conceivable in the abstract, there was nothing in the logic of the economic system itself, or in the wider historical process, that guaranteed their appearance at the right time.

Baran and Sweezy did not pursue this line of thought any further in *Monopoly Capital.* Yet Sweezy was to extend the analysis in his later writings, elaborating on themes that he had developed decades earlier, both in his discussion of new industries as a countervailing factor to underconsumption in *The Theory of Capitalist Development,* and in a subsequent inquiry into the problem of capitalist maturity in his 1952 essay, "A Crucial Difference Between Capitalism and Socialism."[104] Returning once again to these issues in recent years, beginning with the publication of *Four Lectures on*

Marxism (1981), Sweezy, along with Harry Magdoff, situated the theory of monopoly capitalism and the question of epoch-making innovations within the larger historical "problematic" of industrial maturity, employing the analytical apparatus of Marxian economics to develop deeper insights into the long-run concerns raised by Alvin Hansen, on the basis of hints made by Keynes, during the secular stagnation debate of the late 1930s.[105]

The general underconsumptionist argument had stressed the fact that the tendency for Department I (the investment goods sector) to expand faster than Department II (the consumption goods sector) was deeply rooted in the conditions of overexploitation intrinsic to the capitalist system, and was a possible cause of economic crises. But whether or not a realization crisis actually surfaced depended on the degree to which Department I, in any given period, was relatively autonomous from Department II. In other words, this particular crisis tendency had a definite historical dimension where its concrete materialization was concerned, which could not be derived from the logic of capital in and of itself.[106] It is in this context that Sweezy and Magdoff have advanced a general argument on the "maturation process" in a capitalist economy. Although the initial stages of industrialization, they argue, were characterized by the building up of basic productive capacity in both departments (with the first industrial revolution centering on Department I, and the second, or scientific-technical, revolution, centering on Department II), there eventually came a time, in the early decades of the twentieth century, when a state of "maturity" began to manifest itself, in the sense that "Department I" was "sufficiently built up to supply all the needs of replacing worn-out means of production, and, in addition, to provide the inputs for an ample expansion of Department II."[107] Under these circumstances, a Tugan-Baranovsky path of investment that was in some sense self-sustaining became increasingly unlikely, and any substantial expansion of Department I, the mainspring of the capitalist economy, became more and more difficult to achieve, producing a condition of enduring stagnation. As Sweezy has explained:

> In the absence of new stimuli (wars, opening of new territories, significant technological or product innovations), this stagnant condition will persist: there is nothing in the logic of the reproduction

> process to push the economy off dead center and initiate a new period of expansion.[108]

In fact, wars have been perhaps more important than major technological innovations as external stimuli to the system in its present stage, helping produce the long wave upturns that belong to the larger history of the system.[109]

Nevertheless, while the concept of maturity and the related notion of long waves (in a fairly loose and noncyclical sense) give us some clues to the deeper historical contradictions behind stagnation, which form the setting in which the pattern of monopolistic accumulation takes place, none of this of course "closes" the theory of accumulation; nor, according to Magdoff and Sweezy, is there any hope in doing so as far as pure economic logic is concerned. At bottom the problem is historical rather than economic. This was the dilemma that Kalecki faced from a purely economic standpoint when he wrote in 1968:

> Why cannot a capitalist system, once it has deviated downwards from the path of expanded reproduction, find itself in a position of long-term simple reproduction? In fact, we are absolutely in the dark concerning what will happen in such a situation so long as we have not solved the problems of the determinants of investment decisions. Marx did not develop such a theory, nor has this been accomplished in modern economics. Some attempts have been made in the development of the theory of cyclical fluctuations. However, the problems of the determination of investment decisions involving . . . the long-run trend are much more difficult than in the case of the "pure business cyle." . . . One thing is clear to me: the long-run growth of national income involving satisfactory utilization of equipment is far from obvious.[110]

However, if we view the problem as one that is ultimately unresolvable in terms of strict economic logic, we have at least this answer to turn to: in its widest possible definition, monopoly capitalism is the imperialist stage of the world economy.

The Problem of Capital Accumulation Revisited

In the opening pages of this chapter it was acknowledged that there was a limited degree of truth to Erik Olin Wright's statement that "The most serious weakness in the underconsumptionist position is that it lacks any theory of the determinants of the actual rate of accumulation." In Wright's favor, there were at least three senses in which this statement was not entirely unfounded. First, the neo-Marxian theory of investment was only presented in skeletal form in *Monopoly Capital,* allowing for the interpretation that the theory itself was incomplete.[111] Second, the role of unproductive expenditures in a monopoly capitalist economy, where "formal use values" have come to play a central part, has posed enormous difficulties with respect to the determination of the magnitude and modes of utilization of potential surplus product. Third, the theory of monopoly capital has suffered from the "weakness" that the determination of the secular trend ultimately depends on certain historical "imponderables," extending far beyond the strict logic of economics as normally understood.

Nevertheless, if we place our emphasis on the word "actual" in Wright's statement, quoted above, it can be convincingly argued that the great strength of the current "underconsumptionist position," in comparison to other economic models, is that it does in fact have "a theory of the determinants of the *actual* rate of accumulation." Here it is important to note that Wright's critical comments were based on the additional observation that "falling-rate-of-profit theorists have a specific theory of the determinants of the rate of accumulation," which ultimately rests on the notion that "the rate of profit and the rate of accumulation are equivalent." Yet in the underconsumptionist theory, he goes on to state, "the rate of profit and the rate of accumulation cannot be equated. If they were, there would not be a tendency for underconsumption (i.e., there would be no need for the rate of unproductive spending to increase)."[112] There is a sense in which Wright in not quite correct even here. It would be more accurate to say that in neo-Marxian theory the potential rate of profit, as determined solely at the point of production, generally exceeds the realized rate of profit, as determined by the level of spending on capitalists' consumption, investment, and waste. In any case, it would appear to be wrong to classify the theory of accumulation associated with the classical falling rate of profit model as a theory of the determinants of the *actual* rate of accumulation in a contemporary historical context; and this for the simple reason that it presupposes the existence of conditions roughly analogous to those stipulated in Say's purported Law of Markets (the erroneous notion that supply, if forthcoming, creates its own demand).[113] Thus, once it is assumed—in line with Say's law—that the entire social accumulation fund potentially available for investment is *automatically* invested, it is absolutely correct to associate the rate of accumulation with the theoretical rate of profit at the point of production. Under these circumstances, the rate of accumulation is determined by supply-side factors alone, and the entire discussion in the present chapter becomes irrelevant. But to argue in this way is to lose sight of the distinctive contradictions of the twentieth century.

Although it was a perfectly reasonable operating assumption in the nineteenth century, when conditions of capital scarcity were the general rule, to suppose that the level of investment was a direct result of the level of savings *(ex ante),* this is hardly the case in the contemporary economy, where vast amounts of excess capacity are continually present. Here the appropriate assumption is the Keynesian and Kaleckian one that investment determines savings rather than the other way around.[114] This means that the *actual* rate of accumulation has to be understood in terms of both the rate of exploitation at the level of production, and the effective demand gap at the level of realization. And a "special theory of the demand side of the investment process" becomes necessary.[115] It is a sad fact but true that what divides Marxian as well as liberal economics, almost half a century after the publication of Keynes' *General Theory,* is the Keynesian revolution itself.

5

The Issue of Excess Capacity

Idle Capacity

"According to our model," Baran and Sweezy wrote,

> the growth of monopoly generates a strong tendency for surplus to rise without at the same time providing adequate mechanisms of surplus absorption. But surplus that is not absorbed is also surplus that is not produced: it is merely potential surplus, and it leaves its statistical trace not in the figures of profits and investment but rather in the figures of unemployment and unutilized productive capacity. If, as most economists and historians seem to agree, we can date the growth of monopoly capital in the United States from approximately the end of the Civil War, we ought to be able to demonstrate our model's effectiveness in explaining the economic history of the past century.[1]

One of the virtues of the theory of Baran and Sweezy (and, considering the performance of other Marxist economic theories in this respect, this is no mean achievement) is that it can be backed up by considerable empirical evidence. This despite the fact, as they point out, that "in the analysis of society even a very good theory is not likely to find direct and obvious confirmation in the historical record."[2] In this section, therefore, we will try to examine the theory against the backdrop of historical reality to see exactly how it stacks up, particularly with reference to the capacity utilization factor.

Thorstein Veblen, writing in 1919, was almost certainly the first major economist to highlight underutilization of productive capcity. In his usual sardonic manner he indicated that production *during wartime* might actually be as low as 10 percent of capacity, but "to avoid any appearance of an ungenerous bias" he estimated it at 50 percent. This estimate was formed, he emphasized,

> on the basis of what should ordinarily be accomplished by use of an equally costly equipment having the disposal of an equally large and

> efficient labor force and equally good natural resources, in case the organisation were designed and managed with an eye single to turning out a serviceable product, instead of, as usual, being managed with an eye single to private gain in terms of price.[3]

Veblen's estimate, it should be noted, was intended to indicate what would be possible from a technical standpoint if society were transformed and production decisions, *including the structure of output,* were no longer controlled by business interests. According to this argument, even in wartime "incapacity by advisement" is the general condition.[4] During times of peace and normal business, however, the contradiction is even more obvious:

> It may be conceded that production in the essential industries, under pressure of the war needs, rises to something like 50 percent efficiency. At the same time it is presumably well within the mark to say that this current output in these essential industries will amount to something like twice their ordinary output in time of peace and business as usual. One-half of 50 percent is 25 percent; and so one comes in sight of the provisional conclusion that under ordinary conditions of business-like management the habitual net production is fairly to be rated at something like one-fourth of the industrial community's productive capacity; presumably under that figure rather than over it.[5]

As usual, it is difficult to determine to what extent Veblen should be taken seriously. There can be little doubt, however, that his comments in this respect are very much in line with his critique of the "vested interests" of the business community, and with his preoccupation with the problem of waste. He was clearly a very important influence on Baran and Sweezy.[6] Furthermore, his figures, while obviously not based on any real statistical analysis, are far less improbable than they may appear at first glance. Industrial capacity and its utilization must be defined as an economic concept if it is to have any real value as an analytical category. Veblen's engineering approach, however, demonstrates the extent to which physical possibilities under capitalism can be restricted by the need to obtain a "reasonable rate of return" on capital. Technological possibilities constantly overshoot economic possibilities. It is important to remember, for example, that the fact that much of existing plant and equipment is worked only one out of three possible shifts per day is in large part the result of social and economic conventions.[7] Obviously, there is a limit to the intensity with which machinery can be practically utilized, but there are reasons to suppose that actual use very seldom approaches physical capacity. Moreover, Veblen clearly implies that irrationalities are built into the very structure of production.

Veblen's speculations on capacity utilization, due to the seeming improbability of his estimates, obviously raise the issue of how one is to determine capacity and its degree of utilization. This immediately presents us with two general alternatives: capacity can be defined in either engineering or economic terms. As Ron Stanfield pointed out in *The Economic Surplus and Neo-Marxism* (1973), "Capacity, and therefore excess capacity, is difficult to define meaningfully. This ambiguity stems from the juxtaposition and interrelation of the social and technical factors involved."[8] Stanfield illustrates this by reference to a 1935 study of national productive capacity directed by Harold Loeb.[9] Loeb's *Report* claimed that there were three general ways in which capacity could be defined:

> The capacity of the existing plant with operation governed by existing customs and traditions.
>
> The capacity of the existing plant if production were limited solely by physical factors and knowledge (i.e., resources, manpower, and technology).
>
> The capacity of the nation to produce goods and services if full advantage were taken of existing resources, manpower, and knowledge.[10]

The first definition is a historically determinate one. It is relatively conservative in the sense that it makes existing practice the basis of the determination of capacity. The latter two definitions, however, are technical (engineering) ones. The first of these (definition 2) explains capacity as what is technically possible with existing resources, knowledge, plant, and equipment. The third Loeb definition, in contrast, refers directly to the output of goods and services that is technically possible if resources and knowledge were the only limitations; it thus operates with a much wider conception of potential output than that which is determined by available fixed capital alone.[11]

These general definitions, while not indicating by any means all of the ways in which capacity may be derived, do cover virtually the full range of the concept. As Stanfield tells us:

> Stated extremely, the technical definitions strip the capacity concept of its social content and render it of dubious value to the analysis of production, which is after all a social process. Stated likewise, the

> custom-oriented definition casts an aura of inscrutability around tradition, myth, customary practice. This veil of their being the natural order of things robs the capacity concept of utility in the analysis of social change.[12]

In what follows we will frequently refer back to the Loeb definitions in order to place particular approaches to the capacity concept in relation to the range of possible definitions. These definitions can be seen in terms of a value-laden continuum, from the first, which is the most "conservative," to the last, which is the most "radical." While the first definition presupposes that capacity can be viewed only according to the laws of the present social order, the third clearly, in the words of the Loeb *Report,* "would be a running inventory of our approach to perfection."[13] Indeed, both of the technical definitions of capacity would probably require significant sociopolitical transformation, even social revolution, to become in any way a reality (outside of war production). In this sense they recall Baran's notion of planned surplus, i.e., the amount of surplus that could be achieved given the creation of a more rational social order and the full utilization of labor and productive capacity. Within the existing order, use of productive resources is clearly limited by the profit-maximizing needs of capital, and thus the "economic definition," with its bias toward existing practice, will engage most of our attention.[14]

The Loeb *Report* itself adopted the second definition of capacity, according to which capacity is limited solely by existing plant, resources, and technical knowledge and therefore is *not* determined by traditional practices associated with the current socioeconomic organization of production. Yet the Loeb study, as one might expect, stands out as an exception within the literature on productive capacity. Almost all other studies proceed along the lines pioneered by the well-known Brookings Institution study, *America's Capacity to Produce* (1934). This study, which deeply influenced Steindl, adopted a conception of capacity similar to the first Loeb definition, i.e., it emphasized restraints imposed by long-standing economic conventions and "necessities." Thus it conceived of potential output in terms of "practical capacity," which it defined as "what would be practicably attainable under conditions of 'sustained simultaneous operation.'"[15] It is significant that the Brookings calculation of "practically attainable" capacity—adopting a procedure that was to become standard practice—excludes all plants that have been shut down, which therefore do not enter into any estimation of excess capacity. The difference between the Loeb and Brookings methods of estimating capacity output is best revealed by the fact that the Loeb calculation of potential output for 1929 was over $50 billion higher than the corresponding estimate by the Brookings Institution.

Most economic notions of capacity conceive it, in line with the Brookings concept, as that level which is "practically attainable." Thus the Census Bureau in its new index of capacity utilization describes "practical capacity as the greatest level of output that a plant can achieve within the framework of a realistic work pattern, assuming a normal product mix and an expansion of operations that can be reasonably attained in the particular locality and considering only equipment in place."[16] The McGraw-Hill business survey of capacity and capacity utilization, upon which the Federal Reserve Board's index of capacity utilization has been partially based, avoids the obvious difficulties, and at the same time creates even greater ones, by not defining the concept and thus leaving it up to firms to respond according to their own individual definitions.[17] The Wharton index defines the concept as follows:

> The capacity of an industry at a particular time is the maximum sustainable output the industry can attain within a very short time if the demand for the product were not a constraining factor, when the industry is operating its existing stock of capital at its customary level of intensity.[18]

Economists have also traditionally seen capacity output as a cost-related concept; they have therefore defined it as the optimum level of production or as the point at which average total costs are minimized. This also corresponds to the long-run equilibrium point for perfect competition (itself a myth). Yet, as Steindl argued, "in practice the determination of this point is not unambiguous. The optimum capacity is not constant for a given physical equipment because it depends also on organizational factors."[19] Hence the point of "optimum" production depends on the normal organization of production within the firm. Yet the level of production that is "practical" for a given firm is also dependent on the larger socioeconomic organization of the market; and in this sense too it goes far beyond a simple cost concept. As John Cremeans, of the Bureau of Economic Analysis, recently indicated:

> To the economist, capacity is a cost-related concept and should be determined independent of the price of the output. To the factory operator, the optimum level of production is both price- and cost-related. How much can I profitably produce—given both the prices I pay and those I receive? Thus, to the factory operator, capacity is not fixed. If the price goes up, it will pay to produce more even if unit costs are rising.[20]

More relevant from our point of view (the theory of monopoly capital), and quite understandably overlooked by Cremeans, is the fact that oligopolistic or monopolistic firms may find it possible under existing demand conditions to raise prices by restricting output, and will do so *"even if unit costs are rising"* (though increasing marginal costs is unlikely to be a widespread condition except under times of war).

Those who are primarily concerned with the measurement of capacity and its utilization are forced, like Cremeans, to disregard any simple cost approach and rely on some fairly arbitrary notion of "practical capacity" —though they may, it is true, continue to have faith in the economic ideal of optimum production under perfect competition. "How do we measure capacity?" Steindl asked. His answer, as usual, was penetrating:

> Ultimately this is a matter of convention. The type of question to be answered is: how much more *can* the industry produce in this year as compared with an earlier year? If we have any convention for measuring capacity which can be applied consistently so as to make possible (a) comparison over time and (b) comparison between firms and perhaps, assuming certain price relations, between industries, then we should be on firm ground.[21]

The search for the elusive firm ground in this area is the problem, however. Existing methods allow for some comparison over time but little in the way of comparison between firms. It is perhaps possible to develop some comparison between industries based on existing capacity statistics, *but only through an extended inquiry in which the capacity statistics only play a part.* To this day, the most comprehensive study of productive capacity and its utilization remains the Brookings Institution study, and this is true in spite of the fact that the actual statistics on capacity were extremely limited in comparison to the quantity of indicators available today. Yet it is only in the Brookings study that a comprehensive industry by industry analysis is made readily available; it is only in that study, in fact, that there is some attempt to relate labor and productive capacity statistics in order to determine the total capacity of the nation.

One of the earlier and cruder attempts to analyze capacity utilization in the 1950s was provided by Daniel Creamer, working for the National Industrial Conference Board. Creamer devised his estimates by comparing the capital-output ratio from a given year to that of a benchmark year (1953) taken to represent full capacity output. Fixed capital was defined as "the value (net of depreciation) placed on these assets by manufacturing enterprises in their balance sheets."[22] There are a number of very serious objections to such a technique. First, there exists no set relationship between a given stock of capital measured in value terms on the one hand and output on the other. Quite to the contrary, as Baran and Sweezy argued, increases in the efficiency of a dollar's worth of capital have probably been the main source of capacity expansion in the post-World War II era.[23] Thus the Creamer approach underestimated capacity by overlooking productivity advances which were not directly reflected in the value of capital stock. Second, the designation of any benchmark year as full capacity output tends to inflate the actual levels of utilization. Thus Creamer established the year 1953 as the benchmark year of full (100 percent) capacity output, while the Federal Reserve Board calculations for the same year indicate that more than 10 percent of capacity was idle. Third, one would logically expect that a particular benchmark year would become increasingly inaccurate as an indicator of full capacity output over time.

An approach to determining productive capacity that has proven to be a good deal more accurate, and certainly more useful, was developed by Donald Streever in his *Capacity Utilization and Business Investment* (1960). Ron Stanfield summed up Streever's technique as follows:

> Donald Streever's study for manufacturing and mining covers the period 1920–1955. He takes the Brookings' 83 percent utilization rate as his benchmark. By assuming equal degrees of utilization in 1923 and 1948, he computes a "scaling factor" which is then applied to annual changes in the capital stock to arrive at the change in capacity. By adding the change in capacity to the benchmark figure he arrives at an estimate of total capacity.[24]

While this method is also subject to certain objections—though not to the same extent as Creamer's technique—it nevertheless provides us with the very best estimates that are available (or likely to be so) with respect to the 1920s, 1930s, and 1940s, when there were virtually no survey data available. Streever's data, which were verified and refined in the work of V. Lewis Bassie, are especially important in that they provide a bridge of sorts between the Brookings study in the 1920s and post-World War II estimates.[25] Streever had placed the Federal Reserve Board's index of industrial production next to his index of capacity for 1920–55. Baran and Sweezy, in *Monopoly Capital,* were among the first to deduce utilization rates by dividing the FRB index by Streever's capacity index. In this way they derived their estimates for the 1920s and 1930s.[26] Stanfield later used the Streever figures to determine utilization rates for 1943 and the early 1950s. The average utilization rate of 85.8 percent obtained by this method for the years 1950–55 is remarkably close to the average of 84.6 percent provided by the Federal Reserve Board index for the same years (the period in which the two indexes overlap).[27] These two facts certainly give a great deal of credence to Streever's calculations.

There currently exist a number of prominent establishment indexes of capacity utilization—those of the Wharton School, the Board of Governors of the Federal Reserve System, McGraw-Hill, and the Bureau of Economic Analysis—but some of the difficulties that one can run into through the indiscriminate use of any one of them are aptly revealed by the following anecdote related by Cremeans:

> Speaking in the first debate of the campaign between Ford and Carter, before an audience estimated to be in the neighbourhood of 90 million persons, Carter referred to the low utilization of productive resources, at that time about 73 percent by the Federal Reserve Board measure, and the high unemployment rate. Had candidate Carter chosen to pursue the capacity issue further, he would have had to tell his audience that at the same time the McGraw-Hill capacity figure was 77 percent; the Bureau of Economic Analysis' figure was 82 percent; and the Wharton School was using an 85 percent figure. Considering the mouthful that would have been and the audience listening, Mr. Carter could hardly have been expected to go further.[28]

To list some of the higher estimates as well would not only have been a "mouthful," but would certainly have weakened Carter's argument. Thus the plethora of indexes adds a great deal of confusion to the study of capacity utilization. As George Perry reported to the Brookings Institution, "The answer to the crucial question of how much unused capacity exists in American industry depends to an altogether unacceptable degree on which of the widely used measures one looks at."[29] Further, Perry argued, the discrepancy between the utilization estimates sometimes "corresponds to the difference to be expected in manufacturing operating rates between the trough and peak of a mild business cycle."[30] As we shall see, much of this discrepancy can be eliminated by discarding the Wharton utilization series. Nonetheless, the other indexes also have significant weaknesses, the most important of these being the fact that they all seriously inflate the level of operating rates. It is not possible here to deal completely with the very complicated problem of how these measures are constructed and their relative worth.[31] Instead, we will simply mention a few of the more important points.

The McGraw-Hill and Bureau of Economic Analysis (BEA) indexes are based entirely on survey data. The virtue of such an approach is that it lets businesspeople decide what their capacity output is for the current period and thus it implicitly integrates into the concept all price and productivity changes. It is, after all, businesspeople who make the decisions about investment and there is a certain rough logic to relying on them for estimates of the relationship of actual to potential production. Baran and Sweezy in *Monopoly Capital,* in fact, came out strongly in support of the McGraw-Hill measures.[32] These estimates show little tendency to drift over time and are not subject to revision.[33] In addition, these indexes, especially the McGraw-Hill index, generally show lower utilization rates than the others and thus, from our standpoint, seem to lie a bit closer to reality. There are, however, a number of major stumbling blocks to these survey techniques. First, it may be argued, as Stanfield seems to have done, that the custom element is introduced to a disproportionate degree through the back door of market perceptions, with respect to the survey method. Businesspeople tend to create individual and somewhat arbitrary notions of capacity based on very narrow and traditional conceptions of what is possible.[34] Furthermore, these estimates tend to level out the cyclical swings in utilization because of the well-known tendency of firms to "forget about" marginal capacity in the trough of the cycle and to "rediscover" it under boom conditions.[35] Nevertheless, these indexes seem to give us a reasonably accurate, though understated, indication of the shortfall in utilization and its alterations over time.

The odd man out among the capacity measures is certainly the index of utilization provided by the Wharton school. While the FRB and BEA provided figures of 86.2 and 85 percent, respectively, for 1969, the Wharton estimate was 95 percent. The Wharton figures have always exceeded those of McGraw-Hill, often by as much as 8 percentage points.[36] While the other leading measures are closely correlated, the Wharton index has shown an increasing tendency to deviate upward. All of this is due to the peculiar nature of the Wharton method:

> The Wharton index of capacity is based on the "trend-through-peaks" method. Output, as measured by the Federal Reserve Board's series on industrial production, is plotted for each of the major manufacturing industries, e.g., primary metals, electrical machinery, and chemicals. Successive cyclical peaks are then joined together with straight line segments. The resulting series of connected linear segments is the industry's capacity measure. To obtain the industry's utilization rate, output is simply divided by capacity. The utilization rate for manufacturing is derived by summing the industry utilization rates, each weighted by the fraction of total national income contributed by the industry at full employment.[37]

The difficulties associated with the index so derived are well known. Even more than the other prominent capacity measures, the Wharton index tends to inflate the level of utilization. Since *each* cyclical peak in an industry's production is defined as capacity output (100 percent), there is no way to determine variations in the intensity of production between different peaks.[38] Thus the Wharton method tends to hide the surplus capacity that is usually present even at the top of the cycle, by simply defining it out of existence. Hence, while the BEA estimated utilization to be 87 percent in the primary metals industry in 1969, the Wharton school, in contrast, showed an operating rate of 97 percent in the same industry. The different rates of utilization which do appear in the aggregate index published by Wharton, and the fact that the aggregate figure always falls short of 100 percent, is less a reflection of variations in the intensity of production and much more an indication of the fact that different industries do not reach the top of the cycle in the same quarter.[39] Furthermore, current estimates of the Wharton index are always likely to be revised. Since in the case of current production the future cyclical peak is unknown, it is impossible to *properly* utilize the normal trend through a peaks method, i.e., it is impossible to draw a straight line segment from the last peak to a cyclical peak that has not yet presented itself. The usual Wharton method for current estimates, therefore, is to extrapolate a level of capacity from the most recent peak. If actual output, however, exceeds the line drawn in this way, it is necessary to redefine capacity and revise the figures downward.

These weaknesses are so serious that for the most part the Wharton index should be set aside. There are, however, a number of traits peculiar to this index that make its retention *in qualified manner for limited purposes* advisable. First, utilization figures are not only useful as a means of determining the actual, absolute *level* of utilization in relation to capacity but also the trend in this regard over time. From the standpoint of cyclical fluctuations in the rate of utilization, irrespective of the actual level of utilization involved, the Wharton index corresponds very closely to the other three prominent indexes.[40] This is of course partly because all four indexes have industrial production as a common numerator. Nevertheless, the Wharton measure can serve to verify trends that appear in the other indexes as simply one more piece of proof. Second, the simplicity of the Wharton method allows comparison between different countries, which is certainly not true of any of the other indexes. Third, the fact that the Wharton School provides statistics on both an aggregate and an individual industry basis, combined with the fact that its method of measurement leads it to inflate operating rate levels to an even greater extent than is true for the other indexes, can in certain cases be extremely useful. For example, while the BEA statistics show a 65 percent level of utilization in the aircraft industry in 1971, it is certainly possible to argue that this estimate is too conservative; any such argument is virtually silenced, however, by the fact that the notoriously inflated Wharton index shows a lower estimate (63.5 percent) for the same industry in that year.

In the words of Perry, "The Federal Reserve Board index of manufacturing capacity is the most eclectic of the indexes in construction, relying on three distinct sources of information."[41] These sources include (1) the McGraw-Hill capacity survey which the FRB uses for its long-run benchmark (2) yearly changes in a separate McGraw-Hill utilization survey, together with (3) estimates of the size of capital stock, as short-term indicators of changes in capacity. The Federal Reserve's index of industrial production for a given year is divided by the capacity data so derived in order to determine the level of utilization for that year.[42] Thus the FRB index reflects both the judgments of businesspeople and investment patterns. The FRB index of materials capacity is constructed in a similar way, although the initial information is provided by trade associations instead of surveys. The FRB index of manufacturing is almost certainly the most quoted of all the indexes and hence derives a certain amount of credibility by fame. Baran and Sweezy considered the FRB index (next in their scale of approval to that of McGraw-Hill) to be generally free of any systematic distortions other than its implicit reliance on what is "normal" for business rather that on what is possible. Sweezy has, in fact, relied solely on the FRB index in his later articles on the subject in *Monthly Review.*

The Federal Reserve index, however, like that of Wharton—although to a lesser extent—is open to the rather singular objection that it is subject to fairly frequent revision. As James Ragan indicated:

> Based on the statistical relationship which the Board has estimated in 1971, capacity utilization in 1976-III was originally placed at 73.6 percent, which was low by historical standards. But when the statistical relationships for capacity were reestimated this year, substantially different results emerged. The Board now estimates capacity utilization for 1976-III to be 80.9 percent, which is about midway between the historical high and historical low of the new series. Thus, the Board has revised considerably its assessment of current capacity utilization.[43]

The reasons for these rather substantial modifications in the figures relate back to our discussion of Creamer's approach. The FRB index relies to a certain extent on data on fixed capital investment without taking full account of the fact (prior to such revision) that there is no direct relationship between capital spending and capacity expansion. Thus the FRB technique at times distorts utilization figures by a heavy reliance on value changes that do not take into consideration historical alterations in productivity relationships. Nonetheless, it can be assumed that the FRB index is a relatively good indicator of capacity utilization, with the important reservation that capacity is understated due to the traditional reliance on definitions and to a general methodology that highlights what is *normal under existing conditions of production.*

A number of theorists—such as Leon Keyserling, James Knowles, Ron Stanfield, and Thomas Weisskopf—try to skate around the obvious difficulties by using a potential output approach. Using various techniques they derive estimates of potential output over a given period and divide this into actual output in order to determine utilization rates. While such a method may seem elegant at first glance, its validity in relation to direct estimates of capacity utilization is highly questionable. In order to generate any trend line of potential output, an estimation of capacity output must be made at some point. Stanfield, in a critique of the Keyserling and Knowles methods, shows the inadequacy of their estimates.[44] Keyserling assumes full capacity output in 1929 and generates estimates of "full employment" output over time by calculating the rate of capacity growth, given changing productivity relationships. These results are somewhat misleading, however, since 1929, far from being a year of full capacity output, was a year in which at least 17 percent of total productive capacity was idle.[45] Knowles, in contrast, does not even pretend to be measuring capacity output in his estimation of so-called potential output. Thus he posits from the start a minimum unemployment rate of 4 percent.[46]

Stanfield's own technique is more interesting but also of dubious value.[47] He also takes the year 1929 for his base but adopts the estimate for that year provided by the Brookings study. He then generates growth rates and adds them to 1929 in order to construct a trend line of potential output from 1929 to 1970. It can hardly be expected, however, that capacity output can be accurately determined over four decades largely on the basis of one estimate made in 1929. To do so is to understate the effects of a large number of economic factors which are not necessarily fully accounted for in growth estimates. Hence his figures represent only a very crude estimation of potential output over the period. From these estimates, which seem fairly in accord with the FRB estimates for the 1950s and 1960s but not with Streever's for the 1930s and 1940s (where one would expect the closest correspondence), Stanfield determined that Baran and Sweezy's argument on utilization was neither confirmed nor contradicted. Yet while Stanfield's figures often correspond to what might be expected, they cannot be considered as definitive as the more credible indexes of capacity derived on a yearly, and even quarterly, basis.

This imperfection of existing capacity measures is a problem that is shared—although perhaps not to the same degree—by most statistics on aggregate economic activity. It is noteworthy in this regard that the importance of capacity utilization statistics, coupled with many of the unavoidable problems in compiling such statistics, has led in recent years to the proliferation of such indexes. Over the last decade or so, for example, four new indexes have appeared: the industrial materials series published by the Federal Reserve, and indexes of manufacturing capacity utilization provided by the Bureau of Economic Analysis, the Bureau of the Census, and Rinfret-Boston Associates. Though one must always be careful about the limitations with respect to the valid comparison of such indexes, since the concepts that they measure are not entirely the same, it is nevertheless obvious that the social analyst can, at the very least, strengthen a particular argument concerning capacity utilization by verification through two or more of these indexes. Thus the very proliferation of such indexes, in addition to the negative effect it has of generating confusion, can also have the more positive consequence of providing, in certain cases, a high degree of certainty.[48]

The usual way of examining the issue of shortfalls in production and unused productive resources is to observe the current level of unemployment. Such an approach is convenient, fits in with political considerations, and corresponds closely to the full employment orientation passed on by Keynes. Unemployment figures are clearly very important and are essential to the industrial reserve army concept in Marxian analysis. Yet in many respects the examination of excess industrial capacity can be an even more useful way of understanding what is going on in the economy. There are three overwhelming reasons why this is so. First, there can be little doubt that the two most important factors affecting business investment are profit expectations and the current level of surplus capacity, and the latter factor increasingly affects the former. In the modern period, during which insufficient aggregate demand has been a continual constraint on capital expansion, the fear of excess capacity, it may be safely assumed, is much greater. This is reinforced by the fact that prices are inelastic in a downward direction so that there is relatively little possibility of the safety valve of Schumpeter's competitive "creative destruction" asserting itself.[49] Thus business is constantly aware of the relationship between its capacity to produce and its capacity to sell. George Perry of the Brookings Institution was, therefore, able to write that "high operating rates have generally produced high levels of business outlays, and the extent of such an investment boom is one of the important determinants of the length and strength of any economic expansion."[50] This statement is equally true in reverse: low rates of utilization can help to explain why business does not see fit to invest in additional capital stock. According to *Business Week*, "Capital spending plans accelerate when operating rates move significantly above the 80 percent level and decelerate when they dip below it."[51] Thus utilization statistics are especially significant in that they reflect what is a determinant for investment and hence can be used to explain the reasons behind the existence or nonexistence of unemployment.

Second, it can be argued that capacity utilization statistics, imperfect as they are, give a better indication of the actual shortfall from full utilization of resources than do currently available unemployment statistics. Thus it is much more enlightening to know that, according to FRB and BEA calculations, excess capacity stood at approximately 25 percent in 1975 than it is to know that the official rate of unemployment in the same year was 8.5 percent.[52] Third, while except over a very short time span it is virtually impossible, for obvious reasons, to ascertain the amount of unemployment in any given industry, it is, on the other hand, quite possible to determine the amount of unused capacity on an industrial sector basis. Thus it is feasible on this basis—and business is well aware of this—to see where the weak links in the economy are and to find this information in black and white terms.[53]

After this long and rather technical discussion of the various capacity utilization measures, it is only natural to wonder what they indicate about the modern economy. According to the utilization data computed by dividing the industrial production index by Streever's capacity estimates, the average level of utilization of industrial capacity in the United States in the decade of the 1930s was 63.4 percent (a low of 42 percent in 1932 and a high of 83 percent in 1937), while unemployment, conservatively estimated, averaged around 18 percent.[54] A former Commissioner of Labor Statistics for the U.S. Department of Labor, Isador Lubin, declared in 1938 that roughly 43,435,000 human hours were lost in the years between 1930 and 1938 (setting aside population and productivity changes).[55] War, as is commonly known, pulled the United States out of the Great Depression. The Federal Reserve's Industrial Production Index indicates that production of machinery, for example, more than quadrupled between 1939 and 1943.[56]

We therefore find that capacity utilization at the high point of World War II, according to Streever's estimates, was no less than 136 percent.[57] In the post-World War II era the phenomenon of surplus capacity continued to be typical. Not even in the Korean war peak of 1953, when capacity utilization (according to the FRB index) reached 89.2 percent, nor in the Vietnam peak of 1966 when it reached 91.1 percent, did monopoly capitalism achieve anything like full capacity output.[58] In fact, the inability of capitalism to generate anything like full employment in these years led to a redefinition of "full employment" as unemployment that, according to official statistics, was not higher than the 4 percent level that had become the usual case. The first two and one-half decades of the post-World War II era, despite the massive economic stimulus generated by two hot wars and a cold war, were clearly characterized by a tendency for productive capacity to remain far ahead of profitable outlets for surplus absorption. As Stanfield concluded, "Whether or not one can precisely distinguish equilibrium and disequilibrium excess capacity, it is apparent that something on the order of 10 to 15 percent of capacity, conservatively defined, remains idle in peacetime conditions."[59] In fact, *according to official statistics* the amount of idle capacity has been much closer to 20 percent through much of this period. If we exclude the Korean war years (1951–53) and the main Vietnam war years (1965–68) from our calculations, we find that the average utilization of productive capacity between 1948 and 1977, as indicated by Federal Reserve Board statistics, was approximately 81 percent.[60] There can be little doubt that much of the post-World War II era has been a high tide of prosperity for capitalism, but there is also no denying the fact that the prevalence of surplus capacity in relation to effective demand has put severe constraint on accumulation throughout this period. Periods of decisive expansion have occurred largely through the stimulus of government expenditures on the military, the great automobile push of the 1950s, and a formidable extension of the debt structure.

In the mid-1970s, as the post-World War II economic hegemony of the United States began to fade, the tendency toward economic stagnation began to reassert itself. The landmark in these hard times was the business trough of 1975, during which approximately 25 percent of productive capacity was idle (as demonstrated by both FRB and BEA calculations). At the same time, unemployment rose to between 8.5 and 11 percent.[61] Not since 1939 had the level of unused productive capacity been as high. Even then, the depressionary condition of the mid-1970s hit foreign states harder than it did the United States itself.[62] Operating rates and production levels recovered rather quickly in the United States after the 1973–75 slump. Sweezy explains this as the result of "a veritable explosion of public and private debt." The federal government carried a deficit of nearly $50 billion in 1978 alone. Such contrived solutions to the crisis of accumulation will not, however, hold back the flood for long. As Sweezy commented, "It may turn out that the cure creates problems no less serious than the disease."[63] The decade of the 1970s was a clear demonstration of capitalism at work without war, and over this period approximately 20 percent of total U.S. fixed capital was left inactive. Hence the conspicuous fact that excess capacity is not simply a cyclical factor but has been a continual spectre haunting capital in its monopoly stage.

More can be learned by looking at the data with respect to individual industries. A case in point is the aircraft industry, where capacity utilization from 1965–79 (which includes the Vietnam war years) was only 72 percent on the average (again using BEA calculations). Many other industries, such as electrical and electronic equipment, show large amounts of surplus capacity throughout these years. Indeed, the petroleum industry, which was the only major industrial sector to show anything like full utilization throughout the 1960s, demonstrated a very marked tendency toward surplus productive capacity at increasing levels in the 1970s.[64]

It should be evident by now that the Baran and Sweezy argument, which claims that an overextension of productive capacity in relation to demand is a chronic problem of capitalism, is clearly borne out by the facts themselves. But the "facts" we have referred to so far are the *official* statistics, with their conservative bias. It would therefore be useful to examine briefly what a more realistic view of capacity output would tell us about monopoly capitalism. To do so requires the use of wartime production as a reference point.

Veblen's seemingly outrageous statement that 75 percent of industrial capacity remains unused in times of peace was, it will be recalled, based on the extremely unorthodox (but not therefore incorrect) hypothesis that in times of war the operating rate in industry as a whole seldom rises above 50 percent of its potential. For Veblen, then, potential or capacity output goes far beyond what is likely to be the case even in times of war. Thus his notion of capacity is probably similar to the third Loeb definition, which implies changes in the structure of output. Veblen's conception of capacity as *physical* capacity and serviceable use values represents one extreme in the range of possible definitions. Most of the established measures, however, understate potential output, in line with the first Loeb definition, tying it to normal conditions of monopoly capitalist production, i.e., to what can be produced with "normal costs" and "normal profits." To define capacity in this way is to seriously understate what is possible—not only what is possible in terms of a more rational social order, but also what is sometimes possible within the context of monopoly capitalism itself.

A conception of capacity output based on levels actually achieved during war makes a certain amount of sense, and we should not be deterred by cries that a comparison between capitalism at peace and capitalism at war is "unfair." Capitalism works more efficiently during wartime because *profitability* is enhanced. Capitalism during peacetime—at least during the monopoly stage—works comparatively poorly because accumulation is dampened by a lack of *profitable* investment outlets. Lewis Robb, in "Industrial Capacity and Its Utilization," was one of the first to use the example of war production in order to demonstrate the tendency of existing statistics to inflate utilization estimates through correspondingly low estimates of capacity output. Robb, who influenced Baran and Sweezy, argued that if the actual level of output in 1943 were taken to be capacity output, equal to 100 percent utilization, then the level of utilization in 1952 could be interpreted as being roughly 55 percent.[65] In fact, if we take Robb's assumption that 1943 was a year of 100 percent utilization, apply it to Streever's figures, and adjust accordingly, the year 1932 would have its utilization figure reduced from an estimated 42 percent to 31 percent.[66] In this way Veblen's "wild" assumption of a 25 percent utilization rate no longer seems entirely absurd. As Baran and Sweezy, referring to the figures on capacity utilization for the 1930s derived from Steever's capacity estimates, eloquently argued:

> The figures tell us that in 1939, as the decade came to an end, nearly a fifth of the country's labor force and over a quarter of its productive capacity were idle. From this, one would tend to conclude that output could not have been increased much more than, say, a third even if additional workers were drawn into the labor force and capital equipment worked with more than normal intensity. And yet during the next few years, under the impact of war and with the inherent restraints of the capitalist market temporarily removed, industrial production more than doubled and real Gross National Product went up by more than two thirds. Moreover, these increases occurred during a period when virtually no net investment was taking place and more than 11 million men in the most productive age groups were being mobilized into the armed forces. While of course neither manpower nor equipment could continue indefinitely to be operated at the wartime pitch of intensity, still we think the tremendous expansion of output achieved between 1939 and 1944 conclusively proves that the official unemployment estimates and the figures on capacity utilization derived by widely accepted statistical methods understate the extent to which human and material resources are underutilized in a monopoly capitalist economy.[67]

It is to be expected, Baran and Sweezy point out, that while bourgeois social science cannot afford to ignore totally the shortfalls of the system, it will tend to minimize the degree of unemployment and unused capacity in its statistics.

There are a number of criticisms commonly leveled at any attempt to judge the current economic system by reference to wartime production standards which should be briefly addressed. The most important of these is the contention that the higher levels of production and efficiency are the result of a "forced draft" of resources (primarily labor). Robb, however, discounted this argument by highlighting the fact that "in 1943 nearly 10 million men—the most productive segment of the labor force—were in the armed forces, unavailable for the production of goods and services."[68] Furthermore, he added, the labor force between 1945 and 1952 had increased by about 1 million workers per year and was accompanied by steadily growing productivity. Therefore the failure of U.S. capitalism to reach its wartime level of production by 1952 was not due to a reassertion of the "normal scarcity of resources" but had to be the result of inefficiency in peacetime.[69]

Some economists try to argue that defining productive capacity in terms of wartime output measures physical capacity, not economic (cost-based) capacity. Hence, Cremeans of the BEA wrote:

> In wartime, the nation may want the maximum physical output of some goods regardless of cost. . . . The thing that makes our wartime case different is that one more tank or airplane is priceless—i.e., the price is so high that only the physical limitation applies.[70]

Arguing essentially the same point but from the peacetime angle, Cremeans asks the rhetorical question: "What does it mean to say that the physical capacity of U.S. steel mills is x tons if the owners of those mills are predicting mill closings because of foreign competition?"[71] What does it mean, we might ask, to claim that war production is *not* "cost-related," i.e., that an additional airplane is "priceless"? Clearly it does not mean that corporations during war produce irrespective of cost. This would diminish profits and it is well known that profits are not lowered but generally enhanced through wartime production. It can only mean that altered conditions of supply and demand (reinforced by the government) make capital expansion and a more efficient level of output profitable where it was not before. Rising prices associated with a given quantity of production raises the marginal revenue associated with a marginal unit of output. Effective demand is enlarged, and increased production encouraged, by massive government expenditures and this allows capitalism to transcend normal market conditions. As to the second question posed by Cremeans, it is surely enough to answer it directly: It (the real threat of mill closings) signifies that there is world overproduction of the capacity to produce steel in relation to demand (the so-called buyer's market). This is the current dilemma of capitalism.

One aspect of the capacity utilization issue that certainly needs to be studied further is the relationship of utilization to measured productivity. Obviously, any system of monopoly capitalism in which profits are maximized through monopoly rents at the expense of cost efficiency (particularly with respect to overhead) will result in relatively low rates of measured productivity which are partly, but *only* partly, compensated by the administrative rationalization of production within the oligopolistic firm. Thus one can tentatively expect low rates of measured productivity to be a consequence of excess capacity. This seems also to be borne out by existing facts. In most sectors of the economy, if one compares the 1948–67 period with 1967–78, the rate of measured productivity growth has sagged considerably in the last decade. Several studies by Edward Dennison and George Perry of the Brookings Institution attribute anywhere from 36 to 65 percent of the "productivity slow-down" to low rates of utilization of productive capacity.[72] While such relationships demand a great deal more study, it is sufficiently clear at this point that monopoly capital's attempt to prevent profit rates from being squeezed from without in the face of insufficient demand has resulted in an overabundance of productive capacity which, through lowered efficiency, increased costs, and reduced productivity growth, causes profits to be squeezed from within.

Yet this condition, aggravated by the tendency of the surplus to rise, is unlikely to generate any ultimate, catastrophic economic breakdown in the immediate future (or at all), since monopoly capital is also provisioned and fortified—in a way that "competitive capitalism" never was—to outlast virtually any siege. What it does imply is a tendency toward stagnation in which the prosperity of the few is clearly at the expense of the social totality. It is to be expected that under such a situation capitalism will become more transparently flawed and irrational. Corporations such as Chrysler and U.S. Steel will become increasingly dependent on government support as it becomes ever more difficult to maintain the corporate status quo. The "new" bourgeois ideology of corporatism is designed to preserve the control exercised by the ruling class through the development of a more political capitalism. Whether it will succeed depends largely on the strength of the counter-ideology and radical politics from below.

6

The State Economy

Financing the State

The widely heralded "fiscal revolution in America," supposedly unleashed by the Keynesian revolution, was neither as complete nor as lasting as the economic pundits once imagined. Rising deficits, demands to "balance the budget," cutbacks in federal programs for the poor, coupled with low growth and rising unemployment and excess capacity, have brought the "crisis of the tax state" back to the center of economic discussion. And yet there is a tendency to focus on what is merely symptomatic of the larger illness of monopoly capitalist society.

By far the most influential study in this area by a radical economist is James O'Connor's widely read book, *The Fiscal Crisis of the State* (1973). Adapting Marx's reproduction schemes to the problem of the state, this model divided government expenditures into two categories: "social capital" and "social expenses." Social capital consists of those state expenditures that promote accumulation by subsidizing either capital formation (e.g., spending on transportation) or the reproduction of labor power (e.g., social insurance programs). In contrast, social expenses (e.g., "welfare state" spending) do not increase productive capacity or reproduce labor power (although they do increase effective demand), and are required mainly for purposes of legitimation. Out of this type of analysis, O'Connor then derives his central thesis:

> The socialization of costs and the private accumulation of profits creates a fiscal crisis, or "structural gap," between state expenditures and state revenues. The result is a tendency for state expenditures to increase more rapidly than the means of financing them. While the accumulation of social capital indirectly increases total production and society's surplus and thus in principle appears to underwrite the expansion of social expenses, large monopoly-sector corporations and unions strongly resist the appropriation of this surplus for new social capital or social expense outlays.[1]

Some of the weaknesses in O'Connor's argument were brought to light by Hugh Mosley in an article entitled "Is There a Fiscal Crisis of the State?" O'Connor's almost exclusive attention to the "structural gap" in the state budget, Mosley argued, was "a significant shift of emphasis from the recent Keynesian and American Marxist (e.g., Baran and Sweezy, *Monopoly Capital*) emphasis on the problem of surplus absorption and state maintenance of aggregate demand."[2] Moreover, for O'Connor, Mosley wrote,

> the fiscal crisis is essentially a deficit in transactions between the state and the other [i.e., monopoly and competitive] sectors of his model of the economy. It is a structural gap which he attributes to the fact that the state socializes more and more costs of production while profits continue to be appropriated privately. But the capitalist state can and does appropriate profits or surplus value in the form of tax revenues. O'Connor would have to argue that there is a crisis (structural limits) in the basic form in which the capitalist state raises revenues to meet its expenditures. This he does not do. He merely argued that there are political limitations on restructuring or increasing state revenues.[3]

Mosley was undoubtedly correct in his observation that O'Connor's analysis was far less convincing with respect to the limitations on state revenue than with regard to the tendency of state expenditures to rise dramatically as monopoly capitalism "progressed" (a fact that few would be disposed to contest). O'Connor's argument on the revenue constraints of the state centered on a dialectic of "tax exploitation" and "tax revolt," in which the burden of taxes on those without any (significant) access to economic surplus continued to expand, generating ever more frequent tax revolts. As far as the taxation of capital itself is concerned, O'Connor made his point of view quite clear in his comments on the incidence of the corporation income tax:

> Although the problem is highly complex and hotly debated, it is generally agreed that "when measured from changes in the rate of return (profit), shifting is close to 100 percent." In both the monopoly and competitive sectors (which cannot absorb the tax because profits are so meager) the corporate income tax is similar to a general sales tax levied at a rate in proportion to the corporation's profit margin.[4]

In other words, the ability of the state to increase tax revenue by levying higher taxes on capital is circumvented—at least where the corporate income tax is concerned, but O'Connor's argument would also seem to give the proposition a much wider significance—as a result of monopoly capital's power to pass on the tax increases to the consumer in the form of higher prices. Although this may appear to be irrefutable at first glance, the issue requires much closer attention that O'Connor himself gave it if the thesis of a "structural gap" in government finance under monopoly capitalism is to be understood in its fullest sense. Furthermore, the problem is inseparable from the larger question of the generation and absorption of economic surplus.

Surplus and Taxation

The classical and early neoclassical view of taxation was succinctly expressed by Schumpeter in his 1918 essay on "The Crisis of the Tax State":

> Here we have arrived at the fact which can become the leading principle for the theoretical understanding of the economic capacity of the tax state. In the bourgeois society everyone works and saves for himself and his family, and perhaps for some ends he has chosen for himself. What is produced is produced for the purposes of the private economic subjects. The driving force is individual interest—understood in a very wide sense and by no means synonymous with hedonistic individual egotism. In this world the state lives as an economic parasite. It can withdraw from the private economy only as much as is consistent with the continued existence of this individual interest in every particular socio-psychological situation. In other words, the tax state must not demand from the people so much that they lose financial interest in production or at any rate cease to use their best energies for it.[5]

What Schumpeter had in mind here was brought out even more clearly in the subsequent discussion. Here he explained that (1) "Only one thing is important for us: that there is a limit to the taxation of entrepreneurial profit beyond which tax pressure cannot go without first damaging and then destroying the tax object"; and (2) "In the case of interest and wages the tax cannot penetrate too deeply into the tax object."[6] As Ricardo had written much earlier,

> It should be the policy of governments . . . never to lay such taxes as will inevitably fall on capital; since by so doing, they impair the funds

for the maintenance of labour, and thereby diminish the future production of the country.[7]

The entire argument was couched in terms of what can be broadly defined as the "supply-side perspective" that has dominated liberal economics during most of its history—pointing to a general shortage of profits, savings, and capital as the fundamental constraint on accumulation. Since virtually all profits were thought to be automatically plowed back into investment, whatever the government took from this was bound to reduce the rate of economic growth. Moreover, as Schumpeter had suggested, it would also have a long-term effect of inhibiting technological progress by dampening the incentive for entrepreneurs to innovate.

Although logically unsound to the extent that it was based on Say's "law," this argument was not *simply* "childish babbling" in the nineteenth-century environment of industrial revolution and competitive enterprise. But with the coming of the twentieth century, conditions had changed. That this was so was widely appreciated during the Keynesian interlude. Keynes argued, in *The General Theory of Employment, Interest, and Money* (1936), that a leakage in the expenditure stream in the form of savings would have a negative effect on aggregate demand and the level of output unless it was also injected back into the expenditure stream in the form of investment in new productive capacity. However, there was no automatic mechanism (such as the rate of interest in the traditional neoclassical system) that ensured that all intended savings would necessarily be invested—particularly when accumulation, under modern conditions of rapid productivity growth, expanded savings out of profits faster than primarily wage-based consumption. A drop in the level of income due to oversavings would inevitably bring total savings *(ex post)* back into conformity with actual investment, but under conditions of "unemployment equilibrium" deemed impossible in orthodox thought at the time. It was under these circumstances that Keynes suggested that the state could, by injecting its own spending, make up for any shortfalls in effective demand resulting from the oversaving proclivities of capital (or the well-known "dilemma of thrift").

In fact, Keynes' entire "general theory," as Paolo Sylos-Labini has indicated, can be thought of as an endeavor to refute the idea, resurrected in our time, that public spending can "crowd out" private investment. To quote Sylos-Labini:

> Before completing his *General Theory* Keynes made several attempts to discredit the traditional position that every increase in public spending, and the more so if it was deficit spending, produced an equal reduction in private spending without effect on either income or employment because borrowing by the government for public works implied a reduction in the fund of private savings available for investment. These attempts had met with little success and he eventually became convinced that he could only prevail by going to the roots of traditional theory. It is probable that this is the immediate origin of the *General Theory*. One of the most important ideas to emerge from the book is that in conditions of widespread unemployment neither additional investment nor additional private sector deficit spending take away from available savings, rather they generate savings. Only in conditions of near full employment would increased savings be necessary to avoid inflation and what is called "crowding out."[8]

It was with these discoveries of Keynes before their eyes that Baran and Sweezy opened their chapter on civilian government spending in *Monopoly Capital*. Thus they began their analysis of the state's economic role by noting that, although it was reasonable to assume under conditions of competitive capitalism—when full capacity utilization could generally be taken for granted—that the state was essentially a drag on the private economy, consuming surplus that would otherwise be used for private accumulation, this was not equally true in modern times. "Under monopoly capitalism," Baran and Sweezy wrote,

> the normal condition is less than capacity production. The system simply does not generate enough "effective demand" (to use the Keynesian term) to insure full utilization of either labor or productive facilities. If these idle resources can be put to work, they can produce not only necessary means of subsistence for the producers but also additional amounts of surplus. Hence if government creates more effective demand, it can increase its command over goods and services without encroaching on the income of its citizens.[9]

This, as we have seen, was the real, *practical* lesson of the Keynesian revolution. At this point Baran and Sweezy merely attempted to clarify the fact that the crucial element in generating demand was not the level of deficit spending (as some economists had previously supposed), but rather government expenditure itself, since the stimulative effect of state spending as a component of aggregate demand was also evident, although not to an equal extent, in the case of a balanced budget. In other words, whether the increased state spending was actually financed through deficits or taxation was a secondary matter as far as the problem of surplus absorption was concerned. Since taxation cut into consumption, the taxation multiplier was smaller than the multiplier of equivalent spending financed through deficits. Yet government spending promoted national income irregardless of the mode of financing adopted.

The whole approach adopted by Baran and Sweezy deemphasized the differences between the various forms of public finance in order to clear the way for an examination of the composition of government spending. But in downplaying the former issue they ended up obscuring certain logical and historical implications of their analysis. Indeed, while searching for an explanation for the fact that business had finally learned to accept the need for enhanced government spending, Baran and Sweezy went so far as to suggest that

> the modern Big Businessman, though he sometimes speaks the traditional language, no longer takes it so seriously as his ancestors. To him, government spending means more effective demand, and he senses that he can shift most of the associated taxes forward onto consumers or backward onto workers.[10]

But if monopolistic firms could "shift their tax burdens," wasn't it true that the growth in government was "squeezed out of . . . the underlying population"? The answer provided in *Monopoly Capital* was *No:* "If what government takes would otherwise not have been produced at all, it cannot be said to have been squeezed out of anybody."[11] From the standpoint of Baran and Sweezy's own theoretical framework, this answer, while correct, was somewhat unsatisfactory. For if workers normally consumed almost their entire incomes, it could hardly be said, with respect to the great proportion of taxes deducted from wages, that "what the government takes would otherwise not have been produced at all," so that the main proviso of their argument in this respect did not hold.

The problem that this posed for their theory in general is more easily understood if we recognize that in arguing in the aforementioned way in *Monopoly Capital,* Baran and Sweezy were adopting a Keynesian rather than a Kaleckian emphasis.[12] Kalecki's clearest discussion of the problem of taxation is to be found in his 1937 essay, "A Theory of Commodity Income and Capital Taxation."[13] Starting with the familiar formula that profits equal capitalists' consumption plus investment, or $P = C_c + I$, Kalecki suggests that any attempt to finance an expansion of state expenditure *by taxation of wage goods* (assuming that workers do not save, that all government spending goes to either officials' salaries or for doles to the unemployed, disabled, etc., and that there is a lag before a change in basic data has any effect on the rate of investment) will only serve in the short run to redistribute income from one portion of the underlying population to another and will not increase the level of profits in the economy. In other words, the sales tax on wage goods simply constitutes "a new kind of prime cost" and is likely to intensify struggles for higher wages. And besides not having any immediate, short-run effect on capitalist income, this type of taxation is unlikely to produce any systematic long-run effect either.

The case was quite different, Kalecki contended, where an income tax directed at capitalists was concerned. "It is obvious," he wrote,

> that these taxes are not prime costs, but form a part of gross profits. The entrepreneurs continue to maximise the difference between sales and prime costs, e.g., wages, cost of raw materials, commodity prices, etc.; for the greater this differential, the greater the income from the enterprise remaining after the payment of income tax.[14]

Under these circumstances, total profits will equal capitalists' consumption plus investment plus income tax revenue from capitalists, or $P = C_c + I + T_i$. If T_i is financed initially through the potential savings of capitalists and C_c and I remain the same, the immediate effect will be to increase profits in the economy by an amount equal to T_i (Kalecki is assuming that tax revenue is immediately spent by the government). In the longer run, however, the rate of interest could be expected to rise in order to protect the net return for lending, thereby reducing the inducement to invest.

Because of this negative long-run effect, Kalecki argued that the most efficient way to finance an expansion in state spending would be to impose a tax not on capitalist *income,* but on capital itself. The formula then becomes $P = C_c + I + T_c$.[15] Again, the first effect is to raise total profits by the amount of increase in taxes. "Here, however," Kalecki wrote,

> the course of events does not follow the same path as in the case of income taxation. It is not difficult to see that the increase of the rate of capital taxation does not tend to lower the net profitability of investment (which covers the risk) or to raise the rate of interest. Indeed, if somebody borrows money and builds a factory, he does not pay a greater capital tax. And if he ventures his own means, he also pays the same tax as he would if he abstained from investment. Thus the net profitability of investment is unaffected by capital taxation. Unlike income tax, the capital tax is not a cost of production in the long run either.
>
> In the same way, everybody is ready to lend at the current rate of interest; for whether he lends money or not does not affect the capital tax he pays.[16]

Moreover, the inducement to invest is only strengthened, Kalecki pointed out, under a regime of capital taxation. Hence it follows that taxation of capital has all the advantages, in terms of its income and employment effect, of deficit financing, while not having the disadvantage of the state becoming indebted (and on a cumulative scale). Why then has the taxation of capital never been introduced? As O'Connor noted in 1973, "Monopoly capitalists pay no general business tax and their unrealized capital gains go tax free" (a fact that is equally true for all capitalist countries up to the present day).[17] Kalecki's answer to this question, in which he introduces a quote from Joan Robinson, goes a long way toward explaining his own political perspective:

> It is difficult to believe, however, that capital taxation will ever be applied for this purpose on a large scale; for it may seem to undermine the principle of private property, and therefore in this case, as in general, "any government which had both the power and the will to remedy the major defects of the capitalist system would have the will and the power to abolish it altogether."[18]

Kalecki was to carry his general approach to public expenditure and finance to the empirical level in his important essay, "The Economic Situation in the United States as Compared with the Pre-War Period," first published in 1956. By carefully sorting through the U.S. national income accounts in order to separate real private accumulation from the consumption of the underlying population for the years 1937 and 1956, Kalecki was able to show that the increase in "the relative share of gross private accumulation in the national product" was "more than accounted for by the increase of the relative share in national product of two items: export surplus and taxes on corporate profits." In addition, he noted that both of these elements of private accumulation were associated with the growth of the "armament-imperialist complex."[19]

As Steindl was to write twenty years later, in the introduction to the second (1976) edition of *Maturity and Stagnation in American Capitalism:*

> How did it come about that American capitalism, seemingly very sick before 1939, had become vigorous again, providing high levels of effective demand and employment? The answer is (at least in part): vastly increased public expenditures provided additional effective demand, although these outlays were not deficit-financed, but in large part financed by taxation of profits. . . . Kalecki distinguishes wage earners and profit receivers, and in this way makes it obvious that the expansion occurs only to the extent to which the tax hits the profits and not mass consumption.[20]

In writing *Monopoly Capital,* Baran and Sweezy, as we have seen, did not take account of the effects of state financing on the generation and absorption of economic surplus, in line with the Kaleckian theory recounted above. And other leading radical economists like O'Connor clearly relied on a view opposite to that of Kalecki, insisting that the expansion of government during the post-World War II period was financed almost entirely by direct and indirect taxes on wages, and by budget deficits—with corporate taxation amounting to little more than a "general sales tax" because of the ability of the larger corporations to pass on their taxes in the form of higher prices.

An indication of the confusion that all of this caused can be found in Michael Bleaney's contention that he had discovered a major flaw in Baran and Sweezy's argument in this respect. In an important critique of Luxemburg, Kalecki had pointed out "She consistently makes . . . the mistake of treating the *whole* of government expenditure, for instance on armaments, without paying due consideration to its financing, as absorbing the economic surplus." But this, Kalecki argued, was misleading, since expenditures financed through taxation of workers would "have no effect on the absorption of national product because the new 'armaments markets' are offset by an equal curtailment of workers' consumption."[21] Noting Kalecki's criticism, Bleaney went on to argue in his book, *Underconsumption Theories* (1976), that Baran and Sweezy had made the same "mistake" as Luxemburg. As Bleaney put it:

> Baran and Sweezy do not believe that deficit financing has been of great significance in the post-war world, and since the great bulk of taxes are paid by workers, they are effectively arguing that it can help absorb the surplus.[22]

Now it might be reasonable to suppose from this that Bleaney's criticism was directed at demonstrating—as Kalecki had in the case of Luxemburg—that Baran and Sweezy's theory was, in certain respects, weaker than it needed to be, since taxation of workers could make the problem of surplus absorption all the more difficult. But Bleaney arrived at an altogether different conclusion. On the above grounds alone, he argued that

> Baran and Sweezy's easy addition of the whole of the state budget into the process of surplus absorption seems unjustified. And without it, their attempt to demonstrate with statistics the rise of the surplus as a proportion of GNP from 1929 to 1963 is jeopardized.[23]

The argument is logically fallacious. Baran and Sweezy had noted that the multiplier of government spending financed by taxes (which cuts into consumption) is smaller than that of government spending financed by deficits (which does not). Assuming that the composition of taxation and its incidence is such that it falls entirely on the working population, and thereby reduces consumption by an equal amount, there is no immediate increase in profits or income in the economy as a whole.[24] But it would be a mistake to take this to mean that the government's expenditure of its tax revenues does not absorb surplus or constitute an element of effective demand. Rather, it simply means that *on balance* the reduction in consumption cancels out the increase in government demand.

Indeed, far from ignoring the whole problem, Baran and Sweezy, in writings published prior to *Monopoly Capital,* had both dealt with the issue of state finance and its relation to the generation and absorption of surplus in terms that were much more consistent with—and, in Baran's case, actually went beyond—Kalecki's approach. Thus Baran went to great lengths to examine the question of government finance in *The Political Economy of Growth* (1957). After examining the various contradictions of deficit financing, Baran wrote:

> Therefore, as a matter of longer run policy, the government expenditures required for the maintenance of a decided-on level of income and employment have to be at least approximately matched up by tax revenues. This means, however, that government spending has to remain within more or less circumscribed limits. For it is in the nature of the tax mechanism normally employed under capitalism that while it siphons off some of the employed surplus (in the form of business profits and personal savings), it necessarily also cuts into consumption. Hence, the paradox that the larger the amount of surplus the government must spend in order to maintain the desired level of income and employment, the larger it tends to make the surplus itself by seizing income that would have been spent on consumption.[25]

The thrust of Baran's analysis seems clear. Whatever the state can extract from wages can be viewed as an *addition* to economic surplus. (Any additional taxation of capitalists, it can be safely assumed, would have no significant impact on their own consumption and would merely involve the appropriation of available surplus by the state.) Nor is the basic argument only relevant to tax *increases:*

> As tax rates are raised, some economic surplus—part of profits and saving—is seized by the government. At the same time, however, additional income is "transferred" to the economic surplus—part of what would have otherwise have been spent on consumption. Indeed, it has always been the essence of taxation policy under capitalism to minimize the share of tax revenue which confiscates privately appropriated economic surplus and to increase simultaneously the proportion constituting additional economic surplus. This basic principle underlies all *reductions* of taxes under capitalism. They are so calculated as to *maximize* the amounts returned to privately appropriated economic surplus and to *minimize* the sums that are released, as it were, from the economic surplus and made available for consumption.[26]

Thus because of their regressive character, tax reductions also have the effect of enlarging the economic surplus at the expense of workers' income (and hence consumption). It would seem to follow from Baran's analysis that any tax system, once established, will become gradually more dysfunctional in terms of the problem of surplus absorption, as time progresses, since any shifts in taxes (in either direction) from that point on will be directed at maximizing the amount of additional surplus appropriated through the phenomenon of tax exploitation. Furthermore, by making it clear that whatever was appropriated from workers in the form of taxes belonged to the economic surplus, and thus incorporating the marginal factor of workers' savings, Baran went somewhat beyond Kalecki's own explanation (though remaining consistent with the logic of the latter's analysis).[27]

Only a year after Baran's death in 1964, and before the publication of *Monopoly Capital,* Sweezy had clearly begun to rethink the whole problem of state finance in the context of changing historical circumstances. In a 1965 article on "The Kennedy-Johnson Boom," written with Leo Huberman, the authors rejected the idea that the type of rapid growth then observed could be attributed to deficit financing in and of itself.[28] Instead, one had to focus on the underlying meaning of the form of deficit financing adopted, by examining the tax cuts that had been put into place. On this, Huberman and Sweezy quoted then Treasury Secretary C. Douglas Dillon, who had written:

> It was necessary to get the major increases in defense and space spending behind us before we could safely implement our full program of tax reduction. But rather than wait, we promptly undertook two major moves to improve the climate for business investment—moves that could be instituted without any excessive loss of revenue. They were the Revenue Act of 1962, with its central provision of a 7 percent investment tax credit, and the administrative liberalization of depreciation—both landmarks in our drive to spur the modernization of our capital equipment. Together they increased the profitability of investment in new equipment by more than 20 percent. This was equivalent in terms of incentives to invest to a reduction in the corporate profits tax from 52 percent to 40 percent.[29]

Following the actual tax reductions of 1964, the total effect on the after-tax returns to corporations, as calculated by ultraconservative economist George Terbough and related by Huberman and Sweezy, was equivalent "either to a cut in corporate income tax rates from 52 percent to 34 or 29 percent (depending on the ratio of equity to total capital), or to a reduction in the cost of new capital equipment of 16 percent."[30] The result was a rapid growth in profits and a drop in the share of wages in national product. And despite the sharp upturn, real unemployment and excess capacity remained serious problems.

Although Huberman and Sweezy did not go any further into the theoretical implications of all of this with respect to the realization problem, it was clear from the argument that the reduction in effective levels of corporate taxation, combined with increasing deficits (meaning larger interest payments to the capitalist class), was swelling corporate coffers. It would therefore be reasonable to assume that the ability of capital to pass on *all* of its taxes (particularly the corporate income tax) had been considerably overestimated.[31]

In the years that followed deficits grew ever larger, while the rate of effective taxation of corporations and the wealthy steadily declined. Some of the more serious contradictions of this process were first evident in Britain. As Dudley Jackson, H. A. Turner, and Frank Wilkinson indicated in *Do Trade Unions Cause Inflation?* (1972), the percentage of British corporate profits taken in taxes (including the tax on dividends, and figuring in the effect of tax exemption allowances of various kinds) dropped from 45.6 percent in 1949–52 to 30.9 percent in 1965–68, while the percentage of all wage and salary income taken (also figuring in tax exemptions) rose from 9.8 percent to 15.5 percent in the same years. Thus it is not at all surprising that total corporate profits as a percentage of aggregate wages and salaries *after taxes* rose from 25 percent in 1949–52 to 30.2 percent in 1965–68. Moreover, the shift in taxes and tax incidence hit the poor the hardest. For those single men earning real gross income of £600 or less at 1960 prices, the increase in the average tax rate was 40 percent during 1960–70, while for those earning £20,000 or more the rate of increase was 4 percent. Most of the attacks on trade unions for allegedly squeezing profits during the 1960s and 1970s could be discounted on precisely these grounds.[32]

Steindl's *Maturity and Stagnation in American Capitalism,* which had developed much of the "basic theory" that Baran and Sweezy were to take as their own point of departure, had been written at the outset of the post-World War II era to explain the decline in the rate of private accumulation and stagnation of production that had gradually emerged along with monopoly capitalism, becoming a full-blown contradiction in the depression decade. Faced with the reemergence of stagnation in the 1970s, Steindl returned to the problem in 1979 in an essay entitled "Stagnation Theory and Stagnation Policy," which was designed to deal with the entire post-World War II era and its relation to stagnation theory by accounting for both the period of relatively high growth that existed up to 1969 and the period of stunted growth that has followed.[33] In doing so, Steindl once again placed emphasis, along with a number of other historical factors already emphasized by Baran and Sweezy, on the changes in state policy with regard to the taxation of profits. Following Kalecki, he contended (as he had in the introduction to the second edition of his book) that accumulation would be promoted by government spending financed through the taxation of corporate profits, to the extent that the budget deficit was not correspondingly reduced (since that also constituted a form of finance based on the savings of capital). Indeed, in relation to the United States Steindl called attention to this fact:

> Profit taxes as a percentage of national product were much higher after the war, especially in the 1950s, than before. Budget deficits were lower than before the war, but not so much as to compensate for the increased taxation of profits. On balance, therefore, the budget was expansionist and increased utilization in industry. This, I maintain, has contributed to the high postwar investment activity.[34]

Yet from the early 1960s on there was a steady decline in the taxation of income from capital, which was a contributing factor in the shift from a period of high growth to one of stunted growth. Thus Steindl argued, along the lines of Jackson, Turner, and Wilkinson, that the rise in the tax burden on the working class had been the main cause of the so-called wage explosion in the final years of the long boom, and that the real net wages of the underlying population had declined, intensifying the tendency toward stagnation.[35]

Within the U.S. left, the relationship between stagnation theory and the taxation of capital was brought to the fore in the fall of 1984 when Craig Medlen's influential article, "Corporate Taxes and the Federal Deficit," appeared in *Monthly Review.* Medlen's contribution was intended to be an explanation of why the federal deficit had been expanding so rapidly in recent years, but the theoretical basis for his argument was the "monopoly-stagnation viewpoint" as presented by Baran and Sweezy. As Medlen forcefully explained:

> Viewed through the lens of stagnation theory, the earlier Keynesian understanding that high taxes on the upper classes promote growth corresponds not just to the requirements of "depression" economics but to the requirements of a corporate system that tends to sink by reason of its very foundations. By raising revenue through taxation of corporations, the state diverts a stream of purchasing power that would otherwise have gone into nonproductive spending (advertising and the like, mergers, land acquisition, financial assets) rather than new investment. By spending these funds directly, or redistributing them to the lower and middle classes, the state can prop up the final-demand markets that entice new investment.[36]

Having laid the theoretical foundations for his argument in this way, Medlen proceeded to examine the record on the U.S. corporate income tax. As a consequence of accelerated depreciation allowances and investment tax credits, the corporate income tax had fallen from 52 percent of corporate tax flow in 1957 to 9 percent in 1983, and from 26 percent of total federal revenues in 1957 to 6 percent in 1983. Moreover, Medlen calculated that if corporate taxes had remained at their 1957 level, the *additional* taxes collected in the years 1980-83 would have been $302 billion, as compared with a total deficit in the same years of $424 billion. And since some of the deficit was "passive," or the result of the decline in the level of production, this would have been more than enough to take care of that section of the deficit which the Council of Economic Advisors had designated as "structural."[37]

This did not mean, of course, that a sudden reversal of the trend in taxation that has existed over the last two decades would provide a magic solution to most of the problems besetting the U.S. economy, even in the short run. Complicating the whole matter was the fact that in the meantime—and partly as a consequence of speculation in Treasury securities—the corporations had accumulated a massive debt of their own. Total outstanding debt in the U.S. economy grew from $3.3 trillion at the end of 1977 to $7.1 trillion at the end of 1984, with the federal debt rising only about a third as fast as private debt during this period. In 1984 alone total debt in the economy rose at a rate of 14 percent—the largest annual increase in post-World War II history.[38] Obviously, as Medlen pointed out, these circumstances complicate matters. But it is equally clear that the present state policy of shifting taxes more and more on the backs of the poor is likely to have the effect of intensifying stagnation, as well as class struggle within the U.S. system.

Still, this entire argument might be considered vulnerable to the criticism, consistent with O'Connor's argument and even supported (in an aside) by Baran and Sweezy in *Monopoly Capital,* that the corporations can pass any additional taxes on in the form of higher prices. The "classical" response to this, in the words of Brookings Institution expert on federal taxation Joseph A. Pechman, is that:

> In the short run a tax on economic profit should make no difference in this decision [on price and output]. The output and price that maximized the firm's profits before the tax will continue to maximize the firm's profits after the tax is imposed. (This follows from simple arithmetic. If a series of figures is reduced by the same percentage, the figure that was highest before will still be the highest after.)[39]

In line with this type of argument Medlen added, in a 1985 reply to criticisms that had been directed at his original article, a more concrete one of his own, refuting the notion that the incidence of the corporate income tax fell almost entirely on the backs of the poor:

> In the case of present-day capitalism the appropriate model is oligopoly. The oligopolistic corporation seeks to set prices at the point where profits are maximized, i.e., where the total revenue from sales exceeds total production costs by the maximum possible amount. Hence any tax that directly affects costs (inventory taxes, payroll taxes, sales taxes, value-added taxes) can induce a change in prices designed to pass on as much of the tax as possible. But the corporate income tax is of a different kind; it doesn't directly affect either revenue or costs. It is calculated as a *percentage of profits,* and this is the key to understanding why the corporate income tax falls mainly on the rich. . . .In levying a corporate income tax the government is in effect saying to corporations: go ahead and price at whatever level you wish; make as much money as you can; and after you've done your best, pay *x* percent of your profits in taxes. If *x* percent were raised to *y* percent or *z* percent, corporations might try to hike prices to retrieve some of the lost profit. But such a move would be self-defeating if the assumption that we have made is correct, i.e., that the corporation has already set the price at the profit-maximizing level.[40]

It will be noticed that Medlen's analysis here is akin to Kalecki's earlier point (examined above) that "these taxes are not prime costs, but form a part of gross profits." If we assume that the giant corporations, with their corespective behavior, normally set a price that approximates that of a single firm monopoly (taking into account such factors as the elasticity of demand), it follows that it would be irrational for them to raise their prices in response to a tax levied as a flat percentage of profits, since this would reduce their receipts without altering the *percentage* of taxes taken.[41] In this respect, a tax levied on profits falls into a different category from one that directly affects production costs, such as payroll taxes. What is argued here in relation to the corporate income tax would obviously hold as well for a general tax on capital assets, as proposed by Kalecki.

"Why," Medlen asks, "is there such widespread sentiment that corporations have the ability to pass on their income tax?" In the case of business executives the answer may seem obvious: "The argument that raising corporate taxes would simply raise prices is the self-serving corporate argument that taxing them is at best fruitless and at worst harmful to the underlying population."[42] Where the left is concerned things become a bit more complicated. The idea that corporations simply pass on their taxes by increasing the price to the final consumer has a certain "seductive appeal," since it once again reaffirms "the subservience of politics to economics." "But again," Medlen asks,

> what is the mechanism of escape? Even our best theorists on the left have neglected to specify the shift dynamics. James O'Connor informs us that "from the outset, business leaders have favored taxing their corporate rather than personal income because monopoly sector corporations control prices and thus can shift the corporate income tax to consumers." (*Fiscal Crisis of the State,* pp. 206–7). But O'Connor does not tell us how a percentage tax can be passed on. Instead he presents evidence that despite a huge increase in the corporate tax from 1920 to 1955, the aftertax return on assets remained relatively constant. Seen from the vantage point of stagnation theory, the continued ability to extract profits might, in good part, be *because of* (not despite) the high rates of post-Korean taxation.[43]

Indeed, monopoly-stagnation theorists like Magdoff and Sweezy were quick to build on the foundations that Medlen had raised, suggesting—in an article entitled "The Need for Tax Reform"—that it provided a partial explanation for the cumulative rise in the federal deficit. Under circumstances of deepening stagnation and larger and larger tax breaks to the rich, they contended,

> the only practical way for the government to pump up demand is to spend more than it takes in, i.e., by running deficits. The stimulating effect of a given deficit, however, is reduced by the dampening effect of a regressive tax structure, i.e., one that transfers income from lower income people (spenders) to higher income people (savers). And when, as in recent years, there is a trend toward an increasingly regressive tax structure, it follows that deficits have to grow just to maintain a given level of stimulation. Pumping up demand through deficits is thus like pumping up pressure in a leaky tire. And if the leak is getting bigger (i.e., if the tax structure is getting more and more regressive), you have to pump harder to stay even and still harder to get ahead.[44]

Needless to say, there is a cumulative aspect to deficits, quite apart from the question of tax structure, since what is borrowed has to be returned *with interest* and thus the deficit must constantly grow if it is to have the *same* effect in stimulating demand. But the leaky tire metaphor serves to point out that the tax structure itself contributes to the massive growth of federal deficits. In the terms earlier employed by Baran, it serves to increase the *additional* surplus appropriated from the underlying population, and thus to cancel out much of the positive effect of government spending in closing the realization gap.

The facts, in any case, are startling. As Gabriel Kolko has indicated, "Real wages of workers in the entire private, nonfarm sector began a sharp long-term decline after 1972, dropping 15 percent by 1983."[45] And it is in this context that the tax burden on those at the bottom has increased. In the words of Robert Kuttner:

> Between 1953 and 1974, direct taxes paid by the average income family doubled, from 11.8 percent of income to 23.4 percent of income, while the tax burden of a family with four times the average income went from 20.2 percent to 29.5 percent, an increase of less than half. Between 1969 and 1980, social security taxes increased by 92 percent. And since social security taxes apply to only the first $37,700 of wages, the major portion of this increase was on the nonweathly. During the same period, corporate income tax collections fell 14 percent, and capital gains rates were cut by 20 percent.[46]

Some of the larger implications of this become apparent when comparison is made with Japan. While corporate income taxes correspond to about 6 percent of federal revenues in the United States, and only 3 percent in Britain, they add up to 28 percent of central government revenues in Japan, where the corporations pay the highest rate of effective taxation of profits in the world. Given this very high rate of corporate taxation, the Japanese central government is able to balance its budget while allowing the bottom third of the population to escape paying income taxes altogether.[47] One should, of course, be careful not to draw too many inferences from partial comparisons of this kind, since taxation is just one of the factors affecting the economic growth pattern of a country. But the case of Japan gives some plausibility to the argument that a high level of corporate taxation, under conditions of monopoly capitalism, is more likely to promote than obstruct the process of economic growth.

Comparison with Japan may be relevant in another way as well, since it suggests that "the crisis of the tax state" is also tied to the composition of its spending. This was recently emphasized by Sylos-Labini, who wrote:

> In the long period—this is a very important point—the gap between the growth in spending and the growth in revenues depends, at least in part, on the composition of spending itself. If the share of expenditures destined to productive uses is high, income will tend to increase at a higher rate than it would have had there been a lower share of productive spending. Remember that Japan alone among the industrialized countries avoided the "fiscal crisis of the state," not so much because public expenditures grew at a lower rate than in other countries, or at a lower rate than income, as from the fact that the share of expenditure directed to productive ends was higher than that observed in other countries.[48]

State Expenditures in a Class Society

Unlike O'Connor's *Fiscal Crisis of the State,* which divided state spending into "social capital" and "social expenses" in order to demonstrate the fundamental thesis of a "structural gap" between the growth of spending and the growth of revenues, Baran and Sweezy's *Monopoly Capital,* with its focus on surplus absorption, approached the composition of state spending primarily in terms of the systematic bias away from those areas that could be considered reproductive, from the standpoint of society as a whole, and toward those areas, like military spending, that belonged to the nonreproductive utilization of social surplus.[49] Hence the issue of state expenditures in U.S. class society was introduced in the following way:

> During the interval 1929–1957, total government spending increased from roughly one-tenth to one-quarter of GNP, most of the difference representing the absorption of surplus which would not otherwise have been produced. Of this proportionate increase in the ratio of government spending to GNP, almost nine-tenths was transfer payments and defense purchases, little more than one-tenth non-defense purchases. How are we to interpret these figures?[50]

The most important thing to recognize here was that "government's direct contribution to the functioning and welfare of society is almost entirely subsumed under nondefense purchases."[51] This includes not only education and highways (the two biggest expenses), but also commerce, housing, health, sanitation, police and fire protection, the justice system, prisons, administration, and so on. What is noteworthy is that in spite of a vast expansion in the highway system in particular, associated with a doubling of the number of automobiles over the period, nondefense purchases made "almost no contribution to the solution of the surplus absorption problem."[52]

Transfer payments, which had grown from 2 percent to 6 percent of GNP over the period, had, Baran and Sweezy contended, probably "made a significant contribution" to staving off stagnation. Nevertheless, the regressive nature of the payroll taxes on which social security was based, and the fact that some 12 percent of transfer payments were actually interest payments to banks, corporations, and wealthy individuals, diminished the extent to which such payments were part of the "solution" rather than the problem.[53]

It was in the area of military spending, however, that the real expansion had taken place, rising "from less than 1 percent of GNP to more than 10 percent, accounting for about two-thirds of the total expansion of government spending relative to GNP since the 1920s." Moreover, without the prop of military spending, they contended, unemployment would be back up to levels of 15 percent or more, "such as prevailed in the 1930s."[54]

But was this an intrinsic feature of U.S. capitalism, or could military spending simply be replaced by civilian spending if the voters so decided? The answer lay in the "modalities of political power in a monopoly capitalist society, and more specifically in its particular American version."[55] For Baran and Sweezy this had two aspects: (1) the theory of the state as such, and (2) the social limitations on civilian spending.

Baran and Sweezy's analysis of the state is closest to the instrumentalist approach of theorists like Lenin, Luxemburg, and Ralph Miliband in that it places its emphasis on the fact that the state in capitalist society is, first and foremost, the state of the capitalist class. Its "primary function" is to guarantee conditions of private appropriation.[56] Yet their approach was probably best characterized in the typology of Marxian state theories presented by David Gold, Clarence Lo, and Erik Olin Wright, as a form of "economic structuralism" in which the state is viewed largely in terms of the imperatives of accumulation, rather than as a by-product of unmediated ruling class initiatives.[57] Thus the role of the capitalist state in the economic growth process is limited by the determinant character of accumulation itself.

This is best understood by looking first at the argument on the "prospects of liberal capitalist reform" developed by Sweezy in *The Theory of Capitalist Development* and at the critical analysis of "laborism" provided by Baran in his 1952 essay on "National Economic Planning." Only then will we be in a position to appreciate the political argument in Baran and Sweezy's essay-sketch.

Generally speaking, Sweezy wrote in *The Theory of Capitalist Development,* genuine programs for social control over consumption and investment based on the work of Keynes could not be faulted in terms of economic logic, "either on their own ground or on the basis of the Marxian analysis of the reproduction process."[58] What mainly distinguished the left-Keynesian and neo-Marxian approaches to the issue of reform, then, was the former's emphasis on economic growth and popular sovereignty, and the latter's stress on accumulation and class. Thus while economic theory after Keynes was generally couched in terms of the broad concept of growth, abstracting from most institutional characteristics of the system and implying little more, from a developmental standpoint, than increases in output of goods and services per unit of time, Marxian analysis suggested that growth under capitalism was synonymous with capital's own self-expansion, and thus had a determinate historical character associated with class-based accumulation.[59] This meant that high-minded, left-Keynesian proposals for massive increases in social consumption and for redistribution of income from the rich to the poor were utopian fantasies as long as capital retained its hegemony over the state. "The Keynesians," Sweezy wrote, "tear the economic system out of its social context and treat it as though it were a machine to be sent to the repair shop there to be overhauled by an engineer state."[60]

But the role of the state could never be reduced merely to the immediate interests of the capitalist class, or even to the imperatives of capital accumulation. And this was doubly true since the normal political structure under capitalism, bourgeois democracy, carried a "latent contradiction" associated with the electoral process.[61] As Marx had written of the 1848 French constitution in *The Class Struggles in France:*

> The classes whose social slavery the constitution is to perpetuate, proletariat, peasants, petty bourgeois, it puts in possession of political power through universal suffrage. And from the class whose old social power it sanctions, the bourgeoisie, it withdraws the political guarantees of this power. It forces its rule into democratic conditions, which at every point help the hostile classes to victory and jeopardize the very foundations of capitalist society.[62]

What possibility, then, was there of a genuine labor party arising that would act in the interests of society as a whole rather than in the interests of capital and accumulation? While not ruling out the possibility altogether, Sweezy argued that three conditions were necessary: (1) the reform movement must stay entirely "free of capitalist influence"; (2) it must manage to obtain control over the state and remove capitalists and their retainers from all positions of power, by nonrevolutionary means; and (3) it must somehow secure so strong a hold over the political economy as to make economic sabotage by vested interests futile. If these requirements were not overdrawn, Sweezy argued—and he pointed to the Chartist movement of nineteenth-century Britain and to the various social democratic and labor governments, popular fronts and new deals of recent history, as evidence that they probably were not—then "a rather surprising conclusion follows, namely that the elimination of the contradictions of capitalism via the road of liberal reform is, viewed from a political standpoint, no less than the gradual achievement of socialism."[63] Needless to say, any genuine political threat to the system would tend to generate an authoritarian response, and thus a revolution stopping short of "socialist consummation" might suddenly find itself facing a fascist counterrevolution.[64]

"Reforms," Sweezy wrote, "may modify the functioning of

capitalism but never threaten its foundation."[65] And yet the very reforms necessary to overcome the deep-seated contradictions of the accumulation process, if carried out in sufficient magnitude, would have to attack the class basis of accumulation itself.

Although sharing the same general view as Sweezy, Baran was to give the argument greater focus in his 1952 essay on "National Economic Planning." Following Schumpeter in adopting the term "laborism" for the type of social democracy that was evident in Britain and northern Europe in the years following World War II, Baran sought to explain, in a systematic manner, why such political movements would run into fundamental contradictions.[66] In his own words:

> A trade union administration determined to abolish bargaining over the distribution of the social product by eliminating one of the two decisive claimants would have to be a much stronger government than a regime sponsored and supported by the business class, since its task would be considerably more complex. Indeed, the claimant whom it would wish to "abolish" would be the economically and socially ruling class in society, entrenched in traditional positions of property and power, resting upon an elaborate structure of custom, habit, and prevailing social values. Compared with the magnitude of this undertaking, the task of fascism was easy. . . . [The latter] did not disturb . . . the basic socioeconomic structure of the capitalist order. It was in other words a *political* revolution neither accompanied nor followed by what could be termed a social transformation.
>
> What is envisaged in "laborism's" advent to power is, however, precisely the opposite: with the continuity of political institutions maintained, with the structure of social values and ideologies unaffected, the prevailing *economic* and *social* system is expected to be radically altered. To make matters still less realistic, this drastic overturn in the basic economic order of a capitalist society is expected to be carried out by an organization [the trade union] that by its very nature constitutes an integral part of that society.[67]

Were a laborist government to rise to political preeminence, Baran argued, its practical dissolution would be almost certain, since it would generally be "unable to adapt" the state to its "original plans and purposes." On the other hand, if "a 'laborist' administration were to succeed in squaring the circle, in 'suppressing' the capitalist class in a capitalist society, the contradictory nature of the resulting situation is easily visualized." By promoting aggregate demand in the form of state consumption and tax relief to the poor, it would generate inflationary pressures which could only be countered "by freezing wages on some level agreed upon with the trade unions and by the enactment of suitable measures to enforce stable prices."[68] Private investment, under these circumstances, would plummet due to lack of confidence. And "confronted with an 'investment strike' on the part of the capitalist class," Baran explained,

> the laborist administration would find itself compelled either to retreat and to grant such concessions to the business community as may be needed to restore the confidence of the investor or else to undertake on an ever expanding scale investment and operation in the field of productive enterprise.[69]

In either case, the laborist experiment, in itself, would have come to an end: in the former case, by simply "yielding to 'economic necessity' "; in the latter instance, by a bold attempt to follow the path of "all-out socialization."[70]

In *Monopoly Capital,* Baran and Sweezy set the terms for their discussion of the state by arguing that bourgeois democracy "was democratic in form and plutocratic in content." In any first approximation to the truth, then, it had to be recognized that while "the people exercise sovereign power," in actual fact "a relatively small moneyed oligarchy rules supreme."[71] Again, this did not mean that the rule of the capitalist class was an unmediated one. Instead, Baran and Sweezy suggested that political institutions in the United States constituted a highly structured class environment. Here they pointed to the fact that:

> The nation's Founding Fathers were acutely aware of the latent contradiction in the democratic form of government, as indeed were most political thinkers in the late eighteenth and early nineteenth centuries. They recognized the possibility that the propertyless majority might, once it had the vote, attempt to turn its nominal sovereignty into real power and thereby jeopardize the security of property, which they regarded as the very foundation of civilized society. They therefore devised the famous system of checks and balances, the purpose of which was to make it as difficult as possible for the existing system of property relations to be subverted.[72]

"For these and other reasons," Baran and Sweezy wrote, "governmental institutions which have taken shape in the United States have been heavily weighted on the side of protecting the rights and privileges of minorities: the property-owning minority as a whole against the people, and various groups of property owners against each other."[73] On top of this there was the evolution of political parties as "vote-gathering and patronage-dispensing machines without program or discipline." Given the resulting power structure, even the New Deal administration, with its vast popular support, had failed dismally to come up with the kind of civilian spending needed to lift the United States out of the Great Depression, providing a concrete indication of the enormous power of vested interests.

The reason that the United States did manage to increase its GNP by more than two-thirds in the half-dozen years beginning in 1939 and ending in 1945 was of course World War II.[74] What the New Deal could not achieve the war "proved to be within easy reach."[75] For Baran and Sweezy, civilian spending had reached its "outer limits" as a proportion of GNP, "given the power structure of United States monopoly capitalism," by around 1939. After that its share of GNP remained fairly constant while further increases in government spending were generally attributable to enhanced transfer payments and the growth of military expenditures.

What specific barriers to civilian spending were involved here? In the case of those programs that generally competed with the private market, such as river valley development (i.e., the Tennessee Valley Authority), public housing, public hospitals, and public transportation, no answer was necessary.[76] Statization of the private sector in advanced capitalist societies is steadily resisted by the powers that be except in those cases where the market has already collapsed.

In the more difficult case of education, Baran and Sweezy explained, there is an analogous conflict between the private educational system serving the offspring of the wealthy and the public educational system serving the larger population. Moreover, the system of public education is divided along class and racial lines, reflecting the stratification of education with respect to suburbs, inner cities, and ghettos. Nor is this hierarchical system an accident. Instead, Baran and Sweezy argued, such inequality in educational opportunities is "vitally necessary to buttress the general inequality that is the heart and core of the whole system."[77] And given the fact the private schools and colleges are already well-endowed financially, all that the privileged elements have to do, in order to maintain this crucial degree of inequality, is to make sure that the federal government does not step in to create real equality of educational opportunities through its immense spending power. All of this was heavily documented and detailed in *Monopoly Capital,* in the context of an extended critique of the educational system in the United States as a concrete, cultural manifestation of an antagonistic class society.[78]

"There is just one major exception," Baran and Sweezy claimed, to the generalization that all major forms of civilian spending conflict with powerful vested interests, "and it is very much the type of exception which proves the rule: government spending on highways."[79] This was tied to "the frightful havoc wreaked on American society by the cancerous growth of the automobile complex."[80] And for Baran and Sweezy this was, in large part, a form of economic waste, when judged from the standpoint of society as a whole.

On paper, Magdoff and Sweezy wrote in 1975, it is a relatively simple matter to draw up plans that will solve many of the more glaring irrationalities of monopoly capitalism within the framework of capitalism itself. But those who fall for such "paper dreams" overlook the fact that each of these irrationalities "is the fortress or hiding place of vested interests which wield enormous political power and have absolutely no intention of making the least sacrifice for the common good, even if that somewhat elusive concept is defined wholly in capitalist terms."[81] Thus the added problems that distinguished monopoly capitalism—although not a part of the abstract concept of capitalism—had become part of the historical logic of the system.

But if the obstacles to substantive social change, within the framework of the system, could be traced to history and politics and not to economics in any conventional sense, then a much more general theory of *social* crisis was needed. Recognizing the enormous difficulty of this task, Baran, Sweezy, and Magdoff carefully refrained from any attempt to provide an explanation of the political history of American capitalism that would complement their largely economic (or socioeconomic) thrust. Instead, they confined their analysis of political phenomena to what was absolutely necessary to "close" their basic model. Although institutional obstacles, erected by both the capitalist class in general and by various segments of that class, were emphasized, their origins were not discussed. Nor was the crucial issue of recurrent opportunities for political rebellion at certain critical conjunctures ever addressed in any detail, although Baran, Sweezy, Huberman, and Magdoff always kept their eyes firmly fixed on the New Deal as a historical landmark. Hence, while their analysis suggested that the dilemma of maturity and stagnation could not be surmounted short of revolution, it left many of the more immediate political questions unanswered.

The most sophisticated approach to this problem is to be found in Gabriel Kolko's analysis of the course of modern U.S. history in terms of what he designates as "political capitalism," or the "utilization of political outlets to attain conditions of stability, predictability, and security—to attain rationality—in the economy."[82] He demonstrates that the great merger movement of the last decade of the nineteenth century and the first two decades of the twentieth resulted in an economic order that, at least at the outset, was anything but stable or rational. Hence the giant corporations had no choice but to resort to extra-economic means to protect their profits, their investments, and sometimes their very lives. The misnamed "progressive movement" that resulted led to the formation of a "new Hamiltonianism" in the form of a regulatory system controlled by the firms that were ostensibly being regulated.[83] And along with this went the penetration of a new business ethos into the very heart of American government.

Kolko's conception of the turn-of-the-century period as a state of crisis for capital and its profitability, despite the relatively rapid rate of economic growth, corresponds to the position taken by Sweezy, who has repeatedly emphasized the "nearly universal complaints of economic crisis and unrelieved depression" by business firms in the period of "cut-throat competition," when "the wholesale price index (1823 = 100) plunged from 139 in 1873 to 74 in 1898."[84] In Sweezy's analysis, the dominant change that occurred in this period, allowing for the consolidation of monopoly capitalism, was the banning of price competition. In Kolko's more complex case, stress is placed on the political solutions devised with the rise of a regulatory system controlled by the corporations that it ostensibly regulated.

The dilemma of "political capitalism" is that it is essentially a static, ad hoc solution to an extremely dynamic problem. The political solutions to monopoly capitalism's first period of political crisis were undermined by the destabilizing features of the business cycle itself. The 1920s saw a gradual rise in excess capacity, along with a long-run decline in liquidity, the combined effect of which led to the disastrous downturn of the 1930s. It was in the midst of World War II, according to Kolko (and Magdoff and Sweezy), that a new institutional order of politico-military capitalism was devised, one that was to become the basis for the post-World War II expansion. But in the end these political arrangements proved "all too finite," with the reemergence of chronic overcapacity in the 1970s.[85] Thus the recurrent crisis of political capitalism in Kolko's terms has presented itself again, manifesting itself this time in an attempt to reconstruct U.S. hegemony in the world economy, while developing various political strategies to overhaul the supply side of the economy.[86]

What should be clear from the foregoing analysis is that the theory of monopoly capitalism requires a dynamic conception of political change and its relation to the accumulation process, such as that provided by Kolko, if it is to be anything like a complete theory of *social* crisis. Unless "the connections between the theory of the capitalist economy and the political situation in the advanced capitalist countries—however mediated . . ." are "established, and their implications explored," theorizing on economic crisis is a vain endeavor.[87]

In any case, Kolko's analysis, like that of Baran and Sweezy, points to the fact that, "The military budget became . . . the sponge which absorbed much, if not always all, excess industrial capacity, thereby putting a floor under the capitalist economy."[88] Baran and Sweezy's own argument on state expenditures in the United States led them to the conclusion that military spending would remain the dominant form of government-promoted surplus absorption. It is by no means insignificant that this view continues to stand up to the test of time. Although the share of military expenditure dropped somewhat in the early 1970s, these were also years of deepening economic stagnation in the United States and war preparations have now regained what small ground they lost. In 1983 the federal government spent $274.8 billion on purchases of goods and services. Of this, $74.5 billion went to education, highways, hospitals, commerce, health, sanitation, police and fire protection, the courts, prisons, administration, etc. The remaining $200.3 billion was spent on direct military expenditures.[89] A further indication of the social priorities embedded in government spending is indicated by the fact that the United States spent some $600 billion on direct military spending in 1967–75 and only $6 billion on public housing in the same period.[90] Direct military spending (actual rather than acknowledged), as calculated by James Cypher, formed an average of 13.2 percent of GNP in the 1947–71 period (with a multiplier of 1). Adopting the still conservative assumption of an actual multiplier of 2, direct and indirect military-induced expenditures accounted for something like 26.4 percent of GNP during the years of undisputed U.S. hegemony.[91]

For U.S. monopoly capitalism, the advantages of such vast state-financed military outlays are multiple. The demand for war expenditures is primarily a product of the need to maintain a worldwide system of imperial domination, the more warlike aspects of which are justified as a "fight against Communism." Such expenditures also have the benefit, as Veblen sardonically remarked, of helping "to direct the popular interest to other nobler, institutionally less hazardous matters than the unequal distribution of wealth or creature comforts."[92] Finally, there is the economic effect on surplus absorption. As stated, with what Baran and Sweezy called "brutal candor," in a *U.S. News and World Report* article in 1949:

> Government planners figure they have found the magic formula for almost endless good times. . . . *Cold War* is the catalyst. Cold War is an automatic pump primer. Turn a spigot, the public clamors for more arms spending. Turn another, the clamor ceases. Truman confidence, cockiness, is based on this "Truman formula." *Truman era of good times,* President is told, can run much beyond 1952. Cold War demands, if fully exploited, are almost endless.[93]

After pointing out the role that military expenditures played in promoting economic growth under the current regime of U.S. capitalism, using evidence of this kind, Baran and Sweezy went on to devote a whole section of their chapter on "Militarism and Imperialism" to the idea that "the effectiveness of arms spending," in this sense, was likely to diminish over time. The reasons for this were twofold: economic and military. The economic limitation had to do with the fact that the shift in arms production from "mass-produced military hardware" to high technology weapons tended to reduce the favorable impact on investment and employment. The military limitation, noted by Baran and Sweezy, was that the piling up of endless amounts of weapons of immense destructive power was irrational in the sense that it might lead to the kind of full-scale nuclear war that the country would not be able to survive, so that sooner or later concrete steps toward arms control would have to be taken.[94] Unfortunately, with the benefit of historical hindsight, it is possible to say that Baran and Sweezy seriously underestimated the degree of irrationality that the system could sustain in this respect. Twenty years after the publication of *Monopoly Capital,* there is no sign at all that the armament process is likely to slow down due to the overaccumulation of means of destruction. The "Star Wars" initiative is but the latest demonstration of just how far the U.S. government is prepared to go in this respect.

There is, however, a third possible argument on the effectiveness/ineffectiveness of military spending as a means of staving off stagnation, one that Baran and Sweezy did not discuss in *Monopoly Capital* but which has received some attention from Sweezy in more recent writings. It is only to be expected that state spending devoted to nonreproductive forms of output like military purchases is bound to have its long-run costs. This issue was raised most fully by Veblen, who remarked:

> A disproportionate growth of parasitic industries, such as advertising and much of the other efforts that go into competitive selling, as well as warlike expenditure and other industries directed to turning out goods for conspicuously wasteful consumption, would lower the effective vitality of the community to such an extent as to jeopardize its chances of advance or even its life. The limits which the circumstances of life impose in this respect are of a selective character, in the last resort. A persistent excess of parasitic and wasteful efforts over productive industry must bring on a decline. But owing to the very high productive efficiency of modern mechanical industry, the margin available for wasteful occupations and wasteful expenditures is very great. The requirements of the aggregate livelihood are so far short of the possible output of goods by modern methods as to leave a very wide margin for waste and parasitic income. So that instances of such a decline, due to industrial exhaustion, drawn from the history of any earlier phase of economic life, carry no well-defined lesson as to what a modern industrial community may allow itself in this respect.[95]

Commenting on the above quote, Sweezy has interjected that, "One may legitimately wonder, as we enter the last two decades of the twentieth century, whether this safety margin is not now at long last in grave danger of being used up. This is the question which lies at the heart of the crisis of our time."[96]

It will be recalled that for Sylos-Labini this growth of the nonproductive component in state expenditures could have the effect, over the long run, of slowing down the rate of economic growth in certain countries, as compared with the growth rate in those industrialized countries that were able to devote a larger "share of expenditure . . . to productive ends." Thus the gap between the growth in spending and the growth in revenues associated with the "fiscal crisis of the state" could—insofar as this was the result of a slowing down in the rate of economic expansion itself—be attributed in part to the augmentation of economic waste. In this sense, Baran and Sweezy's treatment of the composition of state spending in terms of civilian vs. military outlays overlapped with O'Connor's model, since the latter clearly believed that the expansion of nonproductive "social expenses" (such as welfare state and warfare state spending) was one of the key factors sending the national government into the red.

State Contradictions and Political Strategy

In 1982, in an article entitled "The Responsibility of the Left," Magdoff and Sweezy introduced a general theoretical principle that could be used to govern socialist political practice in the present historical conjuncture. Pointing to the example of the Works Progress Administration (WPA) during the Great Depression, in which jobs had been created to fit individuals "where they were and as they were," Magdoff and Sweezy argued that the left should advocate "reforms that go against the grain of the present system," rather than allow a sense of what is immediately feasible to force it into positions, like "the phoney promises of politicians," of "short-run impotence and . . . long-run irrelevance."[97] An elaboration of this approach was later provided by Prudence Posner Pace, who distinguished the "anticapitalist" strategy of Magdoff and Sweezy from the "anticorporatist" strategy of certain radical theorists—Samuel Bowles, Thomas Weisskopf, and David Gordon constituting the "outstanding spokespeople."[98] According to Pace, the anticapitalist strategy requires that "the measure of a program" should be whether (1) it is consistent with a theoretical framework in opposition to capitalist relations; (2) it is accompanied by an educational process which ties it to broader social questions; and (3) the process of struggle consciously attempts to separate the participants from the value and ideas of the capitalist class.[99]

In terms of the specific contradictions of the state economy discussed above, two programs (in addition to a new WPA) that fit the foregoing criteria suggest themselves. "The fiscal crisis of the state" can be dealt with most consistently from a *revenue* standpoint by advocating higher taxes on the wealthy. But instead of *simply* pushing for a resumption of effective taxation of corporate *incomes,* the left should also raise the issue of a general tax on capital *assets*—even at the considerable risk of questioning the legitimacy of private property itself—backing this up with the kinds of arguments, in relation to efficiency, introduced by Kalecki. The class-conditioned composition of state spending can be attacked, first and foremost, through insistent demands for arms limitation (and even a general dismantlement of the "defense" industry). But this should not be done on the grounds of the economic costs—which, in any case, are still outweighed, in the short run, by the economic benefits to capital—but as part of a much larger opposition to U.S. imperialism. Programs of this sort, it should be understood, clearly belong to what Sheldon Wolin has called "a long revolution aimed at deconstituting the present structure of power," and are not merely designed to patch up an unworkable and exploitative social order.[100]

7

Imperialism and the Political Economy of Growth

Dependency Theory: The Plaintiff

According to the traditionalist Marxist economist John Weeks,

> Capitalist accumulation in dependency theory is primarily the result of the redistribution of surplus product between developed and underdeveloped areas. This presupposes both the production of surplus product (a precondition for its distribution and redistribution) and accumulation itself. Accumulation is not related to the social relations under which a surplus product is produced or appropriated, with the implicit view that a surplus product is a sufficient condition for accumulation.[1]

This statement clearly expresses the view, fairly widespread among the more traditionalist Marxists, that radical dependency theory is fundamentally opposed to the theoretical framework of historical materialism. Indeed, we are told that "the surplus extraction argument" (associated with such theorists as Baran, Andre Gunder Frank, and Samir Amin) has two theses: (1) "that exploitation can be seen as a relationship between countries," and (2) "that the capitalist mode of production is an incomplete mode of production, i.e., it cannot generate its own reproduction."[2] "Like Proudhon," Weeks and Elizabeth Dore contend, "the advocates of the surplus-extraction thesis are arguing that inequality lies not in commodity production, but in the unfairness of the . . . plundering relationship, i.e., in commodity circulation."[3]

Weeks and Dore are quite right, of course, in suggesting that any theory which (1) considers accumulation in dependent societies to be "*primarily* the result of the redistribution of surplus product between developed and underdeveloped areas"; (2) "presupposes both production of surplus product and accumulation itself"; (3) divorces accumulation from "the social relations under which a surplus product is produced or appropriated"; (4) assumes that "surplus product is a sufficient condition of accumulation"; (5) argues that "the capitalist mode of production . . . cannot generate its own reproduction"; and (6) contends "that inequality lies not in commodity production, but in . . . commodity circulation," has very little in the way of any direct connection with Marxian political economy. But it is quite a different matter to argue that theorists like Baran and Amin (or even Frank), at whom Weeks and Dore and numerous others have directed many of their criticisms, have actually made these "mistakes."[4]

It is no doubt true, as Richard Fagan has usefully observed, that in the process of dealing with such previously neglected issues as the international context of underdevelopment and the phenomenon of superexploitation, much of *"the clarity with which classical Marxism located the question of class struggle at the center of the development and decay of capitalism has been lost."*[5] At the same time, neither exploitation, nor class struggle, nor development, nor revolution can be dealt with in abstraction from "accumulation on a world scale," where third world social formations are concerned. "In this shift (from the capitalist mode to the world scale capitalist system)," Amin has written, "lies the entire subversive power of Marxism in our time."[6]

Arrested Development

There can be little question about the fact that Baran's main object in writing his now classic study, *The Political Economy of Growth* (1957), was to emphasize the very real possibility of substantial development in underdeveloped countries once they had freed themselves from the shackles of imperialism. As Baran explained in a letter to Sweezy, "In addition to what imperialism does, one should consider and indeed emphasize what its role is in the *prevention* of what needs to be done."[7] Thus in introducing the concepts of actual, potential, and planned surplus, Baran was attempting to throw light on the full range of productive resources currently available in a dependent economy—as well as emphasizing the need to radically transform the society if these resources were to be put to use.

The economic basis of his analysis was succinctly expressed in the following précis by Rudolfo Stavenhagen, which relies on much of Baran's own language:

> Economic growth is usually said to be related to the level of investment. This, in turn, depends on the available capital and the level of savings in a given society, and may be called the society's *actual* eco-

> nomic surplus, that is, the difference between society's actual current output and its actual current consumption. The rate of development will then be the result of the size of the actual economic surplus and the way in which it is used. If a good part of the surplus is transferred abroad, as is the case in the underdeveloped countries, then of course the rate of development will be low. But societies also dispose of a *potential* economic surplus, which is the difference between the output that could be produced in a given natural and technological environment with the help of employable productive resources, and what might be regarded as essential consumption. The potential economic surplus is to be found in (a) society's excess consumption, (b) the loss of output due to the existence of unproductive workers, (c) the loss of output due to the irrational and wasteful organization of the existing productive apparatus, and (d) the loss of output due to open and disguised unemployment. Consequently, the chances for economic development in the countries of the Third World depend upon the ways in which they employ their actual economic surplus and successfully tap their potential economic surplus which at present goes to waste. These are problems directly related to social and political organization.[8]

It will be readily perceived from Stavenhagen's summary above that the distinction between actual and potential surplus, insofar as it relates to the underdeveloped countries, is relatively simple when it comes to treating the issue of consumption. For where the mass of the population in the poorer countries is concerned, there cannot be much difference between the "actual current consumption" associated with actual surplus and the "essential consumption" associated with potential surplus—indeed, in many cases actual consumption will be lower than essential consumption. Since the great majority of the population lives at a near physical subsistence level, the potential economic surplus—most of which shows up in the form of the capitalists' consumption, the "take" of foreign firms, and the wasteful organization of industry, and only a relatively small part in recorded savings—is quite large, despite the low level of national income. To quote Baran, "The economic surplus . . . while by comparison with the advanced countries small in *absolute* terms, has accounted for a large *share* of total output—as large as, if not larger than, in advanced capitalist countries."[9] Under these conditions, then, growth becomes dependent on tapping the sizable amount of wasted surplus.

The immediate usefulness of this approach was demonstrated

by the facility with which Baran was able to counter the four central postulates of mainstream development theory: (1) The underdeveloped economies had always been underdeveloped, and were simply in the early stages of economic growth; (2) the main obstacle to development was a "vicious circle of poverty," requiring a diffusion of capital to the third world; (3) less-developed countries suffered from a shortage of entrepreneurial talent, requiring the importation of Western know-how and initiative; and (4) most of the economic difficulties experienced in poor nations can be traced to overpopulation, making educational programs designed to promote birth control a primary need.

Instead of simply assuming that the poorer economies in the capitalist world had always been relatively "backward," Baran approached the issue historically. "The question that immediately arises," Baran wrote, "is why is it that in the backward countries there has been no advance along the lines of capitalist development that are familiar from the history of other capitalist countries, and why is it that forward movement there has been either slow or altogether absent?" The answer is to be found in the way in which capitalism was brought to these regions, during the period of what Marx called "primitive accumulation," characterized by "undisguised looting, enslavement, and murder," and in the way in which this very process served to "smother fledgling industries."[10] In opposition to the presuppositions of liberal development theory, Baran argued that "the peoples who came into the orbit of Western capitalist expansion," beginning in the sixteenth and seventeenth centuries, had not always existed in a state of abysmal poverty. Rather it was the very intrusion of Western capitalism that served to destroy whatever existed in the way of "primary accumulation" in these societies, and to slow down (and even halt) the rate of economic growth.

The "outstanding case" was India. As Marx had pointed out, British penetration into India involved the destruction of the original economic and social fabric of the society, including the forcible destruction of the Indian textile industry, which was at the time nearly as advanced as Britain's own.[11] As Irving Zeitlin, whose work follows Baran in this respect, has written:

> Development of a native industrial capitalism in India was not conducive to the interests of British imperialism. British rulers, therefore, actively sought to prevent its development and, in fact, succeeded in

> doing so. As a result, British industry, particularly textiles, was able to employ an increasing number of British workers in spite of the growing mechanization of production. The destruction of a large part of the Indian weaving industry and the forestalled development of a large industrial working class provided an extended market for British goods and enabled British industry to employ more workers than otherwise would have been possible.[12]

Thus, in the words of Baran, "the violent, destructive, and predatory opening up of the weaker countries by Western capitalism immeasurably distorted their development." If the despoilation of India had not occurred, and its economic surplus had been instead "invested *in India,*" the development record of that country would certainly have been quite different.[13]

The detrimental effects that Western expansion had produced in the third world, Baran argued, could also be seen in the contrary example of Japan, "the only Asian country that succeeded in escaping its neighbors' fate and in attaining a relatively high degree of economic advancement."[14] What was most striking about Japan, in this respect, was that it had largely managed to escape penetration by capitalism during the more vulnerable stages of its development. It was thus able to initiate its own form of bourgeois revolution in the late nineteenth century.

Baran listed three factors that may have enabled Japan to escape imperialist penetration: The first was the early "backwardness and poverty of the Japanese people and the paucity of their natural resources."[15] Second, during the period of most rapid colonial conquest in Asia, Britain, the leading capitalist power, was involved in conflicts over so many regions—China, the Middle East, and Europe itself—that it had no opportunity for imperalist adventures in a relatively uninviting state such as Japan. Like China, and more effectively than China, Japan was able to maintain a certain degree of independence as a result of the struggle between capitalist powers for colonies and spheres of influence. Indeed, as Baran went on to indicate,

> what decisively affected the position of Japan was another characteristic of modern imperialism: the growing rivalry among the established imperial whales, and the arrival on the world stage of a new industrial power, the United States. . . . Although in the case of Japan it was the United States that carried out the initial opening-up and that imposed upon it its first unequal treaty, neither the stage in the

development of American capitalism nor its international status allowed the United States as yet to try to establish exclusive control over Japan.[16]

In the meantime the threat of military and economic penetration was enough to spur Japan to extraordinary state-directed efforts at economic development in the years following the Meiji Revolution. "Less than half a century," Baran stated,

had to pass before the concentrated, monopolistically controlled industry had provided a firm basis for an impressive military potential which, combined with the purposefully nurtured chauvinism of the *samurai* and their descendents, turned Japan from an object of imperialist intrigues into one of Western imperialism's more successful junior partners.[17]

Hence, the case of Japan, like that of India, served to illustrate the fact that "backwardness" ws not to be thought of as an original condition, as bourgeois economic development theory would have it, but as a manifestation of capitalist penetration. Capitalism destroyed native industries, removed a large part of the economic surplus, and created massive social disharmony and disorder, the form and content of which had little to do with the historical requirements of internal development in and of itself.

All of this pointed to the fact that the vicious-circle-of-poverty explanation of underdevelopment was really a means of explaining away a long history of exploitation. Contradicting this second major postulate of modern development theory, Baran argued that the main obstacle to economic growth was not a lack of capital. Even though the amount of actual surplus (or actual savings) in such societies was typically small, the potential economic surplus (or potential savings) was such a large proportion of national income as "to enable them to attain high, and indeed very high, rates of growth."[18] As partial evidence, Baran cited estimates on potential economic surplus and property income in various countries, comparing these to the much lower rates of actual investment. For example, he cited Harry Oshima's "careful calculations" indicating that potential economic surplus was 33 percent of national income in Malaya as of 1974, while gross investment amounted to only 10 percent of the national product. The same ratios for Ceylon (1951) were "30 percent and 10 percent respectively; for the Philippines (1948), 25 percent and 9 percent; for India, 15 percent and 5 percent; for Thailand, 32 percent and 6 percent." Much of this available economic surplus had its statistical trace in "excess consumption of the upper class," "increments to hoards at home and abroad," and the expenses of enormous military establishments. And "a very large share . . . was withdrawn by foreign capital."[19]

Obviously, such estimates are difficult to derive and are open to question on a number of scores. Nevertheless, what evidence is available consistently supports the view that the surplus accounts for a much larger proportion of total income in the periphery of the capitalist world than in the core. Moreover, the huge discrepancy between this high rate of surplus generation and the comparatively low level of investment in these countries is patently obvious. This can be seen in a 1981 study, entitled "An International Comparison of the Rate of Surplus Value in Manufacturing Industry," by Alice H. Amsden. After a detailed country-by-country comparison, Amsden concludes:

> By comparison with the average for the advanced capitalist countries, s/v [surplus value] is almost three times greater in Latin America, twice as great in Asia (excluding Hong Kong), and approximately one and one half times more in Africa (excluding Ghana) and the Middle East. These differences between developed and underdeveloped countries are so sharp that even if the biases enumerated were removed, the overall picture would probably remain unchanged.[20]

It might be logical to assume that countries "enjoying" such a high rate of exploitation would be free from any serious supply-side constraints with respect to accumulation within manufacturing itself. And since basic industry remains underdeveloped there is ample room for classical-type expansion on the demand side, in the sense that investment can increase for relatively long periods of time "independently" from consumption, as contrasted with the more mature capitalist economies.

Consequently, for some theorists the main barrier to development in the peripheral states is not to be found in a dearth of capital itself, but in the absence of creative entrepreneurs (or an industrial bourgeoisie) capable of launching a sustained pattern of rapid growth. Thus Baran pointed to the all-too-common

> lamentation bewailing the lack of "entrepreneurial talent" in the underdeveloped countries, the ample supply of which purportedly must be credited with the economic development of the Western countries.

> Inspired by the work of Weber and Schumpeter—both of whom, incidentally, stand miles above such platitudes—economists identified with this view stress the crucial role played by "the creative entrepreneur" in promoting economic progress.[21]

If this thesis of a missing entrepreneur was not to be reduced to a simple truism—there is no industrial capitalism because there is no industrial bourgeoisie, and vice versa—it had to be based, according to Baran, on one of two propositions: either it was purely pathological, or it was due to the formation of class and corporation monopolies. The very idea that the presumed economic failures of a given underdeveloped country could be traced to a supposed lack of entrepreneurial talent, or to the wasting away of such talent as existed through a psychosomatic preference for unproductive consumption, contained, in Baran's view, strong voluntaristic, nationalistic, and even racist overtones.[22] But to attribute entrepreneurial backwardness to the formation of "monopolistic positions" was to undercut the whole missing entrepreneur thesis and to raise in its stead the problem of accumulation and class:

> It is in the existence of these monopolistic positions, as well as of all the other relations previously discussed [such as the wasting away of potential economic surplus], that one has to look for an explanation of the slowness or absence of industrial growth in underdeveloped countries, rather than in sterile speculations of "inherent lethargy," "preference for the maintenance of family concerns," and "lack of enterprise" supposedly characteristic in backward countries.[23]

Nor did Baran accept the most deeply held Western belief on the causes of underdevelopment: that it could be attributed to overpopulation. This "supreme effort" of bourgeois social science at blaming the victim simply presented the paralytic view that nothing could be done for the "teeming millions" in the so-called basket case countries. The truth of the matter, as Baran demonstrated with detailed statistics, was that it was not population density but the degree of industrialization that was the most important factor conditioning per capita income. Thus he replied with the words of Engels: "The pressure of population is not upon the means of subsistence but upon the means of *employment*."[24] And this in itself could be traced to the modes of utilization of economic surplus. All that the problem of overpopulation signified, in the end, was that there was a crying need for revolution in the imperialized countries of the world. "The problem of underdevelopment, of overpopulation, of want and disease," Baran argued, "could now be solved by a concerted, planned effort of the world as a whole within the lifespan of one generation."[25] That millions continued to die of hunger and want was a sufficient condemnation of the capitalist system as a whole.

If none of these standard liberal explanations stood up under serious scrutiny, the question remained: "How could the backwardness of development in the poorer part of the capitalist world be explained?" The root answer could not be found in vague generalities about dependency, as Baran well knew, but had to be traced to the class structure of underdeveloped societies.

In order to understand Baran's approach to this problem, it is useful to disgress briefly to consider the impressive account of Marx's own conception of class provided in Geoffrey de Ste. Croix's important new work—winner of the Isaac Deutscher Memorial Prize—entitled *The Class Struggle in the Ancient Greek World* (1983). According to Ste. Croix, elaborating on Marx:

> *Class* (essentially a relationship) is the collective expression of the fact of exploitation, the way in which exploitation is embodied in a social structure. By *exploitation* I mean the appropriation of part of the product of the labour of others: in a commodity-producing society this is the appropriation of what Marx called "surplus value."[26]

The significance of this understanding of Marx's conception of class is the primacy that it gives to exploitation, or the mode of appropriation of the surplus product. As Marx wrote, "Only the form in which this surplus labour is extracted from the immediate producer, the worker, distinguishes the economic forms of society, for example the society of slavery from that of wage labour."[27]

Hence at its most *general* level—divorced from *historically specific* conditions, such as the "high capitalism" of nineteenth-century Britain—Marx's conception of class requires an approach that focuses on the process of exploitation, or the expropriation of surplus labor from the direct producer, in order to get at the reality of the class divisions through which this relation of exploitation is socially *expressed*. To quote Ste. Croix again, "The most significant distinguishing feature of each social formation . . . is not so much *how the bulk of the labour of production is done, as how the dominant propertied classes,* controlling the conditions of production, *ensure the extraction of the surplus* which makes their own leisured existence possible."[28] Moreover, as he elsewhere points out:

> *Imperialism,* involving some kind of economic and/or political subjection to a power outside the community, is a special case [of the general class phenomenon] in which the exploitation effected by the imperial power (in the form of tribute, for instance), or by its individual members, need not necessarily involve direct control of the conditions of production. In such a situation, however, the class struggle within the subject country is very likely to be affected, for example through support given by the imperial power or its agents to the exploiting class or classes within that community, if not by the acquisition by the imperial power or its individual members of control over the conditions of production in the subject community.[29]

In other words, imperialism, as understood by Ste. Croix, enormously complicates class phenomena by making possible an extraction of surplus by interests that have no necessary, direct connection with exploitation at the level of production, and by altering the class struggle in the subject community as well. In circumstances such as these, the issue of the expropriation of surplus labor, i.e., the issue of exploitation and class, is less than ever divorced from the issue of the utilization of the surplus product, which stands between the level of production and the reproduction of society as a whole.

Given these aspects of the class "problematic," it becomes clear how Baran's attention to the difference between the high rate of exploitation in underdeveloped countries (as measured by potential economic surplus) and the low level of actual accumulation (as reflected in the actual surplus) is tied to the question of the reproduction of these societies as definite class formations.

In the general analysis of underdeveloped countries, as outlined by Baran, the economic surplus fell into the hands of five fundamental social entities: (1) a semifeudal landlord class, (2) a merchant bourgeoisie, (3) an industrial bourgeoisie, (4) foreign capital, and (5) the state. It was a typical, although not necessarily defining, feature of underdevelopment that agriculture—much of which was devoted to cash crops destined for export—accounted for a large share (often more than half) of total output. This was partly carried out through subsistence-level production by peasant farmers, whose tiny holdings had "to support not merely the peasants' families, but also the payments of rent or taxes (or both)."[30] In another part of the typical agricultural economy, production was carried out on large estates with the help of hired labor. One way or another, a significant proportion of the economic surplus of society was appropriated by a land-owning class, which used up much of the potential accumulation fund that passed through its hands to support excess consumption. "What aroused the ire of Adam Smith, Ricardo, and other classical economists," Baran wrote,

> is still the rule in backward countries. Maintenance of sumptuous residences, lavish living, acquisition of conspicuous luxuries serving as symbols of wealth and status, large numbes of servants, entertainment, and travel—all account for much of what is received and spent by the landowning aristocracy.[31]

Nevertheless, agrarian revolution, if it meant the parcelization of land among the peasants, was unlikely to solve the problem of underemployment, low productivity, and wasted surplus in the agricultural sector. Under capitalist conditions, Baran argued, agrarian revolution can only promote economic growth indirectly, by generating an "agrarian counterrevolution," resulting in a "new concentration" of agricultural production in the hands of capitalist farmers. But for this to happen the position of the feudal-landlord class must be weakened decisively and the bourgeoisie must obtain control of the state apparatus.[32]

Within the nonagricultural part of the economy, a very large share of the economic surplus was appropriated by "merchants, moneylenders, and intermediaries of all kinds, some of them living in rural areas, but by the nature of their activities not belonging to the agricultural population."[33] What was most significant about this "lumpenbourgeois" element of third world social formations was that while it obtained a significant share of the proceeds of exploitation, very little of the surplus it appropriated actually made its way into (or back into) the industrial branches of the economy. Instead, it remained within circulation, or was used up "in buying up land yielding rent revenue, in various undertakings auxiliary to the operation of Western business, in importing, exporting, moneylending, and speculation."[34]

Although part of the surplus was accumulated in the industrial sector itself, and thus constituted a significant contribution to the growth process, it was the "backwardness" of this sector in particular that lay close to the center of the problem of underdevelopment. Much of this could be traced to the early penetration of capitalism into the regions of the third world. At a time when protection of infant industry might have provided the basis for a smooth transition to steady growth, "the countries most in need of such protection were forced to go through a regime of what might be called industrial infanticide."[35] More significantly,

> whatever market for manufactured goods emerged in the colonial and dependent countries did not become the "internal market" of these countries. Thrown open by colonization and by unequal treaties, it became an appendage of the "internal market" of Western capitalism.[36]

Since most of the industrialization that took place was carried out by, or in conjunction with, international capital, the effect was to disrupt the economy still further. For most large ventures, the part actually spent within the dependent country was small, with most of the outlays occurring abroad, on the purchase of machinery, patents, etc. Closely connected to this was the point, to be developed more fully by such later theorists as Samir Amin, that the "multiplier effect" of investment spending on factories and equipment in an underdeveloped country was not usually felt in the underdeveloped country itself but in the economies of the capitalist center, where the actual purchases were normally made.[37] To make matters more complicated, those indigenous firms that did arise, in close connection with international capital, usually took the form of monopolies, dominating the very narrow markets and reducing the competitive stimulus to rapid growth. Thus in most underdeveloped countries, Baran wrote, "capitalism had a peculiarly twisted career. . . . To the dead weight of stagnation characteristic of pre-industrial society was added the entire restrictive impact of monopoly caitalism."[38] Monopolistic firms of this sort did not invest most of the surplus at their disposal; instead, they sent it abroad or utilized it in wasteful ways, much like the landed aristocracy. All of this contributed to the weakness of the relatively small, indigenous industrial bourgeoisie.

In discussing the fourth claimant to the economic surplus of the third world states, Baran noted that the increase in Western assets in the periphery was largely due to the reinvestment of part of the surplus obtained in the periphery itself. "The worst of it is, however, that it is very hard to say what has been the greater evil as far as the economic development of underdeveloped countries is concerned: the removal of their economic surplus by foreign capital or its reinvestment by foreign enterprise."[39] The harmful effect of the so-called repatriation of profits could scarcely be doubted. But, Baran argued, reinvestment of the profits of foreign firms in the domestic economy could also be very damaging. The reasons for this were manifold: (1) While local capital, under the sway of foreign firms, tended to make most of its investment purchases abroad, this was even more the case for multinational capital with its international production and marketing system. (2) Promotion of cash crops for export in the agricultural sector placed these economies in a position of almost perpetual dependency. (3) Quoting H. W. Singer, Baran pointed out that the railways, bridges, ports, and power stations had been constructed primarily for the benefit of raw material exporters and in no way constituted part of the internal structure of the dependent countries themselves, "except in the purely geographical and physical sense."[40] (4) The subsistence wages provided by foreign firms were frequently so low—between 5 and 25 percent of the value of output—as to have very little effect on domestic demand.

However, the most important consequence of foreign enterprise, for Baran, was the way it affected the class struggle in the subject country. Thus there emerges a "group of merchants expanding and thriving within the orbit of foreign capital." Then there are the local "industrial monopolists, in most cases interlocked and interwoven with domestic merchant capital and with foreign enterprise," whose position in society would be very much lessened with the rise of autonomous industrial capitalism. "Concerned with preventing the emergence of competitors in their markets, they look with favor upon the absorption of capital in the sphere of circulation, and have nothing to fear from foreign export-oriented enterprise."[41] Finally, there are the feudal landlords, whose interests "run entirely parallel" with those of the other propertied classes. Thus, the penetration of foreign capital into the subject country takes the form of a class alliance devoted to the common exploitation of a large peasantry and a small working class, and is integrated, via foreign capital itself, with the class struggle on a world scale. In Baran's words:

> What results is a political and social coalition of wealthy compradors, powerful monopolists, and large landowners dedicated to the defense of the existing feudal-mercantile order. Ruling the realm by no matter what political means—as a monarchy, as a military-fascist dictatorship, or as a republic of the Kuomintang variety—this coalition has nothing to hope for from the rise of industrial capitalism which would dislodge it from its positions of privilege and power. Blocking all economic and social progress in its country, this regime has no real political basis in city or village, lives in continual fear of the starving and restive masses, and relies for its stability on Praetorian guards of relatively well-kept mercenaries.[42]

Behind all of this is foreign capital itself, which engages in both direct and indirect exploitation in the underdeveloped countries. The resulting distortions in third world social formations become even more apparent when the subject of the final claimant to the economic surplus—the state—arises. Baran considers three general forms of state structure: (1) colonial regimes ruled directly from the center of the capitalist world, (2) comprador regimes, and (3) regimes of a "New Deal type." Since the nature of colonial social formations is well known and presents no unusual theoretical problems, it is useful to focus on the second and third types. The older type of comprador state, Baran argues, is represented by certain of the oil-producing states of the Middle East, such as Saudi Arabia and Kuwait, where an overclass of feudal sheiks cooperates with foreign capital in the extraction of the riches of their own country. This is ultimately less important, however, than the kind of imperial client state that frequently emerges as an afterword to anticolonial struggles.

The general anticolonial struggle was based on "united fronts of the progressive bourgeoisie . . . intellectuals . . . active elements of the urban and rural proletariat," and, in some cases, "segments of the feudal aristocracy."[43] Once national independence has been achieved, however, the anti-imperialist alliance breaks down and the newly sovereign state follows one of several paths, depending on the constellation of class forces. Where "the peasantry's struggle for an agrarian revolution" continues to gain momentum and is supplemented by the action of the much smaller urban proletariat, the bourgeoisie, the landed aristocracy, the comprador groups, and their "foreign principals" unite, usually with a powerful segment of the military, to suppress any tendencies toward popular revolt and end up re-establishing "the *ancien régime* not *de jure* but *de facto*."[44] In this respect, Baran cited China under the Kuomintang, the Philippines, Pakistan, South Korea, and South Vietnam. Needless to say, this is not the end of the story; such imperial client states soon become dependent on large infusions of armaments and economic aid from the centers of international capital, in a desperate attempt to strengthen their precarious social position.[45] In the case of China and Vietnam, however, these and other more extreme means proved inadequate in the face of a revolutionary upsurge.

The other main path is represented by the strategy of import substitution, the most radical variants of which were introduced in Egypt and India. Here the ground was prepared by the existence of a strong national bourgeoisie and the relative weakness or passivity of the proletariat and peasantry. Writing of Nasser's Egypt, Baran indicated that:

> It may well be that conditions are at the present time most propitious in the case of Egypt for the country's entering upon the road of "Japanese development." That the officers' corps and the army are apparently backing Egypt's national bourgeoisie, that its leaders seem to be determined to overcome the opposition of the feudal and comprador interests, and that the international situation is such as to enable them to conduct an independent policy—all this greatly enhances the chances of success of their current campaign to move the country in the direction of industrial capitalism.[46]

Baran thus conceded that it might still be conceivable (at least in the case of Egypt) for an underdeveloped state with a relatively strong national bourgeoisie and a favorable international environment to proceed along a path of "Japanese development," perhaps under the auspices of an officers' corps.[47]

A far more important case was represented by India, which Baran characterized as a "New Deal-type" third world regime. In India, he noted, the class forces impeding the rise of a developed social formation in the rural and urban environments were as strong as in other underdeveloped countries, so that the only entity capable of mobilizing the economic surplus and using it for productive purposes was the state. What was needed for rapid development, Baran argued, was an investment rate of something like 15 percent, which could conceivably be accomplished by seizing some of the approximately "25 percent of India's national income which that poverty-stricken society places at the disposal of its unproductive strata."[48] But such a mobilization of the potential surplus was bound to generate determined resistance from the propertied classes (including foreign capital), and Baran doubted that "the present Indian government" had the strength or will to accomplish what needed to be done. Thus Baran concluded that while capitalist India might continue along a tortuous growth path, facilitated by its five year plans, it was unlikely to realize "its great historical chance: the peaceful transformation of a great country from a state of squalor and oppression to that of a rapidly advancing socialist democracy."[49]

Hence Baran qualified his general assessment of stagnation, or slow growth, in the third world in a number of ways. Where industrial development was taking place, as he noted in his discussions of the indigenous industrial bourgeoisie and foreign capital, this usually took the form of a presumed "partnership," in the sense of "a rider and his horse," between indigenous capital and international enterprise, creating a strong demand for Western imports.[50] In other words, his analysis pointed to the growing importance of a relationship similar to what more recent theorists like Peter Evans have called "dependent development," or a "special instance of dependency, characterized by the association or alliance of international and local capital," with the state also joining in and converting the connection into a "triple alliance."[51] In addition, Baran's discussion of the development strategies in such states as the Philippines, Egypt, and India raised the issue of what has since come to be known, with some degree of confusion, as the "neocolonial state."

Whatever might be the prospects open to states like Egypt and India, however, it was clear that Baran believed that the chances for rapid development in the majority of third world nations was not very good. "Like all other historically changing phenomena," he wrote,

> The contemporary form of imperialism contains and preserves all its earlier modalities, but raises them to a new level. Its central feature is that it is now directed not solely toward the rapid extraction of large sporadic gains from the objects of its domination, it is no longer content with merely assuming a more or less steady flow of those gains over a somewhat extended period. Propelled by well-organized, ra-

> tionally conducted monopolistic enterprise, it seeks today to rationalize the flow of these receipts so as to be able to count on it in perpetuity.. And this points to the main task of imperialism in our time: to prevent, or, if that is impossible, to slow down and control the economic development of underdeveloped countries.[52]

The flexibility of Baran's assessment here can be seen in the fact that contemporary forms of imperialism, in his conception, only required that the economic development of third world nations be *slowed down* and *controlled,* not that it be *prevented* altogether. In other words, his analysis allowed for the possibility of dependent development in the wider sense of growth within the parameters of dependency.

Baran's extremely influential work produced a whole school of followers. Of these the most important was certainly Andre Gunder Frank. Frank was the first to coin the term "development of underdevelopment" and was largely responsible for the almost universal acceptance of the underdevelopment approach within radical circles in the late 1960s and early 1970s. Although Frank's work on dependency was primarily concerned with Latin America, other theorists proceeded to apply his (and Baran's) framework to Africa and Asia.[53]

Frank's theory had its basis in a number of clearly expressed propositions about certain contradictions that he believed to be inherent in the capitalist world system. First, there was the capitalist contradiction associated with the expropriation of economic surplus by a few to the detriment of the many—particularly evident in the exploitation of the periphery by the center. Frank relied here on Baran's distinction between actual and potential surplus. According to Frank, the "non-realization and unavailability for investment of 'potential' economic surplus is due essentially to the monopoly structure of capitalism."[54] This was not, however, dependent on the existence of a monopoly *stage* of capitalism. It was fundamental to Frank's view that regardless of how competitive capitalism in the major capitalist states has been, it has nonetheless always been monopolistic in relation to the periphery. Thus it was clear that although the leading capitalist powers had found it necessary to maintain direct colonial monopolies during the competitive phase, with the later emergence of monopoly capitalism more subtle forms of monopolistic control had become feasible and even necessary.

Second, the centralization of capital has its counterpart in uneven development. This could be conceived, Frank argued, in terms of the "polarization into metropolitan center and peripheral satellites."[55] The dialectic of development and underdevelopment was a single structurally interrelated process. Extraction of economic surplus from the periphery generated accelerating development in the center and reinforced underdevelopment in the periphery. This global dialectic was mirrored within each society. Yet while the "world metropolis" managed to develop in the true sense, the metropoles of the underdeveloped states remained dependent and were unable to generate snow-balling growth, due to the fact that they were simultaneously "satellites" of the "world metropolis." The implication was that underdeveloped states were trapped in a vicious system of stagnation enforced by the imperialist capitalism of the center. Any weakening of ties between the center and periphery of the capitalist system, as in the 1930s and 1940s, increased developmental opportunities in underdeveloped regions.[56]

Third, this dialectic of development and underdevelopment remained central in spite of the changing nature of the capitalist system as a whole, since it was basic to capitalism's very nature and survival. From a class standpoint it was virtually impossible, Frank argued, for underdeveloped states to develop an autonomous national bourgeoisie. In fact, for Frank the bourgeoisie in these countries was little more than a "lumpenbourgeoisie"—a class whose interests were directly or indirectly, actively or passively, identified with the interests of foreign capital.[57]

All of this should indicate that in Frank's analysis the concept of class was generally less central to the overall analysis of underdevelopment than was the case for Baran. Deriving his conceptual framework from Marxian notions of necessary and surplus labor, Baran had emphasized the dialectical relationship between the production, appropriation, and utilization of the economic surplus in underdeveloped countries, on the one hand, and bonds of dependency externally imposed on these countries on the other. And out of this complex interaction between overexploitation and late imperialism arose the historical imperative of socialist transformation in these countries. However, Frank and certain subsequent dependency theorists, who gave concrete meaning to Baran's analysis by placing it in specific historical settings, concentrated almost exclusively on the second and third aspects of his dialectic, strangely deemphasizing the first. Dependency theory itself became associated with a one-sided, outward-looking perspective that ignored most of the root conditions of accumulation and class. Related to this was the well-known static character of certain early versions of dependency theory. Having detached Baran's analysis of class fractions from its logical roots in the underlying accumulation process, there remained only a Schumpeterian-like view of suppressed industrial entrepreneurship (together with the net outflow of surplus to the metropole) as the unchanging economic context in the periphery. Worse still, the all-too-frequent failure to appreciate the conceptual basis of Baran's theory of accumulation meant that the main point of the "political economy of growth"—the very real possibility of substantial economic progress in postrevolutionary society—was often lost.[58]

Thus, in trying to extend radical analysis to such important problems as international exploitation and internal colonialism, certain dependency theorists after Baran tended to construct theories of development/underdevelopment that were insufficiently rooted in the analysis of *class-based accumulation*. The fact that this was more a problem of inadequate theoretical synthesis than a retreat from Marxian categories, however, could be seen in the subsequent rise of theories of "dependent development," which—in the work of Samir Amin and others—returned to Baran's more dynamic notion of accumulation under conditions of imperialism as essentially a *class phenomenon*.

Dependent Accumulation

Two of the most essential features of dependent development, as characterized by Sweezy, are to be found in (1) the failure to carry out an agricultural revolution in the periphery, and (2) the much higher rate of exploitation that exists in periphery nations. The first point, according to Sweezy, was best expressed in the words of Amin, who had written that, "Unlike the countries of the center, where the 'agricultural revolution' preceded the 'industrial revolution,' the countries of the periphery have imported the latter without having started the former stage."[59] It is the seeming inability to carry out an agricultural revolution, as Baran had earlier emphasized, which lies at the heart of the external orientation and lack of self-sufficiency in these countries.

The second aspect of the difference between independent development in the center and dependent development in the periphery, Sweezy explained in his *Four Lectures on Marxism* (delivered in Japan in 1979), is that:

> The rate of exploitation is and always has been vastly higher in the periphery than in the center. In the center, the rate of exploitation is for all practical purposes the same as the rate of surplus value. This is not so in the periphery, where only a small part of the workforce is employed as wage laborers in capitalist industry, with a much larger proportion being exploited directly and indirectly by landlords, traders, and usurers, primarily in the countryside, but also in the cities and towns. Here all or most of the surplus extorted from the workers not employed in capitalist industry is commercialized and becomes indistinguishably mingled with capitalistically produced surplus value. In these circumstances we can speak of a social rate of exploitation but should not confuse the concept with a rate of surplus value in the usual sense.[60]

These circumstances, which lay at the heart of Baran's analysis, provide the basis for what Sweezy, in conformity with the theoretical distinctions made above, calls "a massive flow of monetized surplus product (in the form of profits, interest, rent, royalties, etc.) from periphery to center."[61] Moreover, the impoverishment of the masses in dependent countries is very much worsened by what might be called the "vicious circle of superexploitation" characteristic of underdevelopment.

Thus it is the excessively high rate of exploitation that prevents the development of "a mass market for consumer goods . . . in a local version of Marx's Department II."[62] And the lack of such a market means that capital has no stake in ensuring—not of course out of its own good will, but in response to class struggle—that the rate of exploitation does not drastically undermine the "propensity to consume."

But to even consider the possibility of a pattern of growth in third world societies in which Department I (producers' goods industry) and Department II (in this case, mass consumption goods industry) are in some way uncoupled is to suggest a radical departure from the conditions of accumulation described by Marx. In fact, it is this insight that provides the basic structure of Amin's theory of "accumulation on a world scale." As he introduced the problem in an elegant explanation of his theory, written for *Monthly Review:*

> The determining interrelation in a self-reliant capitalist system is that which links the sector producing mass consumption goods with the sector producing capital goods. This determining interrelation has been the characteristic feature of the historical development of capitalism in the center of the system (in Europe, North America, and Japan). Thus it provides an abstract definition of the "pure" capitalist mode of production and was analyzed as such in Marx's *Capital.* Marx, in fact, showed that in the capitalist mode of production, there is an *objective* (i.e., *necessary*) relation between the rate of surplus value and the level of development of the productive forces. The rate of surplus value is the main determinant of the pattern of social distribution of national income (its distribution between wages and profit), and hence that of demand (wages being the main source of demand for mass consumption goods and profits being wholly or partly "saved" for "investment" purposes). The level of development of the productive forces is expressed through the social division of labor—the allocation of the labor force, in suitable proportions, to each of its two sectors.[63]

Among the corollaries that Amin logically derived from this understanding of Marx's schema of reproduction was (1) the thesis, discussed above, that the industrial revolution of the late eighteenth century was dependent upon a prior agricultural revolution that released surplus labor in sufficient quantities for a rapid expansion of Department I, and gave rise, at the same time, "to a surplus of marketed foodstuffs necessary for the reproduction of this proletariat";[64] (2) the fact that the main class alliances between propertied interests were internal to the center social formations; and (3) the observation that external economic (and political) relations were subordinated to the needs of internal accumulation.

Along with (and somewhat prior to) the agricultural revolution was a commercial revolution, dating back to the sixteenth century, during which the mercantilist states penetrated into parts of what was to become the periphery of the world system. But the way in which these regions were gradually incorporated into the world economy, under the domination of the leading capitalist states, blocked any progress along the path of independent, self-reliant development.

In Amin's analysis, the basis for the *systematic economic exploitation* of the third world only really emerged with the appearance of "imperialism" (as opposed to colonial expansionism) in the last quarter of the nineteenth century. The immediate source of the qualitative change in the nature of worldwide exploitation was the rise of monopolies, the export of capital, and the creation of a relatively advanced peripheral export sector—all of which could be summed up as the development of capital mobility on a world scale. This had its roots, Amin suggested, in the search for higher profits, as a result of a falling rate of profit (associated with the rising cost of raw materials) in the center.[65] But its main manifestation, and the central contradiction of world accumulation during the imperialist stage, was the rationalization of a system of *unequal exchange* (a concept that Amin adapted from Arghiri Emmanuel, making it virtually synonymous with the whole phenomenon of superexploitation), which exists when "the differences between the returns to labor is greater than the difference between the productivities."[66]

Thus, as Amin wrote elsewhere:

> This point of view allows one to define the peripheral capitalist mode as opposed to its central form. Essentially, the peripheral form has the dual feature of a modern technology (hence high productivity) and low wages within the framework of the capitalist social organization. From this specific characteristic . . . dependency is derived. Integration implies that the balance between the development level of the productive forces and the value of labor power is not to be found at the level of the peripheral social formation but only of the world system into which the latter is integrated. This lack of internal correspondence between the two elements in question results in the vicious circle of peripheral development: in order to reproduce its own conditions of existence, the peripheral formation must still contain precapitalist modes of production or produce noncapitalist modes which, being dominated, provide the capitalist mode with its cheap labor.[67]

In other words, the peripheral social formation is distorted by a constant transfer of value toward the center of the capitalist system due to a greater productivity per unit-wage cost—and hence a greater rate of exploitation—which is not reflected in, and actually precludes, the growth of an internal market. Although the expansion of the export sector eventually results in the emergence of a significant luxury goods market (especially in the larger countries), reflecting the sizable amounts of economic surplus appropriated by local capital, by the feudal-landlord element, and by various auxiliary classes or strata (such as the comprador bourgeoisie, state functionaries, "kulaks," etc.), the internal market nevertheless remains quite limited. Thus even in the contemporary case of Brazil, which some radicals (e.g., Bill Warren) have characterized as a "successful" third world country, "the dynamic at work," to quote Sweezy,

> has produced a most startling result: in the fifteen years since the military coup of 1964, a period frequently referred to as the Brazilian "economic miracle," when the Gross National Product rose at rates as high as 10 percent, the level of real wages *declined* by a third or more. No wonder the president of Brazil on a visit to Washington several years ago was quoted in the press as saying, "In my country the economy is doing fine, but the people aren't."[68]

It is the very "disarticulation" of the country, "split" between "an advanced (and sometimes very advanced) . . . export sector," and a "backward" sector of a precapitalist or noncapitalist type which keeps the system going, since the superexploitation of the periphery by the center is mirrored in the superexploitation of the "hinterland" by the "metropolis" within the periphery itself. The ability of the periphery's center to draw surplus labor from the more backward parts of the social formation allows "the peripheral formation" as a whole, as Amin stated in the passage quoted above, "to reproduce its own conditions of existence," despite the absolute impoverishment of the working population. At the same time, "the smallness of the internal market explains the fact that the periphery attracts only a limited amount of capital from the center although it offers a better return."[69]

The first phase of the imperialist stage of capitalism had its "golden age" between 1880 and 1914, but started much earlier in Latin America and lasted up to the 1950s in some areas of the world, such as sub-Saharan Africa. During this period three factors served to distinguish peripheral social formations from the self-reliant model appropriate to the center. First, capitalism was imported from outside and hence was introduced without a prior agricultural revolution. Second, the class alliances were "not principally internal" but involved "an international alliance between the capital of the dominant monopolies and its (subordinate) 'allies' . . . the 'feudal lords' (meaning the varied range of dominant classes in the precapitalist rural systems) and the 'comprador bourgeoisie.'"[70] Third, external relations became the main source of development, conditioning both its direction and its pace.

The second phase of imperialism, in Amin's view, began with the victory of the anti-imperialist liberation movements, based on an alliance between the superexploited proletariat, the mass of the peasantry, and the "potential" class of the national bourgeoisie.[71] Once the victory was ensured the national bourgeoisie in most cases took over and introduced the development strategy known as "import substitution." Beginning with the already existing structure of consumption, this strategy mainly attempted to manufacture consumer durables, in emulation of the consumption patterns of the wealthiest elements in the capitalist center. Thus this strategy generally served to reinforce the distorted emphasis of the consumption goods market on luxury products (or Department III in the Marxian reproduction schemes). All of this was intensified by the rise to dominance, in the same period, of multinational capital, with its emphasis on production of consumption goods only within the reach of the wealthy propertied classes in a third world setting. In the form of industrialization that took place, therefore, wages had significance for the accumulation process only as a *cost* and not also as a source of demand. Thus the "marginalization" of the third world masses, characteristic of unequal exchange, was simply reproduced in a higher form.

The fact that this second phase of imperialism did not constitute a "stage" in the development of self-reliant, third world social formations could be seen in terms of the three variables that Amin had previously stressed. First, no agricultural revolution (the "green revolution" notwithstanding) had taken place. Second, the ruling-class alliances had remained international in character, with the national bourgeoisie shedding its national character and becoming "compradorized" the moment that it replaced the "former 'feudal lords'" at the top of the social pyramid. Third, domination of the accumulation process by external rather than internal conditions continued essentially as before.[72] The examples of Nehru's India and Nasser's Egypt, which had so fascinated Baran in the mid-1950s, were, Amin argued, nothing more than "the most radical attempts in the capitalist third world" to implement the general line of development associated with the period of import substitution.[73]

Indeed, in what might be considered an interesting footnote to Baran, Amin commented that the "Japanese road" (the rise of a semiperipheral nation to the top echelon of the capitalist class) was forever closed with the consolidation of the stage of imperialism at the end of the nineteenth century. Thus, he argues, "the difference between core and periphery is qualitative, and has been insurmountable since the end of the nineteenth century."[74] In this sense, imperialism *is* the highest stage of capitalism.

Imperialism as History

Theorists like Baran, Frank, Sweezy, Magdoff, and Amin have consistently argued that there is a strong tendency under modern capitalist conditions for the net flow of capital to be unfavorable to the periphery and favorable to the center, in clear contravention of the standard assumptions of liberal development theory. But this implies that there is no simple, functional relationship between the problem of surplus absorption in the core states and the system of superexploitation worldwide.[75] Far from alleviating conditions of crisis in the advanced capitalist states, the net inflow of capital from the periphery that has resulted from the imperial system has tended to make the realization problem much worse. Examining data on foreign investment by U.S. firms between 1950 and 1963, Baran and Sweezy showed that U.S. multinational corporations had exported approximately $17 billion in equity capital over the period, "repatriated" around $29 billion (a net inflow into the United States of some $12 billion), while simultaneously expanding their foreign holdings. They then wrote:

> One can only conclude that foreign investment, far from being an outlet for domestically generated surplus, is a most efficient device for transferring surplus generated abroad to the investing country. Under these circumstances, it is of course obvious that foreign investment aggravates rather than helps to solve the surplus absorption problem.[76]

There was, of course, always the possibility that, for short periods, "abnormally high capital exports from the advanced countries" might serve as a safety valve for the overabundant surplus in the imperialist states; but in the normal course of events, Baran and Sweezy argued, foreign investment had to be viewed "as a method of pumping surplus out of underdeveloped areas, not as a channel through which surplus is directed into them."[77]

This position was called into question on both empirical and theoretical grounds by Albert Szymanski in his book, *The Logic of Imperialism* (1981)—despite the fact that Szymanski shared Baran and Sweezy's general assessment of the pattern of accumulation in the advanced capitalist economies themselves.[78] The statistical data that Szymanski gathered from UN and U.S. Department of Commerce sources indicated that:

> In 1977 the developed capitalist countries as a whole transferred to the less developed $8.6 billion in direct investments, $26.0 billion in new private loans, and $43.4 billion in indirect investments (plus various other payments), for a total input to the less-developed countries from the transnational corporatioins and banks of $78 billion. On the other hand, the less developed countries' balance of payments transfers of repatriated profits on direct investment to the developed countries was $14.6 billion, on interest and principal payments for loans $40.3 billion, and for repatriated profits on indirect investments, royalties, fees, and so forth $59.9 billion, for a total of $114.8 billion transferred (in balance of payments terms) from the less-developed to the developed countries. This represented a net transfer of $36.8 billion from the less-developed to the developed countries.[79]

This hardly proved the point that Szymanski wanted to make: that there was a net transfer of wealth from the developed to the underdeveloped world. Not only had the advanced capitalist countries extracted $36.8 billion more than was diffused to the third world, but they had increased their foreign holdings in the periphery at the same time. But by deducting "repatriated profits of raw materials transnational corporations" (on the puzzling grounds that this did not constitute a real transfer of wealth), and by adding in "foreign assistance" by center governments, Szymanski was able to come up with a reduced figure for the net "transfer of wealth" from the periphery to the center of $13.6 billion. Since this figure was still significant, Szymanski then proceeded to argue that much of the transfer undoubtedly reflected the huge OPEC reserves deposited in U.S. banks; so that, if this was recognized, it could be concluded that "the basic effect of the interaction of all of the advanced capitalist countries with the less developed is now a net transfer of wealth from the advanced to the less developed."[80]

Given the tortuous, and highly questionable path, through which Szymanski arrived at this conclusion, we are perhaps entitled to a certain degree of skepticism. This is doubly the case when we consider the fact that what some interpreted as a more equitable balance in the flow of capital between North and South in the 1970s was to a large extent the product of a vast outpouring of loans to third world countries ($26 billion, as compared with $8.6 billion for direct investment, using Szymanski's figures).[81] The full ramifications of this only become apparent when viewed in the context of the "reverse flow process" inherent in the continuous reliance on foreign debt, as discussed by Harry Magdoff in *The Age of Imperialism* in 1969 (and returned to in "The Two Faces of Third World Debt" in 1984). If a country "borrows, say, $1,000 a year," Magdoff wrote in *The Age of Imperialism,* "before long the service payments on the debt will be larger than the inflow of money each year." Assuming the simple case of an annual loan of $1,000 at 5 percent interest "to be repaid in equal installments over 20 years," it follows that in the fifth year almost 50 percent of the annual loan will go to servicing the debt; in the tenth year approximately 90 percent of the money will be devoted to debt service; in the fifteenth year, the outflow for interest and amortization on the debt will be greater than the loan itself; and in the twentieth year "the borrower is paying out more than $1.50 on past debt for every $1.00 of new money he borrows."[82]

"But why," Magdoff asks, "should a country have to continue borrowing year after year? Won't the borrowed money be used to develop the country so that there will be enough money to pay off the debt?" Part of the answer to these questions lies in the fact—pointed out by Evsey Domar as early as 1950—that, in the words of John Pool and Stephen Stamos, "the economic growth rate of the borrowing nation must exceed the rate of interest in order to avoid a reverse capital flow."[83] Another part of the answer is to be found in the reality, emphasized by Magdoff, that since the repayment has to occur in the currency of the foreign nations, the debt can be repaid (irrespective of the rate of growth) only if there are enough exports to provide the foreign exchange. If the exports prove insufficient, the banks in the center states are under pressure to make further loans (and, as the debt trap becomes more severe, to reschedule loans), to prevent an out-and-out default. "And," Magdoff noted in 1969,

> the fact is that during the postwar period the growth in service payments on the debt of the underdeveloped world has increased much more rapidly than has the growth of exports. Hence the burden of debt has become more oppressive and the financial dependency on the leading industrial nations and their international organizations such as the World Bank and the IMF has increased accordingly.[84]

In fact, the long-run problem is much worse than was implied by Magdoff's 1969 example given above, since interest rates have risen to double-digit figures. After only eight years with an annual borrowing of $1,000 at *10 percent interest,* scheduled for repayment in equal installments over a twenty-year period, the borrower will already be in default, unless payments can be rescheduled or larger loans secured. "Thus," as Magdoff and Sweezy recently pointed out, "if a country's development strategy were to call for a net annual inflow of foreign money, an *increase* in the rate of borrowing would be needed. In other words, a *growing* volume of external debt would become a way of life."[85] Although these observations were based on a simplified model, they were reflected in the actual pattern of third world borrowing, with debt as a percentage of borrowing rising from 56.3 percent in third world accounts in 1972 to 75.3 percent in 1981. Behind this was a general decline in the balance of payments of underdeveloped countries, with the payments deficits for Latin American states (excluding Cuba) rising from *minus* $11.1 billion in 1976 to *minus* $38.8 billion in 1981.[86]

Of course, the "uneasy calm" of third world debt cannot be explained merely in terms of "the simple mechanics of the lending process."[87] This can be seen in the case of Mexico, which in the late 1970s attracted massive amounts of loan capital on the basis of its vast oil reserves. The deepening of worldwide economic crisis, together with the failure of oil prices to keep on rising as expected, brought on a severe structural crisis "with lightning speed." Thus, net proceeds as a percentage of new borrowing in Mexico were 53 percent in 1973 and −213 percent in 1980. This was followed by a massive devaluation of the peso, the imposition of harsh terms of conditionality by the International Monetary Fund, and a rescheduling of the debt.[88]

All of this, of course, implies that what may *appear* to be part of a simple transfer of value, in the form of stepped-up loans to the third world, may actually be a sign—as in the case of Mexico in the 1970s—of deepening financial dependency and of the general phenomenon of unequal exchange (as understood by Amin and Sweezy).

Thus, Szymanski's attempt to demonstrate empirically that the actual data on the international flow of capital contradicted the analysis of such theorists as Baran, Frank, Sweezy, Magdoff, and Amin was not very convincing when judged in terms of the statistical evidence that he presented. His theoretical objection (also raised by liberal critics such as S. M. Miller, Roy Bennett, and Cyril Alapatt) was perhaps more relevant. Taking note of Baran and Sweezy's argument that the export of capital could not be considered an effective means of surplus absorption in the long run, since the net flow of capital was toward the center, Szymanski contended that Baran and Sweezy had failed to demonstrate, at a theoretical level, the actual *necessity* of imperialism. As he himself formulated the issue:

> The traditional link between the theory of capital accumulation on a world scale and the argument for the necessity of imperialism has been severed in the arguments of those affiliated with the journal *Monthly Review.* In its place is put the argument that the process of capital accumulation in the rich countries is facilitated by the exploitation of the poor regions whose capital accumulation process is consequently inhibited.
>
> While maintaining that imperialism is an inherent aspect of advanced capitalism, rather than merely a state policy, the Monthly Review tradition does *not* argue that the accumulation process could not proceed without it, i.e., it is not maintained that imperialism is a necessary condition for the survival of capitalism. This tradition maintains, rather, that imperialism is a natural product or outgrowth of capitalism, a position considerably weaker than that of Lenin.[89]

What are we to make of this argument? It would seem that the real issue is not whether imperialism is "necessary" or not, but revolves instead around two different interpretations of "necessity" and its place in Marxian theory. Szymanski believed that he was operating within the classical tradition of historical materialism in contending that capitalism had no *logical* existence outside of imperialism, i.e., it was incapable of reproducing itself.[90] For theorists like Baran, Sweezy, Magdoff, and Amin, who also claim to be operating in the orthodox Marxist tradition, there is no *internal* contradiction within the accumulation process itself from which the "necessity" of imperialism can be mechanically derived—or, which is merely another way of saying the same thing, there is no *logical* contradiction to an *economic* argument that postulates the existence of "capitalism in one country." But this does not negate the fact that colonialism/imperialism grew up with capitalism, belongs to the *historical necessity* of the system, and is just as much a part of the day-to-day workings of the capitalist mode of production as the drive for profits itself.[91] Indeed, to pose the question "Is imperialism necessary?" on economic grounds, is, according to Magdoff, analogous to asking whether the United States could afford to give Texas and New Mexico back to Mexico and Manhattan back to the Native Americans.[92]

Instead of an abstract and derivative notion of imperialism based on some version of economic crisis theory, the dependency tradition has erected its argument on the wider historical imperatives of the system. Is this a "weaker" approach, as Szymanski seems to believe? The answer is to be found in the fact that while many Western radicals seek to understand imperialism as simply the result of some specific, historically contingent contradiction in the capitalist reproduction process, Baran, Sweezy, Magdoff, Amin, and most third world Marxists have concluded that "imperialism is the way of life of capitalism." The former will be eliminated only when the latter is overthrown.[93]

Dependency Theory: The Defense

"The fundamental error of the surplus-extraction thesis," John Weeks and Elizabeth Dore have written,

> is that its proponents lack any concept of the mode of production. While they may refer to classes in backward countries (particularly Baran), they never find it necessary to consider that "whatever the social form of production, laborers and means of production always remain factors of it . . . but the specific manner in which this union is accomplished distinguishes the different economic epochs of the structure of society from one another" (Marx, 1967, II: 36–37). "The specific manner in which this union is accomplished" determines, within certain limits affected by historical circumstances, the class structure, the nature of the state, the system of laws, and other superstructural forms.[94]

A better idea of what Marx himself had in mind in the statement that Weeks and Dore have cited can be seen in the following passage from another part of *Capital:* "The specific economic form in which unpaid surplus labor is pumped out of the direct producers determines the relationship between those who dominate and those who are in subjection."[95] Thus if Weeks and Dore actually meant to stay true to Marx, they were in effect saying that theorists like Baran and Amin never considered "the specific economic form in which unpaid surplus labor is pumped out of the direct producers."

Obviously, in relation to Baran and Amin (if not for Frank as well), this is absurd. Not only did Baran consider the issue of the generation and absorption of surplus labor, but he actually put it at the very center of his analysis. Moreover—and this is very important—he was the first major Marxist theorist (apart from Marx himself and Rosa Luxemburg) to do so in terms of third world social formations. Nor can it be said that Amin has ignored the "specific economic form" of appropriation of surplus labor, since his entire approach to the question of "unequal exchange" is an attempt to provide an objective explanation for the phenomenon of superexploitation—and thus of the "specific economic form" that *distinguishes* both third world societies and accumulation on a world scale. This, of course, does not mean that these theorists are necessarily right in their understanding of the way in which exploitation takes place, but merely that they (as opposed, perhaps, to Frank) cannot be faulted on the methodological grounds that Weeks and Dore have raised in the foregoing passage.

Indeed, the entire set of criticisms, discussed in the opening pages of this chapter, that Weeks and Dore, as representatives of fundamentalist Marxism, have directed at Baran and Amin (as well as Magdoff, Sweezy, and Frank), has nothing in common with the understanding of the work of these theorists presented in the main parts of this chapter. To take these criticisms in turn: (1) It cannot be said that Baran, Amin, Magdoff, and Sweezy, or even Frank, consider accumulation in dependent societies to be "*primarily* the result of the redistribution of surplus product between developed and underdeveloped areas." What determines accumulation, first and foremost, is exploitation at the level of production. Although there is an international dimension to the exploitation of underdeveloped areas (after all, this is what imperialism is all about),

Baran in particular was careful to explain the various kinds of class relationships (peasant labor vs. feudal-landed elments, industrial capital vs. wage labor, mercantile interests vs. labor of all kinds, as well as the parasitic role of compradors, state bureaucrats, and foreign capital) associated with the generation and absorption of economic surplus. In his analysis (as opposed to Frank's, for example) the *direct* international connection was clearly only secondary—though it was the reality of imperialism that produced the *distinguishing* feature of underdevelopment, i.e., superexploitation (in the sense of unequal exchange). (2) Nor can one reasonably suggest that the approach adopted by theorists like Baran, Frank, Amin, and Sweezy "presupposes both production of surplus product . . . and accumulation itself." The main thrust of their analysis, in fact, was to determine why accumulation was *not* taking place—despite a very high rate of exploitation (and therefore a very high rate of *potential* accumulation) at the level of production itself. (3) As we have already seen, there is no reason to think that sophisticated dependency theorists like Baran and Amin "*divorce* accumulation from 'the social relations under which a surplus product is produced or appropriated." To be sure, they were "guilty" of advancing an understanding of accumulation in a class society that did not stop at what went on within the labor process itself, but also considered the matter in terms of the larger multifaceted context of social reproduction as a whole. And this demanded the scrutiny of various parasitic elements like merchant capital, a deformed peripheral state, foreign capital, etc.—even though the direct connection of these particular interests with production itself was tenuous at best. (4) It is pure fantasy to assert that Baran and Amin (or Sweezy, Magdoff, and Frank) ever made the error of assuming that "surplus product is a sufficient condition for accumulation." While mainstream development theorists argued that the lack of development proved that there was a dearth of capital (a *necessary* condition for economic growth), Baran designed his theoretical framework to show that potential economic surplus existed, but that it was not a *sufficient* condition for growth, as the reality of underdevelopment itself demonstrated. What prevented such development from taking place, of course, was the class basis of peripheral social formations (including class relations introduced from without), which blocked the productive mobilization of economic surplus. (5) There is no suggestion in the work of Baran,

Sweezy, Amin, Magdoff, or Frank (as distinct from, say, Luxemburg) that "the capitalist mode of production cannot generate its own reproduction." Baran and Sweezy, of course, have often been criticized for developing a theory that shows how capitalism in the advanced states can reproduce itself under modern conditions (for the time being). On this Amin has written, "And yet some commentators have reacted vigorously against this contribution of Baran and Sweezy. Why? Because it is awkward for them, since it shows the system *can* function (and yet what is more obvious than that?)."[96] Peripheral social formations have not been very successful at reproducing themselves *on an expanding scale,* and when, as in the case of Brazil, a high rate of growth is temporarily achieved, it is not the kind of development (as Sweezy has observed) that will propel them into the "top echelon" of the capitalist world.[97] To recognize this is not to deny the reality of at least *simple* reproduction in these societies (though there *are* cases of absolute decline). (6) It simply is not the case that theorists like Baran, Frank, Sweezy, Amin, and Magdoff contend that "inequality lies not in commodity production, but in . . . commodity circulation." The truth of the matter is that inequality can *arise* within both production and exchange (although it always has its *ultimate basis* in conditions of production). To recognize that commodity circulation is also important in this sense is not to deny the underlying significance of production. On the contrary, to reject the significance of exchange as a factor in class-based accumulation is to preclude any theory of social reproduction as a whole. It is the radical disjuncture between an extremely high rate of exploitation and an extremely low rate of actual investment that is, perhaps, the most characteristic feature of underdevelopment. And there can be little doubt that exchange or circulation plays an important part in the wasting away of the potential surplus. Failure to understand this means a failure to understand why revolution remains an immediate imperative *for those at the bottom of the underdeveloped social formations.*

8

Some Notes on Socialist Construction and Postrevolutionary Societies

"The Steep Ascent"

Near the beginning of the previous chapter it was noted that:

> There can be little question about the fact that Paul Baran's main object in writing his now classic study, *The Political Economy of Growth,* was to emphasize the very real possibility of substantial development in underdeveloped countries, once they had freed themselves from the shackles of imperialism. As he explained in a letter to Paul Sweezy, "In addition to what imperialism does, one should consider and indeed emphasize what its role is in the prevention of what needs to be done."

"What needs to be done" was discussed by Baran in the final chapter of his book, which dealt with the problem of socialist construction in postrevolutionary societies.[1] His very compressed treatment of this exceedingly complex problem involved combining insights into the size of the economic surplus potentially available for economic growth with observations on its proper allocation, based on a *critical* assessment of the Soviet experience. Hence the crucial issue around which his analysis was structured was the concept of "primitive socialist accumulation," which lay at the heart of the Soviet model of development. As Sweezy wrote much later, in a somewhat different context, "The very foundation of this [the Soviet] model was 'primitive socialist accumulation' at the expense of the peasantry, and its dominant thrust was the building up of heavy industry while concomitantly downgrading the development of light industry and the production of consumer goods."[2]

Baran approached this issue from two directions: mobilization and utilization of economic surplus. With respect to the *mobilization* of economic surplus, he argued, it was impractical in the context of "economic backwardness" for the postrevolutionary society to try to reduce the level of consumption of the peasants below the level that had existed in prerevolutionary times. In fact, development would probably require an *immediate increase* in the income of the peasantry over that which had existed prior to the revolution. Therefore, economic development at the outset could not rest entirely on the generation of new surplus, through higher rates of expropriation directed at the peasantry. Instead, it would have to rely on the mobilization of what had constituted the difference between actual and potential surplus in the period of capitalist underdevelopment, or, in other words, on mobilization of that part of the surplus that had previously remained *dormant*.[3] But a very sizable portion of this surplus, Baran indicated, had been in the hands of rural nonproducers and had been appropriated by the peasantry during the initial stages of the revolutionary transition. It was therefore necessary that this surplus (or a large portion of it) be retrieved, since it constituted an important fund for development, and when divided among the peasants as a whole only had a marginal, nonqualitative effect on their living standards. But this could not be done effectively through an income tax, or through the "opening of the scissors"—i.e., a shift of relative prices in favor of industry and against agriculture—but had to be accomplished through the abolition of subsistence farming and the collectivization of agriculture.[4] This would allow the state to apply principles of planning to the rural sector. Once economic planning predominated in all aspects of the economy, however, it was important to keep in mind, Baran emphasized once again, that the appropriation of a sufficiently high surplus to allow for very high rates of growth did not mean holding down consumption among peasants and workers to its bare minimum. On the contrary, an increase in the level of consumption over prerevolutionary levels was undoubtedly necessary. Thus the *planned* economic surplus, or the amount of surplus available for investment when the population obtained some optimal level of income for consumption, would be much smaller than the *potential* economic surplus, or the amount of surplus available for investment when the income of the populace remained at the level of "bare bones" subsistence. The Soviet experience, Baran argued, had shown that it was not necessary to invest at the maximum rate in order to obtain much higher rates of growth.

Baran's argument from the other direction—that is, with respect to the *utilization* of surplus—was broken into three parts, involving three different kinds of choices in the allocation of surplus to production: (1) agriculture or industry, (2) investment goods (heavy industry) or consumption goods (light industry), and (3) capital-intensive or labor-intensive production. In discussing the first of these issues, on the allocation of surplus to agriculture or industry, Baran reinforced the idea that the consumption of the populace, and the well-being of the peasantry, should not be sacrificed in the irrational hope that growth could be based on the disproportionate expansion of industry at the continuing expense of agriculture. Thus it was necessary to promote both industry and agriculture simultaneously, in order to obtain the highest rates of development over the medium and long term. This was because investment provided technology and material means of production for agriculture, while agriculture provided food for an increasing industrial labor force. One could hardly expect to have a substantial rate of economic progress without a steady increase in the level of subsistence of the population. What was needed was a stretching-out of the material means of production in both agriculture and industry, to the limits of their serviceability. In other words, the kind of utilization of productive capacity relevant to the needs of underdeveloped economies would have to be in line with engineering capacity (falling under the rubric of what is now called "capital utilization"), rather than the extremely low levels of utilization (by engineering standards) characteristic of capitalist market economies. To provide an example of what Baran had in mind here, the degree of capacity utilization (assuming traditional shift patterns) in the chemicals industry in India in 1967 was 53.8 percent, while the degree of *"capital utilization"* in 1967, i.e., the operating rate as calculated in terms of *optimal,* desired shift patterns (taking into account both the durability of equipment and the relative surplus population actually available), has been estimated in International Labor Organization studies as betwen 26.7 and 28.7 percent of full capital capacity.[5]

The problem of the allocation of the surplus between heavy industry and light industry was somewhat more complex. It is clear, as Baran notes, that rapid economic growth under conditions of underdevelopment requires large investment in producers' goods industry (Department I), and since the social accumulation fund is a residual of consumption, whatever is devoted to the expansion of consumer goods industry (Department II) cannot be channeled into investment. Hence, consumption, *beyond some optimal level,* cuts into the optimal rate of growth. Nevertheless, it is important that the two departments grow proportionately over the medium and long run. Although it is possible, in the context of a planned economy, to ensure that funds allocated to investment always increase in step with the output of newly created investment goods (thereby overcoming one of the worst contradictions of the capitalist system), any *drastic* attempt to promote investment *independently* of consumption on a consistent basis results in critical, social dislocations, as the Soviet experience had demonstrated.[6]

On the face of it, Baran's argument here would seem to be somewhat convoluted and even contradictory. But, as Maurice Dobb explained in an article written in Baran's honor, it had its roots in the analysis of "G. A. Feldman of Gosplan,"

> long-neglected but now comparatively well-known (since rediscovered by Domar), who really formalized the notion that investment priority for the capital goods sector was a pre-condition for attaining a high rate of growth. His analysis was based on Marx's famous two-departmental schema of expanded reproduction; but in order to suit them to the purposes in hand, he appropriately adapted these so as to include in the capital-goods sector only the production of what catered for the needs of growth (i.e., represented net *additions* to capital); leaving in the consumers'-goods sector all stages of production (including raw materials and replacement of equipment) necessary to produce "the consumer goods necessary for satisfying an existing level of needs." On the size of the former sector . . . measured in terms of productive capacity, the size of total investment, and hence *growth* in productive capacity, at any date depended. It is to be noted, *inter alia,* that his method of presentation was *not* in terms of the customary antithesis between growth and consumption, but in terms of the necessary condition for achieving a given and desired growth-rate of consumption in future years. To every desired (constant) growth-rate of consumption in the future as a planning objective there corresponded a certain relative size of the capital goods sector at all intervening dates. The higher the desired future growth-rate, the larger, *ceteris paribus,* the proportionate allocation devoted to expanding the capital-goods sector must be. In the course of propounding this, he used an equation formally identical with the Harrod growth-equation, the difference being that it was expressed in terms of productive capacity and supply: namely, the growth-rate was equal to the productive capacity of the capital-goods sector as a proportion of total productive capacity multiplied by the "effectiveness of capital" (the inverse of the capital-

output ratio). The rate of *increase* in the growth-rate depended on the rate of increase in the proportionate size of the capital-goods sector, and hence on the proportionate allocation of current investment between the two sectors.[7]

This model of development in a "backward" postrevolutionary economy, first formulated by the Soviet economist G. A. Feldman (on the basis of earlier work by Marx and Lenin) and later employed by Dobb and Baran (who were familiar with both the Soviet planning literature and the Keynesian growth models of Harrod and Domar), did not see investment and consumption as *alternatives.* Rather, to achieve a desired expansion of consumption it was necessary (assuming full utilization) to increase productive capacity by a certain proportionate amount. On the one hand, this set aside the arguments of certain liberal economists who suggested that "balanced growth" or an "equi-proportional expansion of productive capacity in all sectors" maximized the rate of economic progress.[8] On the other hand, it was consistent with Baran's observation that severe strains in the socioeconomy would arise if the level of investment *exceeded* that which was appropriate to a given level of desired consumption. In other words, growth of "heavy industry" always had to be geared to a planned rate of increase in "light industry."[9]

In dealing, in the next stage of his argument, with the choice between capital-intensive and labor-intensive methods of production, Baran was not responding as much to issues that had arisen out of the Soviet growth model as to certain liberal development economists, like Ragnar Nurkse, who contended that the use of labor-intensive forms of production was desirable in underdeveloped economies because of the very large surplus labor force which existed primarily in the form of "disguised unemployment" in the rural areas. The liberal argument suggested that greater use should be made of this relatively abundant factor of production. But Baran, following Dobb, argued that the real issue was one of investment, geared to a higher rate of consumption in the future, or an immediate increase in levels of consumption; thus the choice between capital-intensive and labor-intensive techniques in a planned economy had, in Dobbs' words, "nothing to do with existing factor-proportions."[10] Moreover, Baran suggested that the use of labor-intensive methods in production could also become a form of disguised unemployment, insofar as the workers did not have enough means of production at their disposal to at least reproduce their own means of subsistence, therefore constituting a drain on the resources of the state. In the end, Baran argued that the kind of strategy developed under an international regime that stressed the importance of each country pursuing its own "comparative advantage" was wholly inappropriate for an underdeveloped postrevolutionary economy trying to break the chains of imperial dependency.

Baran went on to indicate that total self-sufficiency or economic autarky was impractical, even for large states like the U.S.S.R. and China. And in small states, in particular, a unilateral attempt to achieve the degree of diversification or production necessary to industrialize in an autarkic fashion would impose prohibitively high costs, while the ultimate object would remain forever out of reach. Moreover, the shortage of resources in small countries demanded considerable involvement in the world econcomy. But even though trade and foreign loans therefore became an important part of the development strategy of these states, their strength to withstand competitive pressures (both "fair" and "unfair") from the leading capitalist states was limited, putting them in a precarious position. Baran's answer was that the main hope lay in mutually beneficial trade and economic collaboration among socialist states.

All of this should make it evident that, in outlining the main points to be considered in planning economic construction in postrevolutionary societies, Baran had consciously backed off from the strict "laws" of economic development under socialism that had become articles of faith in the Soviet model of development. The two most important of these purported "laws," as explained by Magdoff, were: (1) "Agriculture in the service of industry," and (2) "Priority to heavy industry." In stressing the primacy of industry over agriculture, according to Magdoff, the Soviet Union adopted the extreme strategy of choosing "at each stage in the decision-making process" to ask "what agriculture could do for industry, and not the other way around."[11] A rational approach would have focused on the simultaneous expansion of both sectors, as Baran had emphasized. Thus, to quote Magdoff again:

> Even if priority is placed on industry, two possibilities remain: either to stress industrial products that serve agriculture (e.g., tools, machines, fertilizer, fuel, and consumer goods) or to emphasize develop-

ment of an independent industrial base (e.g., metal manufactures and the production of metal-working machinery).[12]

The Soviet Union's unequivocal choice of industrial development over agricultural development was "complemented" by its unequivocal emphasis on heavy industry over light industry. Baran's approach to this issue was certainly more cautious than that of the Soviet model. In adhering, along with Feldman and Dobb, to the notion that a given expansion of investment must always be geared to a given desired increase in consumption, Baran avoided the error that had induced the Soviet Union to become what Magdoff, following Oskar Lange, has called "a *sui generis* war economy."[13]

During the 1970s, when Baran's pathbreaking work, *The Political Economy of Growth,* was becoming a major target of traditionalist Marxists in the West, a number of radical theorists with a more practical bent were busy applying the type of methodology that he had introduced in order to deepen their understanding of the problem of socialist construction in postrevolutionary societies. One of the chief efforts along this line was to be found in Victor Lippit's *Land Reform and Economic Development in China* (1974). Lippit began his study by noting that net investment as a share of net domestic expenditure had risen from the purely nominal rates existing before the Chinese revolution—1.7 percent in 1933—to 15.4 percent by 1952 and 20.23 percent in 1953.[14] By the standards of any previous historical experience (including, perhaps, that of the U.S.S.R.) the figures were staggering. The obvious question was: Where did the savings for this vast upsurge in net investment come from? Lippit proposed to examine the role that land reform had played in this process. But in order to do so it was necessary to utilize the concept of economic surplus. As he wrote in the preface to his book:

> The question of development finance in underdeveloped countries is ultimately one of the uses of surplus: how can a significant part of that share of national income above a nation's culturally determined subsistence requirements be channeled into investment? In every society an elaborate system of claims on the surplus exists, whether as a material expression of the fealty owed to elders and chiefs in tribal society or the rent, interest, and profits due the owners of capital in capitalist society. These systems of claims are ordinarily so deeply imbedded in the social structure that any effort to redirect the income

> flows associated with them into socially useful investment channels will be severely constrained. Only when the existing claims are eliminated through revolutionary transformation of society does an opportunity arise for massive redirection of the income flows that compose the surplus into development finance.[15]

In specifying the concept of surplus to be used in his study, Lippit used a variant of Baran's notion of potential economic suplus. Thus, "in using the term surplus," Lippit wrote, "I refer to the difference between national output, modified to include the potential output of property owners who do not work, and essential or subsistence expenditures."[16] The most important difference between this formulation and the one introduced by Baran, discussed in Chapters 2 and 7 above, was that Lippit did not include what Baran had called the "essential consumption" of the landowners themselves in the calculation of subsistence needs. "This does not imply," Lippit observed,

> that property owners were deprived of such consumption by the land reform, simply that they had to finance it, like everyone else, by working. This assumption makes it possible to treat the entire property income in the rural sector as surplus. The property share and the surplus are, then, two sides of the same coin . . .[17]

There can be little doubt about the fact that this constituted a slight improvement over Baran's earlier category of "potential economic surplus," and one that brought it more in line with the traditional Marxian concept of surplus product.[18]

Utilizing this methodology, Lippit concentrated his analysis on the crucial period of land reform (prior to the collectivization of agriculture in 1955), when this enormous mobilization of economic surplus had taken place. Land reform had been instituted in the liberated areas prior to 1949, and in 1950-52 swept most of the rural part of the country, with 44 percent of the arable land changing hands in favor of the poorer peasantry.[19] But the land reform in itself did not have the effect of increasing the surplus extracted from agriculture. Here we run into the problem—raised at a theoretical level by Baran in his discussion of socialist economic construction—that most of the previously existing rural surplus would simply have disappeared into the peasantry's own consumption, with no noticeable effect on growth, if the state had not intervened. Hence Lippit laid considerable stress on the all-important fact that:

> Prior to 1955, when the collectivization of agriculture took place . . . the increase in the national savings-investment ratio which may be ascribed to the land reform depended on the extent to which peasant efforts to increase consumption were restricted through agricultural taxation or manipulation of the terms of trade between agriculture and industry. Viewed from this standpoint, any increase in peasant consumption may be regarded as a leakage; the task of the government was to extract as much of the windfall income which land reform brought to the peasants as possible, under the constraints of assuring the basic consumption requirements of the peasantry and not harming production incentives or alienating the class whose interests it represented.[20]

In practice, as Lippit pointed out, this meant that the consumption of the peasantry had to increase somewhat, out of the surplus previously used up in luxury consumption and various forms of dissaving by the landlord class. Thus while "government policy was successful in withdrawing some of the benefits of institutional change from their recipients,"

> . . . the high marginal income elasticity of demand for food and other necessities on the part of the poor peasants, as well as the government's desire to retain their support and improve their living standards, put limits on the portion of the gain which could be extracted. As a consequence, the land reform brought both higher real incomes to most of China's peasantry and an increase in the national savings ratio.[21]

All of this is, of course, consistent with Baran's argument that much of the windfall surplus gained by the peasantry as a result of land reform could be extracted by the state for purposes of investment, while leaving the peasantry better off than before. Thus some of the more harsh effects of a strategy of "primitive socialist accumulation" were avoided.

In this way land reform in China was successful at mobilizing a large part of the surplus that had been dormant in the prerevolutionary society. Taxation of the rural sectors alone contributed 10.3 percent of net capital formation in 1952, while manipulation of the terms of trade between agriculture and industry led to the appropriation of another 34.5 percent of net investment expenditures. And, as noted above, the consumption levels of the peasantry rose at the same time.[22]

Nevertheless, if the institutional changes in the agricultural economy that were brought on by the revolution allowed the available surplus to be utilized in a more rational manner, it did not solve the problems associated with the low levels of surplus generation, i.e., the backwardness of productivity, in the agricultural sector. In Lippit's words, "Small, fragmented, undercapitalized forms dominated the countryside, and there was no path to facilitate the introduction of new practices and technology."[23] Thus further progress required the collectivization of agriculture. It was only under such circumstances that China was able to direct some of its newly emerging industrial capacity to the service of agriculture itself. Here too the famous Chinese policy of "walking on two legs" was to differ significantly from the earlier Soviet model.[24]

Partly (although not predominantly) as a result of the mobilization of previously dormant surplus from the agricultural sector, as Lippit's analysis demonstrated, China was able to begin to "pull itself up by its own bootstraps" in the 1950s.[25] Much of China's demonstrated ability to industrialize, however, was attributed, by observers representing all political standpoints, to its sheer size and the wealth of resources at its disposal. Thus, like the Soviet Union, it was thought to have benefited from a degree of "economic autarky" that was beyond the reach of most underdeveloped countries. Huberman and Sweezy were probably summing up the view of most socialist economists on the prospects for development in the smaller postrevolutionary societies when they wrote, in *Socialism in Cuba* (1969):

> It became increasingly obvious that Cuba's demand for industrial products was not, and under no conceivable circumstances could become, large enough to justify the establishment of a wide variety of modern, technically efficient industries. By committing herself to a program of industrial diversification, Cuba would in effect be condemning itself to industrial backwardness.[26]

This view was challenged in a formidable way by Clive Thomas in his *Dependence and Transformation: The Economics of the Transition to Socialism* (1974). Working within the same general tradition as Baran, Thomas nevertheless went several steps further. The most coherent strategies for postrevolutionary economic construction thus far, he argued, had been based on the insights provided by Baran's concept of economic surplus, on the one hand, and an understanding of the parameters imposed by Marx's two department reproduction schemes, on the other. The first concept was especially attuned to the problems of underdevelopment. The latter concept, if not deepened to include an intensive study of the interrelationships between resource use, demand, technology, and collective needs, was likely to result in false antinomies between agriculture and industry, or heavy and light industry—as in the cruder versions of the "primitive socialist accumulation" strategy.[27] The great danger was that countries like Cuba or Tanzania would end up trapped within a modified form of the essentially bourgeois strategy of import substitution, which provided little hope that the real chains of dependency (via unequal exchange) would be broken.[28]

Thomas's alternative was to propose a "convergence strategy" based on two "iron laws of transformation": (1) the convergence of resource use and demand, and (2) the convergence of demand with needs. The convergence of use and demand had to start with a recognition of the size of the potential economic surplus that had actually existed in the prerevolutionary social formation. Thus, following Baran, Thomas noted five areas in which the bulk of the surplus available for development left its statistical trace: (1) excess overseas repatriation of profits, (2) conspicuous consumption and dissaving by the landlord class, (3) the economic burdens associated with supporting a wasteful state bureaucracy, (4) luxury consumption by the newly emerging bourgeoisie, and (5) unemployment and underemployment. It was this surplus, hidden in so many ways, that provided the necessary social accumulation fund for the early stages of development.[29]

Like Baran and Lippit, Thomas argued that it was possible to transform agriculture and to extract some of the surplus previously dormant in the rural society without adopting harsh or forcible means that would alienate the peasantry. Substantial economic progress meant that the relative balance of production would "shift decisively in favor of industry and against agriculture." But the adoption of "methods of brutal consolidation and coercion (which characterized the early history of capitalism and socialism in the USSR)" were to be avoided.[30] Moreover, in line with the general strategy of convergence of resource use and demand, the composition of output should be determined not with the intention of promoting exports *as a primary object,* but in terms of serving domestic needs. Thus Thomas argued for centering the planning of agriculture around:

(a) the internal need for its produce to be consumed directly, either as processed or unprocessed foods (mainly meat, dairy products, vegeta-

> bles, grain, etc.); (b) the domestic needs for that part of its output which is used as an input into other agricultural activity (e.g., feed for the cattle industry); (c) the domestic needs for new raw materials as inputs in domestic manufacturing activity; and (d) the overseas demand for those industrial outputs using substantially domestic agricultural inputs (e.g., clothing).[31]

Not only did the production of high protein foods have the advantage of high income elasticity of demand, he noted, but they would also reduce imports of necessary foods into agricultural economies, previously directed toward producing cash crops for export under the aegis of international capital. This, then, would constitute a very different, and more effective, form of "import substitution."

Difficult as these problems were, it was in the area of industrialization that the real issue of development in a small, underdeveloped, postrevolutionary society arose. While agreeing with the argument of Feldman, Dobb, and Baran that the rate of growth of Department I must generally exceed that of Department II in the early stages of development, Thomas objected to the notion, advanced by such theorists as Huberman and Sweezy and Robert Sutcliffe, that the promotion of heavy industry and all-around industrial diversification was impractical in small countries—despite, as he pointed out, "the existence of countries like Sweden, Bulgaria, North Korea, Belgium, etc." Errors of this kind, Thomas contended,

> not only betray the uncritical acceptance of the market notion of demand as a constraint on output, without reference to the needs of the community as distinct from purchases, but also represent common and unsupported prejudices about the real "variety" of modern industry and the impact of size in determining the social costs of establishing it.[32]

There were, as can be seen from the foregoing statement, three issues here. First, Thomas argued that even in a very small country, a self-reinforcing demand structure could be established internally, that would allow for a steady process of industrialization. For example, the development of agriculture itself constituted an important source of demand for industry. Second, examination of "the input/output matrices of industrialized countries" indicated that there were a few basic materials that constituted the strategic inputs (and most of the value added) into nearly all commodities. As Thomas himself put it:

> Two of these—iron and steel, and textiles—form the backbone of modern industrial consumption. If paper, plastics, rubber, glass, leather, cement, wood, fuel, aluminum, and industrial chemicals (primarily the alkalis, chlorine, and sulphuric acid) are added, then we can account for the overwhelming bulk of the basic materials used in industry. Most of the value added in industry is derived from these industries, and as a result they constitute the empirically verifiable range of strategic linkages and should form the cornstone of an industrialization program.[33]

In fact these basic materials, as Thomas noted, corresponded to "Sraffa's concept of basic goods."[34] As an initial strategy, then, these goods, which in Sraffian language "enter into the reproduction of all other goods," should be promoted, while the production of nonreproducible luxury goods should not assume *primary* importance. Such factors as substitutability, renewability (e.g., forest products), new technology for exploiting resources, etc., provided more flexibility in obtaining access to these strategic resources (or basic goods), Thomas argued, than was previously thought. Still, such basic materials are so important that a development strategy might well require selective purchase of these materials from abroad if they could not be produced locally—even when short-run cost calculations (or "comparative advantages") suggest that such a strategy is economically unsound.

Third, much of the argument against the ability of small countries to industrialize was, Thomas suggested, based on confused notions of "economies of scale." This point is dealt with most convincingly by Magdoff, who argues that much of the overemphasis on economies of scale in the planning literature derived from the extremes to which the Soviet Union had gone, in this respect, in its own development. Thus while 62 percent of industrial employment in the USSR in 1963 was in plants with 1,000 or more employees, the equivalent figure for the United States in 1958 was 29.7 percent. In fact, U.S. monopoly capital has demonstrated a tendency in recent years to "decentralize its manufacturing operations."[35] It follows from this that there is a lot more room than traditional economic theory envisioned for efficient production at relatively low levels of employment and output.

It should be evident at this point that Thomas's "convergence strategy" was directed at overcoming what Amin and others have called the "disarticulation" of the social formations in the underdeveloped world. This manifests itself not only in the notorious external orientation of these countries, but also in the closely related fact that the forms of production have little to do with domestic demand. The heart of the unequal exchange problem, as Sweezy has explained, lies in the fact that in the third world both foreign and domestic capital view the working population merely "as costs, not as consumers: the lower their real incomes, the higher the profits from selling to the local upper class and the international market."[36] For Thomas, the problem of economic transformation in the transition period is the overcoming of this systematic distortion:

> If the material manifestations of underdevelopment have been expressed as the dynamic divergence in the pattern of domestic resource use, domestic demand, and needs, in the absence of an indigenous technology to provide the basis for an organic link between them, then the principal material goal must be to seek a dynamic convergence of these relationships. When put in this way, two basic problems of an economic strategy tailored to achieving this goal become clear. The first is to find out how to effect a convergence of the pattern and rate of domestic resource use and domestic demand as it has developed and is likely to develop. . . . The second issue centers on finding out how the community's demand can be structured so that it conforms more closely than at present to domestic resource availability and domestic use. The latter problem essentially means determining how the needs of the community can be made to converge with its demand pattern.[37]

The basic framework for overcoming the divergence between resource use and demand while establishing an indigenous industrial capability and technology has been discussed above. The far more radical agenda of Thomas's second " 'iron law' of transformation"—the convergence of demand with needs—might seem even more intractable. However, it is here that the insights associated with analysis of accumulation under monopoly capitalism become most relevant. Thus Thomas extracts the following quotation from *The Political Economy of Growth*

> Just as it makes no sense to deplore war casualties without attacking their cause, war, so it is meaningless to sound the alarm about advertis-

> ing without clearly identifying the *locus* from which the pestilence emanates: the monopolistic and oligopolistic corporation and the non-price competitive business practices which constitute an integral component of its modus operandi . . . the issue is rather *the kind of social and economic order* that does the molding.[38]

The importance of the critical insight that Baran provides here, and the significance that it has for Thomas's argument, can be seen if we recognize that it is a radical version of the Galbraithian "dependence effect"—or the way in which wants come to depend upon the way in which production itself is conducted.[39] In a radical social order demand can come to depend on needs, allowing for a deliberate narrowing of the range of choice among unnecessary and ultimately unsatisfying luxury goods in order to promote collective goods and collective needs. And the means adopted can be a linking of social needs with the process of production, in a dialectical inversion of the practices of monopolistic corporations. Thus Thomas argues that Baran's point was made even more explicit by Joan Robinson, who wrote:

> The true moral to be drawn from the capitalist experience is that production will never be responsive to consumer needs as long as the initiative lies with the producer. Even within capitalism, consumers are beginning to organize to defend themselves. In a planned economy the best hope seems to be to develop a class of functionaries, playing the role of wholesale dealers, whose career and self-respect depend upon satisfying the consumer. They could keep in touch with demand through the shops; market research which in the capitalist world is directed to finding out how to bamboozle the housewife, could be directed to discovering what she really needs. . . . No one who has lived in the capitalist world is deceived by the pretense that the market system ensures consumer sovereignty. It is up to the socialist countries to find some way of giving it reality.[40]

In this way Thomas is able to argue consistently that the ability of collective consumption to increase the general welfare of the community depends on "public participation and democracy in framing society's consumption patterns."[41] The molding of consumption patterns, as Baran's statement had suggested, could, in another type of social system, serve the realization of actual human needs.

The most difficult problem for the "convergence strategy," as Thomas recognized, lay in the need for exports to obtain the foreign exchange with which strategic basic materials and technological knowledge could be purchased. Although this problem was not easily solved, as the history of all third world societies has demonstrated, a number of guidelines could be established. First, the structure of exports should be derived as much as possible as a by-product of the satisfaction of domestic needs, in line with the self-reliant structure of the advanced industrial economies. This means rejecting "import substitution" strategies focusing on the production of the type of luxury goods (in a third world context) promoted by multinational corporations. Second, any "effective import substitution" would involve the production of essential social commodities—such as high protein foodstuffs—that are generally imported by the disarticulated agricultural economies of the third world. Third, foreign assistance should not be summarily dismissed, but considered on a case-by-case basis.[42] Fourth, increasing reliance on trade and economic cooperation with other "socialist" economies should be encouraged. Fifth, tourism (although not of the "Hilton" variety) should be seen primarily as a means of earning foreign exchange. It follows from the logic of Thomas's argument that the more that imports could be restricted to "basic goods," the better chance there was that certain critical thresholds in the direction of self-reliant development could be crossed.

Historical experience has made it abundantly clear that a formal break with the capitalist system through social revolution only makes self-reliant development *possible;* it does not in itself eliminate the problems of dependent development. And for an economy in the transition to socialism, Thomas pointed out, the dangers posed by the world market and multinational corporations are even greater than they are for postcolonial states in general. This fundamental principle was most forcefully expressed by Preobrazhensky, who wrote:

> If there is sometimes a protective tariff policy in countries with a weakly developed industry, aimed at protecting a particular industry from the competition of a capitalistically more developed country, this has nothing in common, beyond external forms, with socialist protectionism. In the one case it is a matter of protecting one industry from another *belonging to the same economic system.* In the other we have the protection of one mode of production, in a state of infantile weakness, from another economic system mortally hostile to it which even in the

period of its senile decrepitude will inevitably be stronger, economically and technically for a time, than the new economy.[43]

In the neocolonial state, Thomas observed, "the local tariff systems are basically instruments of the expansion and development of the multinational firm."[44] In a newly industrializing postrevolutionary society, a tariff system must be designed not to promote the development of underdevelopment but to allow for its transcendence.

In *The Rise of the Authoritarian State in Peripheral Societies* (1984), Thomas has recently provided us with a strong reminder that the issue of socialist construction is not simply a question of economics but of politics as well. In the periphery, Thomas notes, "dictatorial, despotic, and other antipopular measures are the norm of political behavior" whether "the regimes describe themselves as capitalist" or "claim to be socialist."[45] To understand this phenomenon in terms of the methodology of historical materialism, it is necessary to reject all approaches based on ahistorical notions of "authoritarianism" and to posit the problem in a concrete way. Thus the authoritarian state has the following "essential characteristics": (1) it develops in underdeveloped countries undergoing a postcolonial transformation; (2) the underlying conditions of dependency have their origins in "the colonial manner in which these economies were structurally inserted into the world capitalist system"; (3) "the major classes of the capitalist era (bourgeoisie and proletariat) are underdeveloped; (4) the dominant classes and strata (petty bourgeoisie, feudal-type landlords, capitalists associated with import substitution, the military, etc.) are allied (along comprador lines) with international capital; (5) the petty bourgeoisie retains the "favored role" within the state apparatus that it had within the local state of the colonial system; (6) "the practice of 'bourgeois' ideas of legality and equality" is restricted; (7) the focus on economic development under conditions of dependency has resulted in a rapid growth of state property; (8) the augmentation of state property has enhanced the role of the state as an employer (heightening the visibility of class relationships); and (9) the entire social formation is characterized by periodic crises of an acute kind that arise out of its continuing "economic backwardness" within the world system.[46]

Nevertheless, while the "authoritarian state" is "the most likely development [proceeding from anti-imperialist struggles] in the present conjuncture," according to Thomas, "there is nothing automatic about its rise."[47] Naturally, where national liberation struggles have evolved into a full-scale, democratically based people's war (as in Vietnam, Mozambique, and Nicaragua) there are strong, popular socialist forces preventing the emergence of the more repressive forms of rule.[48] Moreover, "oppression and liberation are dialectically related." The rule of the petty bourgeoisie (and other intermediate strata) is a fragile one, undermined by its own inability to become a cohesive ruling class, by the visibility of its political domination (under its rule state power and class power become almost identical), and by the economic contradictions associated with prolonged dependency. The revolutionary process that will continue to unfold, and that will eventually bring all such societies to an end, will be socialist in thrust, according to Thomas, only insofar as it is democratic in all of its aspects.

Soviet-Type Societies

"In analyzing 'really existing socialist societies,'" according to Sweezy,

> it is necessary for Marxists to pose a very specific question: Are these societies showing signs of moving in the direction of communism, which for present purposes may be thought of as characterized by the elimination of classes and of certain very fundamental socioeconomic differences among groups of individuals (manual and mental workers, city and country dwellers, industrial and agricultural producers, men and women, people of different races)? If they do show signs of moving in the direction of communism, they can be judged to be socialist in the sense of Marxist theory. Otherwise they cannot be considered socialist in the Marxist meaning of the term.[49]

There are four ways in which this question is generally answered, according to Sweezy. First, there are those who believe that Soviet-type societies are essentially socialist, in the sense of representing a transitional phase from capitalism to communism.[50] Second, there are those who continue to assert, following Trotsky's initial assessment, that these societies are degenerate workers' states, characterized by the rule of a parasitic bureaucratic elite, and will only become fully socialist when revolution has occurred in the advanced capitalist states.[51] Third, there are those who have become convinced that capitalism was resurrected in the Soviet Union during the 1920s and 1930s.[52] Finally, there are those, like Sweezy himself, who have concluded that the Soviet-type societies represent a new type of social formation, neither capitalist nor socialist.[53]

Sweezy's conclusion that postrevolutionary societies of the Soviet-type constitute a new kind of social formation appears to be based on a gradual recognition of the fact that the first and second answers were inadequate in light of historical experience, and on a subsequent period of sustained critical reflection on the third answer. At a theoretical level, it is clear that the most important work influencing his views was *Class Struggles in the USSR* by Charles Bettelheim. In Bettelheim's analysis the Soviet Union, since the supposed "restoration" of capitalism in the 1920s and 1930s, has constituted a *specific form* of capitalism, or "party capitalism," that conforms to the *general concept* of the capitalist mode of production.

For some time it has been clear to those Marxists who do not agree with the official Soviet interpretation of its own social formation that the material form of the labor process in actually existing socialism of the Soviet type is quite similar in most respects to that which exists under capitalism. As Braverman noted, one of the more unfortunate legacies of Bolshevik practice after the revolution was to promote the uncritical acceptance of the techniques of scientific management that had emerged along with monopoly capitalism.[54] Furthermore, once it is recognized that the state systematically appropriates the surplus created within the labor process in this way, the idea of a social capital/wage labor relationship, replacing the private capital/wage labor relationship of the original capitalist system, becomes conceivable. From here it is only a small step to the issue of whether or not class-exploitative social relations have been resurrected. And for both Bettelheim and Sweezy the answer is "Yes." Through their unmediated control of the state, the *nachal 'stvo* (or "party capitalists," as Bettelheim calls them) are able to control the surplus appropriation and surplus utilization process; while through its privileged access to material rewards, educational institutions, etc., this same tightly knit body of state administrators and state managers of enterprises is able to ensure the necessary conditions for its own reproduction as a ruling class (though the role played by direct family inheritance—unlike classical capitalism—is miniscule or nonexistent).[55]

But having basically agreed to this extent, Bettelheim and

Sweezy then part company. In Bettelheim's argument the above conditions are sufficient for seeing the USSR as a specific form of capitalism, since all other characteristics, like the role of competition, can be derived from the social capital/wage labor relationship.[56] For Sweezy matters are more complicated. In his conception, capitalism cannot be defined entirely in terms of the capital/wage labor relationship but must also incorporate the relation of capital to itself as other capital, i.e., the role of competition. He doubts that the existence of many capitals can be derived from the social capital/wage labor relationship. Nor can one convincingly argue, as Bettelheim has attempted to do, that the rivalry among state enterprises in the Soviet Union is the counterpart of competition between capitals under capitalism. "If one wants a valid comparison," Sweezy has stated, "it would be between the Soviet managers and the managers of subordinate units of large capitalist corporations like Exxon or General Motors."[57] Writing on the historical locus of competition between capitals under capitalism and its absence in Soviet-type societies, he explains:

> In my opinion it is impossible to exaggerate the importance of this feature of capitalism for an understanding of the subject with which we are here concerned, i.e., the nature of the societies that have emerged from the revolutions of the twentieth century. All the "laws" of capitalism which have been the central preoccupation of political economy—classical, Marxian, and neoclassical alike—have depended in a crucial way on the existence of the social capital in the form of many private capitals. It is the pressure of these capitals on each other, given formal expression in the concept of competition, that accounts for the momentous fact, which has never ceased to amaze social philosophers, that what society needs in order to exist is produced, reproduced, and distributed without anyone anywhere having to take responsibility for seeing the job gets done.[58]

In other words, it is impossible to explain the reproduction of capital as a by-product of independent economic "laws," where competition between capitals is no longer a basic datum of the system. The very drive to accumulate for its own sake (as explained by Marx) required the mediation of competition. For Sweezy, the elimination of competition between capitals—which should not be confused with the kind of rivalry that exists among state enterprises in the Soviet Union—is sufficient to suggest that Soviet-type societies constitute an entirely new, class-exploitative social formation that is neither capitalist nor socialist in character.

Indeed, in contrast to capitalism, where "the state as the ultimate political sphere . . . is basically 'programmed' by the autonomous functioning of the economy," the state in a postrevolutionary society takes the "initiative" in securing the conditions of social reproduction.[59] And this has important implications for the nature and functioning of postrevolutionary societies of the Soviet type. To quote Sweezy again:

> If I am right that in the Soviet system there are no objective economic laws of motion comparable to those of capitalism, it follows that the ruling class lacks a structural framework within which to carry out its self-imposed responsibility to manage the total social capital. It must generate its own goals since it cannot simply internalize and be guided by those of an underlying autonomously functioning economy.[60]

This means that the new ruling class could opt for a policy of accumulation for accumulation's sake, with respect to the total social capital, but the drive to do so would certainly be much weaker than under "the system of inequality and family fortune" (as Schumpeter called capitalism). Minimally, of course, the *nachal 'niki* could be expected to reproduce its own hegemonic class position. But in doing so it faces a severe constraint, one that, while existing under capitalism as well, here manifests itself in a qualitatively new way. The very fact that the *nachal'niki* "derives its power and privileges . . . from the unmediated control of the state" results in "a politicization of the surplus utilization process." Indeed, it is this very fact that accounts for the relatively advanced accomplishments of postrevolutionary societies when compared to capitalist societies at similar levels of economic development, in such areas as "employment, education, health, social welfare, and land reform."[61]

Even more significantly, according to Sweezy, it is from this very *politicization* of the surplus-utilization process—and the partial way in which this has actually been accomplished in class-exploitative societies of this type—that the leading economic contradictions of actually existing socialism arise. Thus the guarantee of full employment that prevails in these societies serves to undermine the normal capitalist "incentive system" within the labor process by eliminating the "sword of Damocles" represented by unemployment. The inner structure of these economies is therefore extremely contradictory. Without the power to treat labor power as a commodity like any other commodity, as under capitalism, the Soviet ruling class has nonetheless had sufficient political power thus far to prevent the growth of substantive workers' control over production (and thus over the social formation as a whole).[62] Consequently, when judged solely in terms of labor productivity Soviet society has come to represent "the worst of all possible worlds." If it continues to perform relatively well (though in lessening degrees) when compared to the advanced capitalist states, this is because it operates at a full employment level (what Western economists like to call "static efficiency").[63]

The obvious solution to this dilemma for Sweezy—if class relations did not stand in the way—would be for the working class to assume control of the organization of the labor process and the society as a whole. But class relations do stand in the way. And the response of the *nachal'niki* thus far has been to attempt, in every way conceivable, to depoliticize the working class. To what extent, and for how long, this strategy can succeed remains unknown.

In Sweezy's view, however, this train of reasoning leads to at least one fairly hopeful conclusion. Since there is no imperative to accumulate within Soviet-type society comparable to the "Moses and the Prophets" under capitalism, it follows that the Soviet Union is not driven toward expansion (particularly in the international realm) to anything like the same extent as under capitalism. Hence, it is clear from logic alone—setting aside the vast amount of historical evidence pointing to the same conclusion—that the real destabilizing force in the second Cold War (like the first) is the United States and company.[64] Moreover, there is at least the hope that if the suffocating pressure imposed by the arms race were eliminated, the Soviet Union might be able to move in the direction of socialism in the fullest sense of the term.[65]

It must be acknowledged that Sweezy's argument, as laid out above, may not appear to conform to Marx's own method of distinguishing social formations (or modes of production). Thus Marx wrote: "The essential difference between the various economic forms of society, between, for instance, a society based on slave-labour, and one based on wage-labour, lies only in the mode in which this surplus-labour is in each case extracted from the actual producer, the labourer."[66] Since Marx always emphasized the mode of appropriation of surplus product as the element distinguishing one type of social formation from another, Sweezy's emphasis on the absence of competition between capitals would seem to be an insufficient basis for departing from Bettelheim's notion that Soviet society represents a specific form of capitalism.

The problem here, however, is mainly one of presentation. Thus, drawing out the implications of Sweezy's analysis, we could say that "the mode in which . . . surplus-labour is extracted from the actual producer, the labourer" is through the unmediated control that the *nachal'niki* exercise over the state apparatus, making it possible for them to appropriate the surplus labor of relatively uncoerced wage workers—with the added features that (1) each stage of appropriation is understood as a separate *political* act, and not the result of invisible economic laws (so that the level of subsistence is *politicized*), and (2) there is no *inner dynamic* to the process that inherently induces accumulation on an expanding scale.[67]

Under these circumstances it becomes necessary for the ruling class to control the level of politicization within society, a task which is partly accomplished at the ideological level by positing false "economic laws." This is the problem that Harry Magdoff took up in his recent article, "Are There Economic Laws of Socialism?" In "all stages of capitalist development," Magdoff argues, "competition is the decisive factor in making the [economic] laws work."[68] Since competition between individual capitals cannot be said to operate under socialism, it follows that the notion of economic laws loses most of its former meaning. Although this was well recognized in the early years of Soviet development, a "180-degree turn" in perceptions occurred with the publication of Stalin's *Economic Problems of Socialism in the U.S.S.R.* (1952). Since then it has been part of the official ideology of the system that there are a number of objective economic laws governing society. One of these is "the basic economic law of socialism," which says that the "direct object" of production under socialism is to satisfy the constantly increasing material and cultural needs of the people through the promotion of the highest levels of production possible, and the use of the most advanced technology available. Another is "the economic law of distribution according to work." A third is the operation of "the law of value" under socialist commodity production, which supposedly demands that commodities exchange in accordance with the relative amounts of socially necessary labor time embodied in them. Obviously, none of these purported "laws" are objective forces in the sense of the inner laws of motion—"the laws of value, reproduction, centralization, and concentration of capital, the creation of relative surplus population, and the general tendencies of accumulation"—characteristic of the capitalist mode of production. Instead, they represent conscious political/planning choices that may or may not be carried out. The first is merely an open declaration of the fact that the highest priority in planning will be given to material expansion. The second "law" is simply a justification for a certain pattern of income distribution.[69] The third "law" can only be true (if at all under socialism) where market relations are dominant, and thus has to do with the line drawn between market and plan, which is itself a political decision.

Essentially the same kind of criticism, as Magdoff demonstrated, can be directed against the fourth "law" commonly presented in the Soviet literature—"the law of planned, proportional development." Insofar as this injunction is theoretically meaningful, it relates to the Feldman principle, advocated by such theorists as Dobb, Baran, and Thomas in the context of an underdeveloped postrevolutionary society seeking rapid industrialization. At one level (the *engineering* of production) it has a certain validity, since it recognizes the need to determine the growth of both producers' goods and consumers' goods industries in accordance with an interdependent relationship of inputs and outputs. But there is no magic rule that determines the proportionality of input-output flows associated with the two departments under socialism, given such changing historical conditions as the cumulative overdevelopment of productive capacity in heavy industry relative to light industry, and the developing needs of a high consumption society. Indeed, if this "law" suggests anything it is the inadvisability of expanding investment goods *independently* of consumption. But the serviceability of this supposed law, in terms of the requirements of the Soviet power structure, lies precisely in the fact that it seems to provide a permanent justification for the exact opposite: the relative growth of plant and equipment at the expense of consumption and agriculture, i.e., the perpetuation into the indefinite future of a developmental strategy akin to "primitive socialist accumulation." In actuality, the initiative for development in postrevolutionary societies of the Soviet type resides, as Sweezy has pointed out, in the political sphere. The idea of economic laws governing these societies, in a manner analogous to economic laws under capitalism, is an ideological ploy that only serves to obscure what needs to be done.

Revolution and Reason

"The trouble with economics," Paul Baran once wrote,

> is not that it does not yet "know enough," as many of its practitioners love to repeat. Its fatal shortcoming is that it does not incorporate in its knowledge the understanding of what is necessary for the attainment of a better, more rational economic order. Hemingway's Old Man was a virtuoso fisherman. If he had a fault, it was his incapacity to realize the overwhelming destructive power of the sharks.[70]

As Baran and Sweezy saw it, the main obstacles to the development of a more rational social system were to be traced, on the one hand, to the existence of a socioeconomic order, monopoly capitalism, that actively promoted social imbalance and irrationality; and, on the other hand, to the existence in the postrevolutionary states of a kind of political exploitation for which there was no longer any real "economic necessity."[71] These views arose out of an outlook that Baran characterized as the "confrontation of reality with reason"; that is, out of the kind of historically informed "utopian" thinking that has always been consistent with—and even integral to—the "philosophy of praxis."[72] Indeed, many of the objections to Baran and Sweezy's general approach to political economy that have been raised by Marxists have centered on this very point.

Thus, voicing some common criticisms of Baran and Sweezy's approach to political economy, Michael Bleaney once referred to their analysis as "third worldism with a strong tinge of Marcuse about it."[73] The reference to Marcuse, of course, had to do with Baran and Sweezy's emphasis on the "irrationality" of the monopoly capitalist system. However, this concept of irrationality did not generally refer to a socio-psychological phenomenon—the main emphasis of the critical theorists—but was a historical analogy suggesting the extent to which capitalism had actually departed from the *quid pro quo* of equivalent exchange and from the production of useful goods.[74]

Moreover, Baran and Sweezy's argument with respect to advanced capitalism was directed at showing the historical limitations of Keynesian thinking. The main failing of the "New Economics," in Baran's view, was that it ignored that very waste and destruction that underlay its entire strategy of trying to solve the problem of effective demand within an antagonistic class society. To quote Baran himself:

> Confronted with persistent overaccumulation and insufficient outlets for the economic surplus, and having grasped the theory of income determination in the short run, Keynesians proclaim as economics' ultimate wisdom that *any* spending promotes prosperity, *any* utilization of the surplus enhances the general welfare, and they rest content with this profound insight. . . . There is probably no better example of the absurdity of "practical intelligence." For what is there to be said for a reasoning that justifies waste of enormous quantities of human and material resources by pointing to the *by-product* of that waste—a certain increase of consumption and an (uncertain) increase of investment?[75]

As Ricardo had written in reply to Malthus (Baran pointed out), "A body of unproductive labourers are just as necessary and as useful with a view to future production [in Malthus' own reasoning] as a fire which would consume in the manufacturers' warehouse the goods which those unproductive labourers would otherwise consume."[76] The logic of Keynesian theory, and the actions to which it led, were of a similar kind.

Hence Baran and Sweezy used a historical perspective to demonstrate the growing irrationality of monopoly capitalism as a determinate social formation. In doing so they employed two critical standpoints: those of global capital and society as a whole (production in general). Moreover, they went beyond all other radical theorists (with the sole exception of Veblen) in scrutinizing the degree to which waste had penetrated into the productive process in late capitalism. Other theorists, notably Kalecki, hinted at the same thing, but remained within the traditional calculus of surplus product by confining their attention, with regard to waste, to Department III and excess capacity. Only Baran and Sweezy extended the concept of waste into the "consumption basket of wage goods."[77] And it seems probable that this is the missing link in understanding the evolution of class relationships under monopoly capitalism.

Marx himself provided us with perhaps the single most important clue as to how capitalism's rise and fall should be understood, while discussing the problem of unproductive labor: "Bourgeois society reproduces in its own form everything against which it fought in feudal and absolutist form."[78] Thus the distortion of capitalism's own inner rationality, through the promotion of economic waste, is a concrete manifestation of the *objective* necessity for social transformation, of the growing conflict between capitalism and production in general. "In its day," Sweezy once wrote, "capitalism was a progressive system."[79] The main purpose of *Monopoly Capital* was to provide a concrete explanation as to why capitalism's day, in this sense, had long since passed, and thus to help prepare the ground for a "long revolution."

The idea of a long revolution is meant to suggest that the revolutionary potential in the advanced capitalist countries in the *forseeable future,* if left to their own devices, is extremely weak. As Baran and Sweezy wrote in *Monopoly Capital,* "if we confine our attention to the inner dynamics of advanced monopoly capitalism, it is hard to avoid the conclusion that the prospect of effective revolutionary action to overthrow the system is slim."[80] But advanced monopoly capitalism, they quickly added, does not exist in isolation, and on the periphery one volcanic eruption after another was occurring; a fact which was already beginning to have some reflection within the capitalist core, in the form of the linking of the struggles of U.S. blacks with third world movements. And given the irrational nature of the system in the center, this was bound to create new inducements to rebellion. In later years, Sweezy has continued to argue along these lines, retaining his commitment to revolution, but writing in "Marxism and Revolution 100 Years After Marx" that:

> Today, a hundred years after Marx's death, it is impossible to make out a reasonable case for the view that the proletariat in the advanced countries is destined to be the agent of revolutionary change.[81]

This does not, he adds in a note, "preclude the possibility that at some time in the future" the working class will again assume a revolutionary role, "but Marxism deals with historical realities, not with futurology."[82] And this means that radicals must be concerned first and foremost with the struggles of "the wretched of the earth."

It is this position that has evoked the criticism of "third worldism" from Western Marxists. As both Sweezy and Amin have pointed out, this type of criticism is actually an indirect reflection of the racism and imperialism that are deeply embedded in the theory and practice of certain forms of Western Marxism itself, as an unfortunate legacy of the mainstream European tradition during its entire history (a legacy from which Marx fully liberated himself only during his final decade).[83] Writing of the crisis of Western Marxism from a "third worldist" standpoint, Amin has stated:

> The "left" version of the social-imperialist position of necessity takes on the appearance of the "ultraleftist" position which, in fact, here as everywhere, links up with the right. It resorts to the most erudite formulations to deny the fact of imperialist exploitation. The debate concerning unequal exchange has shown how words are used to mask realities. There are those who explain, without sensing how ridiculous and odious their arguments are, that the proletarian in the periphery is "less exploited" than the worker in the center, although his wage for operating the same machine and producing the same product (i.e., with the same productivity) is ten or twenty times lower! They pretend not be be aware of the mechanisms of formal domination that make it possible to extract absolute surplus value from peasants transformed into quasiproletarians in their homes. They can then no longer understand that these peoples, by revolting against imperialism, have done more to advance the cause of socialism than anyone else until now.[84]

Commenting on the same problem, Sweezy has remarked, "I think that one thing at any rate is clear, that Western-centered Marxism, like Western-centered thought in general, is rapidly becoming more of a hindrance than a help in getting on" with what needs to be done.[85]

All of the existing postrevolutionary societies, including the Soviet Union, emerged from the periphery (or semiperiphery) of the capitalist world system. In the case of Soviet-type societies, considerable economic advances have been made, and the partial politicization of the surplus utilization process has resulted in certain notable advances in the realm of social welfare. Nonetheless, there is reason to believe that these societies have become class-exploitative social formations of a new kind. A historical materialism worthy of the name must apply the same critical methods to the analysis of all "three worlds" of contemporary history. And only in this way is it possible to develop what L.S. Stavrianos has called "a common vision relevant to the unprecedented peril and unprecedented promise now confronting all humanity."[86]

Appendix: The Early Introduction
by Paul A. Baran and Paul M. Sweezy

The articles which form the contents of this issue are two chapters from a forthcoming work tentatively entitled *Monopoly Capital: An Essay on the American Economic and Social Order.* The first comes from near the beginning of the book, the second from near the end.

All the basic ideas of Marx's great work *Das Kapital* were formulated in the quarter century from 1840 to 1865. This was the heyday of competitive capitalism in Britain, then by far the world's leading economic power, and it was natural and inevitable that Marx should focus his attention on this system. In Marx's work, monopoly appears only occasionally, as a remnant of the mercantilist past or as a shadow cast by a future which he did not expect capitalism to live to see.

As it turned out, capitalism had more staying power than the early socialists attributed to it. In the two decades after Marx's death in 1883, monopoly, in the form of giant corporations linked together by a concentrated network of financial institutions, moved to the center of the economic stage. This momentous fact was recognized by Hilferding, and it was Lenin's genius to make it the foundation stone of his theory of imperialism which, in turn, became the core of the Marxian interpretation of twentieth-century politics, international relations, and social and cultural development. Yet paradoxically enough, the impact of this profound economic transformation was felt least of all in what might have been thought to be the area most immediately affected: Marxian economic theory. Here, despite the pioneering work of Hilferding and

---

This Introduction was originally published, along with the drafts of chapters 2 and 10 of *Monopoly Capital,* in *Monthly Review* 14, nos. 3–4 (July–August 1962): 131–34.

Lenin, Marx's *Kapital* continued to reign supreme. Or, to put the point differently, the model of a competitive capitalist economy continued to serve as the basis of Marxian economic theorizing.

It is, we believe, time to break with this tradition. To follow Marx's own example, and to make the most fruitful use of his powerful analytical method, it has become necessary to shift the focus of attention. For the present stage of world capitalism, and most especially capitalism in the United States, differs in many *essential* respects from the competitive capitalism of old. The *prevalent* capitalist enterprise today is no longer the small firm producing a negligible fraction of a large mass of homogeneous products for an anonymous market; the business unit characteristic of the capitalist economy in our time is the large-scale enterprise responsible for a significant share of its industry's output, manufacturing and selling a product frequently clearly identified by name, and for all these reasons able to exercise a decisive influence on the volume of its output, the level of its prices, and the magnitude and timing of its investments. The fact that this monopolistic (or oligopolistic) concern has become the dominant entity in the modern capitalist economy has an overriding significance for an understanding of the system's *modus operandi.* To put the point in a nutshell: in an attempt to understand monopoly capitalism, monopoly cannot be abstracted from; it has to be put in the very center of the analytic effort.

The purpose of the work from which the two chapters published here are taken is to effect this necessary shift in the focus of attention from competition to monopoly. We are under no illusion that we will have succeeded in exhausting the subject. We have no such ambitious goal. What we do hope to do is help people to see things differently and more realistically, to highlight some of the central problems which need to be solved, and to indicate the direction which further study and thought should take.

The plan of the work as a whole, and the place which the two chapters occupy in it, can perhaps best be conveyed to the reader by a listing of the chapter headings. It should be understood that this is a tentative table of contents, subject to modification as the work nears completion. But neither the overall plan which it reflects nor the location of these two chapters will be significantly altered. The table is as follows:

(1) Introduction
(2) The Giant Corporation
(3) The Tendency of Surplus to Rise
(4) The Problem of Surplus Absorption: Consumption and Investment
(5) The Problem of Surplus Absorption: The Sales Effort
(6) The Problem of Surplus Absorption: Government Spending
(7) The Problem of Surplus Absorption: Militarism and Imperialism
(8) On the Recent History of Monopoly Capitalism
(9) Some Implications for Economic Theory
(10) On the Quality of Monopoly Capitalist Society—I
(11) On the Quality of Monopoly Capitalist Society—II
(12) The Irrational System

The chapters which constitute this issue are those numbered (2) and (10). The first deals with the basic institution of monopoly capitalism, the giant corporation; the second describes some of the social and cultural consequences of this system. Each can be read by itself. But their full significance can be appreciated only when they are seen as an introduction to and corollary of the theoretical chapters which lie between them. For this reason, we supply the following desperately brief summary of the theme of the intervening chapters, hoping that it will aid the reader now and stimulate his interest in the fuller treatment to come. Giant corporations typically act like textbook monopolists, having learned to coordinate their policies so as to maximize attainable profits. Concentration on lowering costs then leads to a steadily widening gap, at any given level of production, between output and socially necessary costs of production. This gap we call "surplus." The central problem of the book is to analyze the various ways in which surplus is absorbed. It is shown that the consumption and investment of corporations and their beneficiaries cannot possibly absorb an indefinitely increasing surplus at capacity levels of output and that failure to discover or provide other channels can lead only to depression and stagnation. In part, business does provide additional channels through an increasingly gigantic (and wasteful) sales effort. Government is also called to the rescue, and much space is devoted to showing how the structure of interests which characterizes monopoly capitalism diverts governmental effort from socially useful channels into the destructive and ultimately disastrous activities of militarism and imperialism. The development of the theory of surplus generation and absorption along lines just indicated occupies chapters 3 through 7. We next apply this theory to the interpretation of the history of American capitalism from the late nineteenth century to the present time, showing that it explains and places in proper perspective many phenomena which have baffled bourgeois economic science, most especially the Great Depression of the 1930s and the creeping stagnation of the later 1950s (Chapter 8). Some implications for economic theory are indicated in Chapter 9. The final chapters deal with the social and cultural consequences of an economic system which has mastered the techniques of unlimited production but which, because of the inner structure of private interests which determine its working principles, is unable, and must remain unable, to promote the well-being and happiness of those who live under it.

Notes

Introduction

1. Paul Samuelson, "The House that Keynes Built," *New York Times,* 29 May 1983.
2. Paul A. Baran and Paul M. Sweezy, *Monopoly Capital: An Essay on the American Economic and Social Order* (New York: Monthly Review Press, 1966). Baran and Sweezy emphasized that their study was merely an "essay-sketch," and not an all-inclusive analysis of advanced capitalism. The most important missing component—the theory of the labor process—was later provided by Harry Braverman in *Labor and Monopoly Capital: The Degradation of Work in the Twentieth Century* (New York: Monthly Review Press, 1974.)
3. See the Appendix to this study.
4. Paul Mattick, *Marx and Keynes* (Boston: Porter Sargent, 1969); David Yaffe, "The Marxian Theory of Crisis, Capital, and the State," *Economy and Society* 2, no. 2 (1973): 186–232.
5. Baran and Sweezy, *Monopoly Capital,* p. 72.
6. The more eclectic response is best represented by the "multicausal" model of Ernest Mandel. See his *Late Capitalism* (London: New Left Books, 1975).
7. The terms "fundamentalist" and "traditionalist" will be used interchangeably to refer to a certain school of Marxian political economy that deemphasizes the need to reformulate the theory provided in the basic texts of classical Marxism in order to account for historical changes in the century since Marx's death. Certain representatives of this tendency, like Ben Fine and Laurence Harris, use the term "fundamentalist" to designate their own approach. The term "neo-Marxist," in contrast, applies to those who believe, in Lukacs' words, that "orthodoxy refers exclusively to method," and who argue that many of Marx's own ideas were historically contingent. "Neo-Ricardian"—a third term utilized here—refers (following Fine and Harris's usage) to those radical theorists who have abandoned the Marxian theory of value and exploitation (as well as the concept of productive and unproductive labor) on "Sraffian" grounds, and thus reduce the problem of "exploitation" to wages vs. property income. See Ben Fine and Laurence Harris, "Controversial Issues in Marxian Economic Theory," *The Socialist Register 1976* (London: Merlin Press, 1976), pp. 141–78; and Paul M. Sweezy, *Modern Capitalism* (New York: Monthly Review Press, 1972), pp. 37–39.
8. Andrew Glyn and Bob Sutcliffe, *Capitalism and Crisis* (New York: Pantheon, 1972); Samuel Bowles, David Gordon, and Thomas Weisskopf, *Beyond the Wasteland* (New York: Anchor Press, 1983). For a critique of the profit-squeeze approach, see Albert Szymanski, *Stagnation: The Normal State of Monopoly Capitalism* (London: Zed Press, forthcoming).
9. See Thomas Weisskopf, Samuel Bowles, and David Gordon, "Two Views of Capitalist Stagnation: Underconsumption and Challenges to Capitalist Control," *Science and Society* 49, no. 3 (Fall 1985): 278–80.
10. Raford Boddy and James Crotty, "Stagnation, Instability, and International Competition," *The American Economic Review* 66, no. 2 (May 1976): 27–33;

Bowles, Gordon, and Weisskopf, *Beyond the Wasteland,* pp. 49, 422. Boddy and Crotty correctly designate Kalecki as a "stagnation theorist," in contrast to the strange tendency of most theorists in the profit-squeeze tradition to characterize Kalecki himself as a profit-squeeze theorist, based on a single eight-page article on the political business cycle, written during the full employment years of World War II when he was most optimistic about the efficacy of Keynesian policies. See Michal Kalecki, *Selected Essays on the Dynamics of the Capitalist Economy* (Cambridge: Cambridge University Press, 1971), pp. 138–45. It was the work of Kalecki and Josef Steindl that provided the "basic theory" on which Baran and Sweezy's analysis was erected. On this see John Bellamy Foster and Henryk Szlajfer, Editors' Introduction to Foster and Szlajfer, eds.,*The Faltering Economy: The Problem of Accumulation Under Monopoly Capitalism* (New York: Monthly Review Press, 1984), pp. 7–22.

11. Paul A. Baran, *The Political Economy of Growth* (New York: Monthly Review Press, 1957), p. xxi; John Bellamy Foster, "Investment and Capitalist Maturity," in Foster and Szlajfer, eds., *The Faltering Economy,* pp. 68–70.
12. Weisskopf, Bowles, and Gordon, "Two Views of Capitalist Stagnation," p. 280.
13. Samuel Bowles and Herbert Gintis, "The Labor Theory of Value and the Specificity of Marxian Economics," in Stephen Resnick and Richard Wolff, eds., *Rethinking Marxism: Essays for Harry Magdoff and Paul Sweezy* (Brooklyn, NY: Autonomedia, 1985), p. 31.
14. Paul M. Sweezy, *Modern Capitalism* (New York: Monthly Review Press, 1972), pp. 25, 41–51.
15. Baran and Sweezy, *Monopoly Capital,* p. 10n.
16. Mario Cogoy, "The Fall of the Rate of Profit and the Theory of Accumulation: A Reply to Paul Sweezy," *Bulletin of the Conference of Socialist Economists* (Winter 1973): 53. Cogoy is quoting from a famous letter by Marx to Engels, written a few days after *Capital,* Volume 1, was finished. See Marx and Engels, *Selected Correspondence* (Moscow: Progress Publishers, 1955), p. 180. Although not actually noted here by Cogoy, Paul Mattick was the first to use this passage from Marx to criticize Baran and Sweezy. See his *Anti-Bolshevik Communism* (London: Merlin Press, 1978), p. 191. See also chapter 2 below.
17. Henryk Szlajfer's work consists of four somewhat different, but overlapping, manuscripts, reflecting various phases of composition, formulation, and publication: "Economic Surplus and Surplus Value: An Attempt at Comparison," *Occasional Paper 78.3,* Economic Research Bureau, University of Dares Salaam (August 1979); "Economic Surplus and Surplus Value: An Attempt at Comparison," *Review of Radical Political Economics* 15, no. 1 (Spring 1983): 107–30 (an edited and shortened version of the earlier monograph); "Economic Surplus and Surplus Value under Monopoly Capitalism," in Foster and Szlajfer, eds., *The Faltering Economy,* pp. 262–93; "Waste, Marxian Theory and Monopoly Capital: Toward a New Synthesis," in ibid., pp. 297–321. Ian Gough's relevant contribution is "Marx's Theory of Productive and Unproductive Labour," *New Left Review* no. 76 (November–December 1972): 47–72.
18. John Bellamy Foster, Editor's Introduction to Henryk Szlajfer, "Economic Surplus and Surplus Value," p. 107.
19. See Paul M. Sweezy, "Some Problems in the Theory of Capital Accumulation," in Foster and Szlajfer, eds., *The Faltering Economy,* pp. 41–42.
20. Willi Semmler, "Competition, Monopoly, and Differentials of Profit Rates: Theoretical Considerations and Empirical Evidence," *Review of Radical Political Economics* 13, no. 4 (Winter 1982): 39–52.

21. John Weeks, *Capital and Exploitation* (Princeton, NJ: Princeton University Press, 1981), pp. 165–68.
22. Ibid., p. 153.
23. Paul M. Sweezy, "Competition and Monopoly," in Foster and Szlajfer, eds., *The Faltering Economy,* pp. 37–39.
24. See especially Yaffe, "The Marxian Theory of Crisis, Capital, and the State," pp. 212–16. For more elaborate attempts to question the underconsumptionist position see Anwar Shaikh, "An Introduction to the History of Crisis Theories," in *U.S. Capitalism in Crisis* (New York: Union for Radical Political Economics, 1978), pp. 226–31; Erik Olin Wright, *Class, Crisis, and the State* (London: New Left Books, 1978), pp. 138–47; Michael Bleaney, *Underconsumption Theories* (New York: International Publishers, 1976), pp. 11–14, 102–19, 225–48.
25. See Rosa Luxemburg, "The Second and Third Volumes," in Franz Mehring, *Karl Marx: The Story of His Life* (London: George Allen & Unwin, 1936), p. 378; Paul M. Sweezy, *The Theory of Capitalist Development* (New York: Monthly Review Press, 1942), pp. 176, 184, 201; Jonathon Penzner, Harry Magdoff, and Paul M. Sweezy, "The Classic Contradiction of Capitalism," *Monthly Review* 33, no. 11 (April 1982): 57–60.
26. Evsey D. Domar, *Essays in the Theory of Economic Growth* (New York: Oxford University Press, 1957), pp. 109–28; Josef Steindl, *Maturity and Stagnation in American Capitalism* (New York: Monthly Review Press, 1976), pp. xiii, 243–46.
27. Sweezy, *Modern Capitalism,* p. 8.
28. Steindl, *Maturity and Stagnation in American Capitalism,* pp. xiv, 127; Keith Cowling, *Monopoly Capitalism* (New York: John Wiley and Sons, 1982), pp. 46–47; John Bellamy Foster, "The Limits of U.S. Capitalism: Surplus Capacity and Capacity Surplus," in Foster and Szlajfer, eds., *The Faltering Economy,* pp. 198–213.
29. Ron Stanfield, *The Economic Surplus and Neo-Marxism* (Lexington, MA: Lexington Books, 1973).
30. Baran and Sweezy, *Monopoly Capital,* p. 142.
31. James O'Connor, *The Fiscal Crisis of the State* (New York: St. Martin's Press, 1973); Hugh Mosley, "Is There a Fiscal Crisis of the State?" *Monthly Review* 30, no. 1 (May 1978): 34–45.
32. Kalecki, *Selected Essays on the Dynamics of the Capitalist Economy,* pp. 35–42; Baran, *The Political Economy of Growth,* pp. 123–29; Josef Steindl, "Stagnation Theory and Stagnation Policy," in Foster and Szlajfer, eds., *The Faltering Economy,* pp. 184–85, 189–96; Craig Medlen, "Corporate Taxes and the Federal Deficit," *Monthly Review* 36, no. 6 (November 1984): 1–9; Harry Magdoff and Paul M. Sweezy, "The Need for Tax Reform," in ibid., pp. 1–9.
33. Joseph A. Schumpeter, *Capitalism, Socialism, and Democracy* (New York: Harper & Row, 1950), p. 419; Paul M. Sweezy, *The Present as History* (New York: Monthly Review Press, 1953), pp. 363–69.
34. John Strachey, *Contemporary Capitalism* (New York: Random House, 1956), pp. 289–94; Sweezy, *Modern Capitalism,* pp. 70, 75.
35. Baran and Sweezy, *Monopoly Capital,* pp. 142–77; Sweezy, *The Theory of Capitalist Development,* pp. 348–52; Paul A. Baran, *The Longer View* (New York: Monthly Review Press, 1969), pp. 116–38.
36. John Weeks and Elizabeth Dore, "International Exchange and the Causes of Backwardness," *Latin American Perspectives* 6, no. 2 (Spring 1979): 62–87; Samir Amin, "Reply to Weeks and Dore," in ibid., pp. 88–90.

37. Albert Szymanski, *The Logic of Imperialism* (New York: Praeger, 1981), pp. 75–80, 289–316; Harry Magdoff, *Imperialism: From the Colonial Age to the Present* (New York: Monthly Review Press, 1978), pp. 237–79, and *The Age of Imperialism* (New York: Monthly Review Press, 1969), pp. 152–55.
38. Baran, *The Political Economy of Growth*, pp. 261–94; Victor D. Lippit, *Land Reform and Economic Development in China* (White Plains, NY: International Arts and Sciences Press, 1974); Clive Y. Thomas, *Dependence and Transformation: The Economics of the Transition to Socialism* (New York: Monthly Review Press, 1974), and *The Rise of the Authoritarian State in Peripheral Societies* (New York: Monthly Review Press, 1984).
39. Paul M. Sweezy, *Post-Revolutionary Society* (New York: Monthly Review Press, 1980), "After Capitalism—What?" *Monthly Review* 37, no. 3 (July–August 1985): 98–111; Charles Bettelheim, "The Specificity of Soviet Capitalism," *Monthly Review* 37, no. 4 (September 1985): 43–56.

2. The Economic Surplus Concept and Marxian Value Theory

1. Paul Mattick, *Anti-Bolshevik Communism* (London: Merlin Press, 1978), pp.191–92.
2. Quoted in Henryk Szlajfer, "Economic Surplus and Surplus Value: An Attempt at Comparison," *Occasional Paper 78.3*, Economic Research Bureau, University of Dar es Salaam (August 1989), p. 3.
3. Ernest Mandel, "The Labor Theory of Value and 'Monopoly Capitalism,'" *International Socialist Review* 29, no. 4 (July–August 1967): 34.
4. Szlajfer, "Economic Surplus and Surplus Value," p. 4.
5. Raymond Lubitz, "Monopoly Capitalism and Neo-Marxism," in Daniel Bell and Irving Kristol, eds., *Capitalism Today* (New York: Basic Books, 1971), pp. 167–68.
6. Anthony Brewer, *Marxist Theories of Imperialism: A Critical Survey* (London: Routledge & Kegan Paul, 1980), p. 138.
7. See E. K. Hunt, *History of Economic Thought: A Critical Perspective* (Belmont, CA: Wadsworth Publishing Co., 1979), pp. 213–14.
8. The neoclassical view is reflected in standard national income accounting practice which deducts rent and interest from profts. The numerator in the key Marxian profit ratio (the so-called value rate of profit), in contrast, is total surplus value (or aggregate profits, abstracting from the problem of unproductive labor). Thus while Marxian theory tends to see gross profits as a category rooted in production, which can be broken down into the profits of industrial capital, the interest of money-lending capital, and the rent of landed (or landlord) capital, liberal theory generally follows one strand of Adam Smith's thought in viewing profits as in some way derivative of (or residual to) total costs: wages, interest, rent, and a "normal" mark-up. Indeed, it is frequently suggested that accounting profits may be reducible, in large part, to implicit wages, implicit interest, and implicit rent. There is also a more intricate neoclassical view that attempts to designate a particular factor of production to which profits can be traced. But since wages are thought to represent the marginal product of labor, rent of land, and interest of capital, it is difficult to find "a factor" for which profit is the marginal product. What is more, the general equilibrium model of neoclassical theory assumes zero profits. The solution, then, is to associate profits exclusively with development, and to trace it to "entrepreneurship," viewed either as a special productive factor, or, in the more usual case, as an element producing a temporary residual—of a "monopolistic" variety in Schumpeterian theory—above the three basic factors of

production. "Entrepreneurship," in turn, is variously associated (depending on whether the authority is J. B. Clark, Alfred Marshall, Joseph Schumpeter, or Frank Knight) with such items as risk, management, innovation, and uncertainty. To make matters even worse, all neoclassical attempts to trace profit to the productivity of the "capital factor" have been undermined by the critique introduced by Piero Sraffa, which demonstrates that the neoclassical definition of capital is logically dependent on some given price and profit structure (making the reasoning circular). All in all, it is difficult to avoid the conclusion that there is, in the strict sense, no such thing as a logically consistent orthodox approach to the source of profits. It is by no means insignificant then that Baran and Sweezy took the classical-Marxian tradition as their starting point. See Mark Obrinsky, *Profit Theory and Capitalism* (Philadelphia: University of Pennsylvania Press, 1983); and Hunt, *History of Economic Thought,* pp. 398–413. On the Schumpeterian theory of entrepreneurship and its conflict with Marxian theory see John Bellamy Foster, "Theories of Capitalist Transformation: Critical Notes on the Comparison of Marx and Schumpeter," *Quarterly Journal of Economics* 98, no. 2 (May 1983): 327–31, and "The Political Economy of Joseph Schumpeter: A Theory of Capitalist Development and Decline," *Studies in Political Economy,* no. 15 (Fall 1984): 5–42.

9. Paul A. Baran and Paul M. Sweezy, *Monopoly Capital* (New York: Monthly Review Press, 1966), p. 10n.
10. Paul M. Sweezy, "Monopoly Capital and the Theory of Value," in John Bellamy Foster and Henryk Szlajfer, eds., *The Faltering Economy: The Problem of Accumulation under Monopoly Capitalism* (New York: Monthly Review Press, 1984), pp. 25–26.
11. Baran and Sweezy, *Monopoly Capital,* p. 10n.
12. This was the entirely unsatisfactory conclusion that the present author had arrived at in 1980, prior to being introduced to Henryk Szlajfer's pathbreaking work.
13. Henryk Szlajfer, "Economic Surplus and Surplus Value under Monopoly Capitalism," in Foster and Szlajfer, eds., *The Faltering Economy,* p. 262.
14. Ibid.
15. See Karl Marx, *Capital,* Volume III (New York: International Publishers, 1967), p. 791, where he pointedly uses the general notion of surplus labor rather than the historically specific concept of surplus value. For the methodological principle involved see ibid., pp. 818–19, and note 32 below.
16. Brewer, *Marxist Theories of Imperialism,* pp. 138–46.
17. In this study the term "social accumulation fund" refers to the total surplus value (and/or surplus product) available for economic expansion. This differs somewhat from Marx's usage in that he sometimes used the term "accumulation fund" with reference to depreciation funds. Moreover, it seems appropriate to follow the general practice of using this term even where the boundaries of capitalism are transgressed. The "social accumulation fund," then, equals aggregate profits (net of depreciation) plus economic waste and constitutes the fund *available* for net investment.
18. Michal Kalecki, "On Paul Baran's Political Economy of Growth," *Monthly Review* 17, no. 6 (November 1965): 59.
19. Paul A. Baran, *The Political Economy of Growth* (New York: Monthly Review Press, 1957), pp. 22–23, 41–42.
20. Ibid., p. 22. Szlajfer, "Economic Surplus and Surplus Value under Monopoly Capitalism," p. 266.
21. Ibid.
22. Baran, *The Political Economy of Growth,* p. 23n.

23. Ibid., p. 24.
24. Victor D. Lippit, "The Concept of Surplus in Economic Development," *Working Paper Series No. 65,* Department of Economics, University of California at Riverside (January 1983): 8.
25. That is, each of the first three categories refers to a different aspect of the general problem of unproductive labor or economic waste in its widest possible sense. The first is concerned mainly with luxury goods production, the second with the output effects of unproductive labor (which in Baran's conception includes the former category), and the third with waste in the productive process (which could be interpreted as including the first two categories, along with the penetration of the sales effort into the sphere of production).
26. Baran, *The Political Economy of Growth,* pp. 41–43.
27. Szlajfer, "Economics Surplus and Surplus Value," *Review of Radical Political Economics* 15, no. 1 (Spring 1983): 112.
28. Henryk Szlajfer, "Economic Surplus and Surplus Value under Monopoly Capitalism" and "Waste, Marxian Theory, and Monopoly Capital: Toward a New Synthesis," in Foster and Szlajfer, eds., *The Faltering Economy,* pp. 262–321.
29. This argument is presented in greater detail in John Bellamy Foster, "The Limits of U.S. Capitalism: Surplus Capacity and Capacity Surplus," in ibid, pp. 198–213.
30. Szlajfer, "Economic Surplus and Surplus Value under Monopoly Capitalism," p. 267.
31. Ibid, p. 288.
32. See, for example, Harry Magdoff and Paul M. Sweezy, "Production and Finance," *Monthly Review* 35, no. 1 (May 1983): 7–8. The methodological issue was best explained by Evgeny Preobrazhensky in his discussion of the "law of value in Soviet economy": "Marx more than once warned against confusing ther concept of surplus value with surplus product. Surplus product is a concept incomparably wider than the concept of surplus value. Surplus product existed long before the development of capitalist production and will continue to exist after the ending of the bourgeois system of society, though no longer as a relation of exploitation. Only at a certain historical stage does the surplus product assume the form of surplus value." Evgeny Preobrazhensky, *The New Economics* (Oxford: Oxford University Press, 1965), p. 185. See also Karl Marx, *Theories of Surplus Value,* Part III (Moscow: Progress Publishers, 1971), p. 370. In this context, it is well worth noting that Baran had studied under Preobrazhensky, as indicated in David Horowitz, *Imperialism and Revolution* (Middlesex, England: Penguin Books, 1969), p. 120n.
33. Baran, *The Political Economy of Growth,* p. 32. According to Hilferding's definition, labor is productive when it is "necessary for the social purpose of production, and is thus independent of the determined historical form"; while, in contrast, "labor which is expended only for the purposes of circulation, i.e., which originates from the determined historical organization of production, does not create value." Quoted in I. I. Rubin, *Essays on Marx's Theory of Value* (Detroit: Black and Red, 1972), p. 174. It is quite likely that Baran, who knew Hilferding and wrote for the latter's *Die Gesellschaft,* was at least vaguely aware of this approach to the question of productive labor, adopted by the author of *Finance Capital.* See Paul M. Sweezy and Leo Huberman, eds., *Paul A. Baran (1910–1964): A Collective Portrait* (New York: Monthly Review Press, 1965), p. 33.
34. Ian Gough, "Marx's Theory of Productive and Unproductive Labour," *New Left Review,* no. 76 (November–December 1972): 56–58.

35. Karl Marx, *Capital,* vol. III, p. 20. As quoted in Gough, "Marx's Theory of Productive and Unproductive Labour," p. 57.
36. Marx, *Theories of Surplus Value,* Part III, p. 505. As quoted in ibid., p. 58.
37. Mike Davis notes that "of the 3.6 million manufacturing jobs added to the American economy since 1948, 3 million were filled by non-production employees and at least half of those were managerial posts." Mike Davis, "The Political Economy of Late-Imperial America," *New Left Review,* no. 143 (January–February 1984): 23. See also Seymour Melman, *Profits Without Production* (New York: Alfred A. Knopf, 1983).
38. Gough, "Marx's Theory of Productive and Unproductive Labour," p. 60.
39. Szlajfer, "Economic Surplus and Surplus Value under Monopoly Capitalism" and "Waste, Marxian Theory, and Monopoly Capital."
40. This corresponds to the most basic conception of unproductive labor adopted by Marx. Although it can be thought of as the perspective of individual capital, it nonetheless constituted a *critical* point of view in the late eighteenth and early nineteenth centuries, in that it represented the viewpoint of the industrial bourgeoisie, confronting the earlier productive relations of feudalism and mercantilist capitalism.
41. The term "unreproductive labor" with respect to the luxury goods sector was introduced in Ian Gough, *The Political Economy of the Welfare State* (London: Macmillan, 1979), pp. 158–61, and was elaborated by John Bellamy Foster, "Marxian Economics and the State," in Foster and Szlajfer, eds., *The Faltering Economy,* pp. 339–43, and Jacob Morris, "Underconsumption and the General Crisis: Gillman"s Theory," *Science and Society* 47, no. 3 (Fall 1983): 323–29. See chapter 4 below.
42. The term "useless labor" is based on Gough's observation that Marx employed the concept of "useful labor" in relation to production in general (independent of the capitalist mode). In both cases the intellectual standpoint is that of society as a whole.
43. Szlajfer, "Economic Surplus and Surplus Value under Monopoly Capitalism," pp. 269–71, 278–83.
44. Paul M. Sweezy, "Japan in Perspective," *Monthly Review* 31, no. 9 (February 1980):12.
45. Baran and Sweezy, *Monopoly Capital,* pp. 9–10, 72.
46. Szlajfer, "Economic Surplus and Surplus Value under Monopoly Capitalism," pp. 269–70; Michael Lebowitz, "Monopoly Capital," *Studies on the Left* 6, no. 5 (1966): 64–67; Otto Nathan in "Marxism and Monopoly Capital: A Symposium," *Science and Society* 30, no. 4 (Winter 1966):490–93.
47. Baran and Sweezy, *Monopoly Capital,* p. 82.
48. Nicholas Kaldor, "A Model of Economic Growth," *The Economic Journal* 67 (December 1957):621; quoted in Baran and Sweezy, *Monopoly Capital,* p. 75.
49. Baran and Sweezy, *Monopoly Capital,* pp. 75–77, 218. Baran and Sweezy could also have pointed to the growth of unproductive labor as another mode of disguise assumed by the economic surplus, as Baran had in an earlier exchange with Kaldor. See Baran, *The Political Economy of Growth,* pp. xviii–xxii.
50. Ibid., p. 82.
51. Harry Magdoff and Paul M. Sweezy, *The Deepening Crisis of U.S. Capitalism* (New York: Monthly Review Press, 1981), p. 148.
52. Thus even as perceptive a student of political economy as Michael Lebowitz found it difficult to sort out exactly when Baran and Sweezy were referring to "actual surplus," on the one hand, and "potential surplus," on the other. See Lebowitz, "Monopoly Capital," pp. 65–66.
53. Baran and Sweezy, *Monopoly Capital,* p. 10.

54. Ibid., p. 112.
55. See the Appendix to this study.
56. Szlajfer, "Economic Surplus and Surplus Value under Monopoly Capitalism," pp. 278–79.
57. Baran and Sweezy, *Monopoly Capital,* p. 125; also Baran, *The Political Economy of Growth,* p. xx.
58. See Szlajfer, "Economic Surplus and Surplus Value," p. 125.
59. Baran and Sweezy, *Monopoly Capital,* p. 112.
60. Ibid.; Marx, *Capital,* vol. II, p. 149.
61. Paul M. Sweezy, *Modern Capitalism* (New York: Monthly Review Press, 1972), p. 50.
62. Baran and Sweezy, *Monopoly Capital,* p. 131.
63. Ibid., p. 114.
64. Ibid., pp. 131–32.
65. Szlajfer, "Waste, Marxian Theory, and Monopoly Capital," pp. 302–4.
66. Foster, "Marxian Economics and the State," pp. 342–44.
67. Ibid. See also Ken J. Tarbuck, "Marx: Productive and Unproductive Labour," *Studies in Political Economy,* no. 12 (Fall 1983):96–98.
68. Baran and Sweezy, *Monopoly Capital,* p. 133.
69. Ibid., p. 134.
70. Ibid., pp. 135–37.
71. Ibid., p. 139.
72. See Gough, "Marx's Theory of Productive and Unproductive Labor," pp. 64, 67–69; Szlajfer, "Waste, Marxian Theory, and Monopoly Capital," pp. 313–14.
73. Marx, *Theories of Surplus Value,* Part I, p. 289.
74. Baran and Sweezy, *Monopoly Capital,* pp. 142–43.
75. Joseph D. Phillips in Baran and Sweezy, *Monopoly Capital,* p. 370; Szlajfer, "Economic Surplus and Surplus Value under Monopoly Capitalism," p. 229.
76. Baran and Sweezy, *Monopoly Capital,* pp. 9, 112.
77. Here the measurement problem is itself merely a reflection of the limitations of the global capitalist outlook. A perspective that emphasizes the potential surplus product lost due to unemployment and waste in the production process naturally goes beyond the conventional forms of measuring national income.
78. Szlajfer, "Economic Surplus and Surplus Value," p. 122.
79. Phillips in Baran and Sweezy, *Monopoly Capital,* p. 389.
80. See Lubitz, "Monopoly Capitalism and Neo-Marxism," pp. 169–70; Ron Stanfield, *The Economic Surplus and Neo-Marxism* (Lexington, MA: Lexington Books, 1973), p. 86.
81. This is a problem of measurement rather than a theoretical problem as such. Since property income in the Phillips calculations is net of taxes, there is no double counting to that extent. There appears to be no clear way of avoiding the overall problem of double counting, however, except by consistently working from one side of the income accounts (or from each separately).
82. Ron Stanfield, "A Revision of the Economic Surplus Concept," in Foster and Szlajfer, eds., *The Faltering Economy,* pp. 251–61, and *The Economic Surplus and Neo-Marxism;* Edward Wolff, "Unproductive Labor and Rate of Surplus Value in the United States, 1947–1967," *Research in Political Economy* (1977): 87–115. Stanfield, using a concept of planned surplus, indicates that the surplus as a percentage of actual GNP increased from 46.3 percent in 1929 to 75.7 percent in 1970. Wolff, using the concept of total surplus value, shows a 5 point increase in surplus value as a percentage of value-added for the U.S. economy

between 1947 (31 percent) and 1967 (36 percent). The Phillips/Baran and Sweezy figures lie between these estimates, with the surplus rising from 46.9 percent of GNP in 1929 to 56.1 percent in 1963.

83. Phillips in Baran and Sweezy, *Monopoly Capital,* pp. 381–84.
84. Ibid., p. 370.
85. Szlajfer, "Economic Surplus and Surplus Value," p. 125.
86. Karl Korsch, *Three Essays on Marxism* (London: Pluto Press, 1971), pp. 16–25.
87. Szlajfer, "Economic Surplus and Surplus Value under Monopoly Capitalism," pp. 281–82.
88. Baran and Sweezy, *Monopoly Capital,* p. 10n.
89. Mattick, *Anti-Bolshevik Communism,* p. 191.
90. William Barclay and Mitchell Stengel, "Surplus and Surplus Value," *Review of Radical Political Economics* 7, no. 4 (Winter 1975): 55.
91. David Yaffe, "The Marxian Theory of Crisis, Capital, and the State," *Economy and Society* 2, no. 2 (1973): 186–87. Here it is interesting to note that Baran actually studied at the famous Institute for Social Research in Frankfurt am Main, where he held an assistantship under Friedrich Pollock. See Sweezy and Huberman, eds., *Paul A. Baran,* pp. 32–33.
92. "Utopian socialism" in traditional Marxist discourse meant the attempt to construct a definite blueprint for a future socialist society, after the examples of Charles Fourier and Robert Owen, without regard to the real social forces developing within the womb of the existing society and without regard to the indeterminacy of much of the future. Naturally, Marx and Engels never meant to deny the possibility that the appearance of new social capacities would allow some further conception of objective possibilities, limited only by the class structure of society, the knowledge of which could provide an additional basis for criticism of capitalism as a determinate historical form. In other words, the criticism of utopianism was never meant to leave the socialist vision foreshortened.
93. Paul M. Sweezy, *The Theory of Capitalist Development* (New York: Monthly Review Press, 1942), p. 22.
94. Paul A. Baran, *The Longer View* (New York: Monthly Review Press, 1969), p. 33, 36–37.
95. Baran was clearly advocating "utopian" thinking in the sense in which that outlook is now promoted by theorists like E. P. Thompson and Rudolf Bahro and not in the sense in which it was originally condemned within scientific socialism.
96. Ibid., pp. 35–36.
97. This, as Szlajfer has demonstrated, is the critical potential of the concept of planned surplus.
98. Sweezy, *The Theory of Capitalist Development,* pp. 52–53.
99. Thomas Sekine, "A Glossary of Technical Terms," in Kozo Uno, *Principles of Political Economy: Theory of a Purely Capitalist Society* (Atlantic Highlands, NJ: Humanities Press, 1977), p. 184; see also Wlodzmierz Brus, *The Market in a Socialist Economy* (London: Routledge & Kegan Paul, 1972), pp. 89–93.
100. The assumption that the law of value worked in what could be thought of as a relatively unobstructed fashion, in Marx's theory of a purely capitalist economy, modeled after the competitive capitalism of his day, was not based so much on the day-to-day reality of the Victorian economy as on what appeared to be its developmental tendency.
101. Szlajfer, "Economic Surplus and Surplus Value," p. 117.

3. Free Competition and Monopoly Capital

1. Paul A. Baran and Paul M. Sweezy, *Monopoly Capital* (New York: Monthly Review Press, 1966), pp. 4–5. See also the Appendix below.
2. Ibid., p. 6.
3. All such interpretations of Baran and Sweezy's work, while not altogether unreasonable when considered in terms of *Monopoly Capital* itself, implicitly assume that Sweezy had in effect repudiated his earlier analysis in *The Theory of Capitalist Development*. There is no concrete evidence, however, to support such a conclusion. It is more plausible to presume, in line with Baran and Sweezy's own indications and Sweezy's subsequent statements, that their essay-sketch was not intended as a comprehensive study of capitalist development in the twentieth century, but focused only on those elements *specific* to the *monopoly stage* of capitalism, which demanded major theoretical modifications but did not call into question the most fundamental aspects of Marxian political economy (the analysis of class, value, and the labor process).
4. Karl Marx, *Grundrisse* (New York: Vintage, 1973), p. 752; quoted in Paul M. Sweezy, "Competition and Monopoly," in John Bellamy Foster and Henryk Szlajfer, eds., *The Faltering Economy: The Problem of Accumulation under Monopoly Capitalism* (New York: Monthly Review Press, 1984), p. 27.
5. Marx, *Grundrisse,* p. 552; quoted in Sweezy, ibid., p. 27.
6. The difference between neoclassical and Marxian theory in this respect is cogently expressed in the following statement by Sweezy: For Marx "competition could not be 'perfect' or 'pure,' nor could it end in equilibrium situations lending themselves to analysis as to their uniqueness, stability, and so on. Fantasies of this kind were imported into economics only much later by those more interested in concealing than revealing the real role of the economy in shaping the history and destiny of bourgeois society. Neither Marx nor the classical economists had any interest in playing such intellectual games. For them, and for Marx most of all, competition was an elemental force, somewhat comparable to the force of gravity, which keeps the parts of the system in place and interacting with each other in intelligible ways." Thus economists in the classical and Marxist traditions commonly employ the *historical* category of "free competition" as a theoretical point of departure.
7. John E. Elliott, *Comparative Economic Systems* (Englewood Cliffs, NJ: Prentice-Hall, 1973), pp. 62–63.
8. Ibid., p. 63n.
9. J. R. Hicks, *Value and Capital* (Oxford: Oxford University Press, 1946), pp. 83–84.
10. See Michal Kalecki, *Studies in the Theory of Business Cycles, 1933–1939* (New York: Augustus M. Kelley, 1966), pp. 50–52; Piero Sraffa, "Laws of Return under Competitive Conditions," *Economic Journal* 36 (December 1926): 510–11; Mark Obrinsky, *Profit Theory and Capitalism* (Philadelphia: University of Pennsylvania Press, 1983), pp. 104–5, 134–35.
11. This is shown most dramatically in Kalecki's work. See Michal Kalecki, *Essays in the Theory of Economic Fluctuations* (New York: Russell and Russell, 1939), p. 27. The same phenomenon of "shortrun average costs" that are "virtually constant over a considerable range of output" is widely appreciated by economists working with the reality of excess capacity. See *Measures of Productive Capacity,* Hearings Before the Subcommittee on Economic Statistics of the Joint Economic Committee, 87th Congress, 2nd Session, May 14, 22, 23, and 24, 1962, p. 94.
12. Hicks, *Value and Capital,* pp. 84–85.

13. John Stuart Mill, *Principles of Political Economy* (New York: Longmans, Green, 1904), p. 147.
14. See James A. Clifton, "Competition and the Evolution of the Capitalist Mode of Production," *Cambridge Journal of Economics* 1 (June 1977): 137–51; John Eatwell, "Competition," in Ian Bradley and Michael Howard, eds., *Classical and Marxian Political Economy* (London: Macmillan, 1982), pp. 203–28; Peter Kenyon, "Pricing," in Alfred Eichner, ed., *A Guide to Post-Keynesian Economics* (White Plains, NY: M. E. Sharpe, 1979), pp. 36–37.
15. Clifton, "Competition and the Evolution of the Capitalist Mode of Production," p. 145; Eatwell, "Competition," p. 218; Philip L. Williams, "Monopoly and Centeralisation in Marx," *History of Political Economy* 14, no. 2 (1982): 238–39.
16. Williams, "Monopoly and Centralisation in Marx," p. 239.
17. Karl Marx, *Capital,* vol. I (New York: International Publishers, 1967), p. 626.
18. Karl Marx, *Early Writings,* trans. and ed. by T. B. Bottomore (New York: McGraw-Hill, 1964), p. 91.
19. Clifton, "Competition and the Evolution of the Capitalist Mode of Production," p. 137.
20. Ibid., p. 145; Marx, *Capital,* vol. III, p. 175.
21. Ibid.
22. Marx, *Capital,* vol. I, p. 626.
23. See Frederick Engels, Preface, in Marx, *Capital,* vol. III, p. 3; Karl Korsch, *Three Essays on Marxism* (New York: Monthly Review Press, 1971).
24. George J. Stigler, "Perfect Competition Historically Contemplated," *Journal of Political Economy* 65, no. 1 (February 1957): 1–17.
25. Eatwell, "Competition," p. 210.
26. Williams, "Monopoly and Centralisation in Marx," p. 238.
27. Ibid., pp. 238–39.
28. Ibid., p. 238.
29. Clifton had initiated this type of criticism of Baran and Sweezy in his own article. See Clifton, "Competition and the Evolution of the Capitalist Mode of Production," p. 143n.
30. John Weeks, *Capital and Exploitation* (Princeton: Princeton University Press, 1981), p. 159.
31. It is true that Smith went beyond most of the other liberal-classical theorists in explicitly accounting for the necessity of a large number of firms. But, in sharp contrast to Marx, there is no sign that Smith considered the issue of economies of scale. He seems to have had only the possibility of collusion in mind. See Philip L. Williams, *The Emergence of the Theory of the Firm: From Adam Smith to Alfred Marshall* (London: Macmillan, 1978), pp. 30–35.
32. Use of the term "imperfection" is itself a sleight of hand. As Galbraith writes, "In one exception, the firm has influence over prices and output; that is the case of monopoly or oligopoly, or their counterparts. . . . But monopoly—the control of prices and production in an industry by one firm—and oligopoly—control by a few firms—are never the rule in this image; they are always the exception. They are imperfections in the system. The use of the word imperfection, which is the standard reference to monopoly and oligopoly, affirms that these are departures from the general competitive rule." John Kenneth Galbraith, *Annals of an Abiding Liberal* (New York: New American Library, 1979), p. 5.
33. One of the paradoxes of the new neo-Ricardian approach is that while they deny the importance of market structure in their theory of competition, they nevertheless adopt the most rigid view of monopoly in terms of market power,

along lines that appear to resemble mainstream theory itself. Neo-Marxian theory, in contrast, tries to use a less rigid and formalized notion of monopoly capital to capture the essential reality of a U.S. economy in which an elite of two hundred nonfinancial corporations—ostensibly competing with some 2 million corporations and some 12 million partnerships and individual proprietorships—controlled 34.9 percent of total nonfinancial assets and earned 38.4 percent of nonfinancial net income as of 1975. See Edward S. Herman, *Corporate Control, Corporate Power* (Cambridge, England: Cambridge University Press, 1981), p. 191; C. L. R. James, "The Characteristics of Capitalism," *Monthly Review* 33, no. 1 (May 1981): 54–55; Reply by Paul Sweezy in ibid., pp. 55–56.

34. Weeks, *Capital and Exploitation,* p. 149.
35. In Marxian terms, this can be expressed by saying that the monopoly element leaves the qualitative value problem largely unaffected (except insofar as the giant corporations are able to promote formal use values), and is mainly relevant to the realization process.
36. John Bellamy Foster, "Is Monopoly Capitalism an Illusion?" *Monthly Review* 33, no. 4 (September 1981): p. 38; Marx, *Capital,* vol. III, pp. 435–41.
37. Baran and Sweezy, *Monopoly Capital,* p. 5.
38. Ibid., p. 4. See also the Appendix.
39. Marx, *Capital,* vol. III, p. 861.
40. Sweezy, "Competition and Monopoly," p. 37.
41. Failing to appreciate the *static* character of Marx's very limited treatment of monopoly price, Ernest Mandel, in his critique of Baran and Sweezy, wrote: "The labor theory of value implies that, *in terms of value,* the total mass of surplus value to be distributed every year is a *given quantity.* It depends on the value of variable capital and the rate of surplus value. Price competition cannot change that given quantity (except when it influences the division of the newly created income between workers and capitalists, i.e., depresses or increases real wages and thereby increases or decreases surplus value). Once this simple basic truth is grasped, one understands that the displacement of free competition by monopolies does not basically alter the problem *in value terms.*" Ernest Mandel, "The Labor Theory of Value and 'Monopoly Capitalism,'" *International Socialist Review* 28, no. 4 (July–August 1967): 34. Mandel's misnomer stems from the fact that once one drops the *static* assumption that value is some "given quantity," it becomes readily apparent that monopoly capital's ability to exercise significant control over price, output, investment, and waste can materially affect the system "in value terms"—altering not only the quantity of value actually produced and realized, but also the rates of productivity and exploitation and relative distributive shares. What remains largely unchanged, of course, is the essential character of the underlying valorization process. See Henryk Szlajfer, "Economic Surplus and Surplus Value under Monopoly Capitalism," in Foster and Szlajfer, eds., *The Faltering Economy,* pp. 276–7.
42. Viewing the matter in static terms, Steve Zeluck assumes that monopoly pricing cannot result in an increased rate of exploitation, since this would mean that wages were reduced below the value of labor power. See Steve Zeluck, "On the Theory of the Monopoly Stage of Capitalism," *Against the Current* 1, no. 1 (Fall 1980): 45–46; John Bellamy Foster, "Marxism and Monopoly Capital Theory: A Reply," *Against the Current* 2, no. 2 (Spring 1983): 48–49.
43. Sweezy, "Competition and Monopoly," p. 37.
44. Paul M. Sweezy, "Marxian Value Theory and Crises," in Foster and Szlajfer, eds., *The Faltering Economy,* p. 242.
45. In neoclassical theory the problem of value presents itself *simply* as a quan-

titative issue of relative prices at the level of exchange. In her book, *The Economics of Imperfect Competition* (written when she still adhered to the neoclassical position), Joan Robinson stated: "The main theme of this book is the analysis of value. It is not easy to explain what the analysis of value is. . . . The point may be put like this: You see two men, one of whom is giving a banana to the other, and is taking a penny from him. You ask, How is it that a banana costs a penny rather than any other sum?" Joan Robinson, *The Economics of Imperfect Competition* (London: Macmillan, 1948), pp. 6–7, as quoted in Paul M. Sweezy, *The Theory of Capitalist Development* (New York: Monthly Review Press, 1942), p. 33n. From a Marxian standpoint, the reduction of the value question to a simple question of exchange value precludes any logically coherent theory of the source of capital or profits. On the circular character of neoclassical analysis see E.K. Hunt, *History of Economic Thought* (Belmont, CA: Wadsworth Publishing Co., 1979), pp. 398–413.

46. Richard Edwards, *Contested Terrain: The Tranformation of the Workplace in the Twentieth Century* (New York: Basic Books, 1979), pp. 44, 226–27.
47. On the historical specifics see Joseph Ernest Bowring, "The Dual Economy: Core and Periphery in the Accumulation Process in the United States," Ph.D. diss., University of Massachusetts at Amherst, 1982, pp. 44–78.
48. This paragraph is adapted from John Bellamy Foster and Henryk Szlajfer, Editors' Introduction to Foster and Szaljfer, eds., *The Faltering Economy,* p. 13.
49. Ibid., pp. 14–15; Frederick Engels, *On Marx's Capital* (Moscow: Progress Publishers, 1956), pp. 118–20.
50. This was the original title of Lenin's pamphlet. See Foster and Szlajfer, Editors' Introduction to Foster and Szlajfer, eds., *The Faltering Economy,* p. 21.
51. Baran and Sweezy, *Monopoly Capital,* p. 5.
52. Ibid.
53. Ibid., pp. 5–6.
54. Sweezy, *The Theory of Capitalist Development,* p. 285.
55. Ibid.
56. For later presentations of the same argument see Paul M. Sweezy, *Modern Capitalism* (New York: Monthly Review Press, 1972), pp. 45–48; Sweezy, "Marxian Value Theory and Crises," pp. 241–42. It seems quite likely that this issue would have been dealt with in the missing "chapter 9" of *Monopoly Capital,* entitled "Some Implications for Economic Theory"—a preliminary draft of which had been written but was not included in the book itself, due to the fact that Baran and Sweezy had not worked out all of their differences at the time of Baran's death. See Appendix.
57. Sweezy, *Modern Capitalism,* p. 41.
58. See John Bellamy Foster, "Investment and Capitalist Maturity," in Foster and Szlajfer, eds., *The Faltering Economy,* pp. 66–67.
59. Sweezy, "Competition and Monopoly," pp. 37–38.
60. Harry Braverman, *Labor and Monopoly Capital* (New York: Monthly Review Press, 1974), pp. 251–56; Paul M. Sweezy, Foreword in ibid.
61. See Roy Coombs, "'Labor and Monopoly Capital,'" *New Left Review,* no. 107 (January–February 1978): 80. John Weeks goes even further, actually criticizing Braverman for being weak on value theory, since he "refers to surplus value on only 7 out of 450 pages." On the basis of this observation, Weeks concludes: "In an underconsumptionist world, the analysis of production has only 'sociological' relevance." John Weeks, "A Note on the Underconsumptionist Theory and the Labor Theory of Value," *Science and Society* 46, no. 1 (Spring 1982): 72.
62. Weeks, *Capital and Exploitation,* pp. 149–69.

63. Willi Semmler, "Competition, Monopoly, and Differentials of Profit Rates: Theoretical Considerations and Empirical Evidence," *Review of Radical Political Economics* 13, no. 4 (Winter 1982): 39.
64. Willi Semmler, "Theories of Competition and Monopoly," *Capital and Class,* no. 18 (Winter 1982): 99; Semmler, "Competition, Monopoly, and Differentials of Profit Rates," p. 43.
65. Ibid.
66. Semmler, "Theories of Competition and Monopoly," p. 100.
67. Ibid., p. 93.
68. Semmler, "Competition, Monopoly, and Differentials of Profit Rates," pp. 43–49.
69. Anthony Brewer, *Marxist Theories of Imperialism* (London: Routledge & Kegan Paul, 1980), pp. 135–37.
70. Zeluck, "On the Theory of the Monopoly Stage of Capitalism," pp. 43, 46.
71. See James F. Becker, "On the Monopoly Theory of Monopoly Capitalism," *Science and Society* 25, no. 4 (1971): 415–38; Paul Mattick, *Anti-Bolshevik Communism* (London: Merlin Press, 1978), pp. 187–88; Paul Walton and Andrew Gamble, *From Alienation to Surplus Value* (London: Sheed and Ward, 1976), pp. 213–17; Peter Bell, "Marxist Theory, Class Struggle, and the Crisis of Capitalism," in Jesse Schwartz, ed., *The Subtle Anatomy of Capitalism* (Santa Monica, CA: Goodyear Publishing Co., 1977), pp. 185, 193.
72. Sweezy, "Competition and Monopoly," p. 30.
73. See V. I. Lenin, *Imperialism: The Highest Stage of Capitalism* (Moscow: Progress Publishers, n.d.), pp. 20–22, 83.
74. Howard J. Sherman, "Monopoly Power and Profit Rates," *Review of Radical Political Economics* 15, no. 2 (Summer 1983): 127; Foster, "Is Monopoly Capitalism an Illusion?" pp. 40, 45; Foster and Szlajfer, Editors' Introduction, in Foster and Szlajfer, eds., *The Faltering Economy,* p. 11.
75. In orthodox economics, "monopolistic competition" generally refers to a market structure in which there are a fairly large number of small or medium-sized firms, together with substantial product differentiation. It excludes, by definition, the case of oligopoly (monopoly capital). In fact, in the rigid formulation that it was originally given by E. H. Chamberlain, "monopolistic competition may be as rare as perfect competition." Mark Blaug, *Economic Theory in Retrospect* (Cambridge, England: Cambridge University Press, 1978), p. 415.
76. Michael A. Lebowitz, "The Theoretical Status of Monopoly Capital," paper presented at the Political Economy Section of the Canadian Political Science Association, Ottawa, Canada, June 7, 1982, pp. 11, 14 (quoted by permission). Lebowitz's views here contrast sharply with those of a neo-Ricardian (or "post-Keynesian") theorist like Peter Kenyon, who argues that in the work of the classical economists from Smith to Marx competition was simply a *process* and did not involve question of *market structure.* See Peter Kenyon, "Pricing," in Alfred Eichner, ed., *A Guide to Post-Keynesian Economics* (White Plains, NY: M. E. Sharpe, 1979), pp. 36–38. It should be noted that the logical "tendency of capital to become one," which Lebowitz has underlined, merely points to what Marx called the "extreme limit" of the concentration and centralization of capital. See James and Sweezy, "The Characteristics of Capitalism." As Bukharin understood, Hilferding's well-known statements on this tendency were of a similar abstract character, and do not necessarily lead toward the more ahistorical notions of world capitalist trusts and ultraimperialism advanced by Karl Kautsky. See Nikolai Bukharin, *Imperialism and World Economy* (New York: Monthly Review Press, 1929), pp. 130–43.

77. Sweezy, *Four Lectures on Marxism,* p. 66.
78. Baran and Sweezy, *Monopoly Capital,* pp. 225n–26n.
79. See Semmler, "Competition, Monopoly, and Differentials of Profit Rates," pp. 43–49; Sherman, "Monopoly Power and Profit Rates," pp. 129–32.
80. Edwards, *Contested Terrain,* pp. 82–83, 219, 221, 231. Bowring gives a more specific breakdown on profit rates for the same period. Defining a small firm as one with less than $100 million in assets, and low concentration as a four-firm concentration ratio of less than 40 percent, he provides the following average profit rates by firm size and industry concentration for 1958–1971 based on U.S. government data: (1) small firms, low concentration—8.2 percent; (2) small firms, high concentration—8.8 percent; (3) large firms, low concentration—7.8 percent; (4) large firms, high concentration—10.8 percent. His fourth category of "core firms" is of course equivalent to the oligopolistic sector of the economy. See Bowring, *The Dual Economy,* p. 169.
81. Ibid., pp. 109–44.
82. Among the more important studies are: Howard J. Sherman, *Profits in the United States* (Ithaca, NY: Cornell University Press, 1968); Bagicha Singh Minhas, *An International Comparison of Factor Costs and Factor Use* (Amsterdam: North-Holland Publishing Co., 1963), pp. 54–73; Josef Steindl, *Small and Big Business: Economic Problems of the Size of Firms* (Oxford: Basil Blackwell, 1947); Kathleen Pulling, "Cyclical Behavior of Profit Margins," *Journal of Economic Issues* 12, no. 2 (June 1978): 287–306.
83. As quoted in Sweezy, *The Theory of Capitalist Development,* p. 270. After making this statement Hilferding goes on to qualify and elaborate on it in various ways. Thus he points to the replacement of the economy-wide average rate of profit by a hierarchy of profit rates among industries and firms, various limitations on monopoly price, and the fact that monopoly profits are based on a redistribution of surplus value. See Rudolf Hilferding, *Finance Capital: A Study in the Latest Phase of Capitalist Development* (London: Routledge & Kegan Paul, 1981), pp. 228–35.
84. Semmler objects that, "From monopoly as a general phenomenon (see Baran/Sweezy, 1966, Ch. I) it follows that the theory of value has to be rejected because laws of prices can no longer be analyzed." Semmler, "Theories of Competition and Monopoly," p. 111. Actually, the general validity of *value* theory does not depend on the unfettered working of the law of value, or, what amounts to the same thing, absolute determinacy in a theory of relative *prices.* While monopoly prices represent upward deviations from values (and prices of production) for which there is no completely unambiguous, general rule, and while the average rate of profit for industry as a whole loses much of its operational meaning under a regime of monopoly capital, the rate of surplus value—the key concept in Marxian economics—loses none of its concrete relevance. See Sweezy, "Marxian Value Theory and Crises," pp. 240–42.
85. Samir Amin, *The Law of Value and Historical Materialism* (New York: Monthly Review Press, 1978), p. 3.
86. Foster, "Is Monopoly Capitalism an Illusion?" p. 45.
87. See Henryk Szlajfer, "Economic Surplus and Surplus Value," *Review of Radical Political Economics* 15, no. 1 (Spring 1983): 117–18.
88. Amin, *The Law of Value and Historical Materialism,* p. 17.
89. Zeluck, "On the Theory of the Monopoly Stage of Capitalism," pp. 50–52; also Foster, "Is Monopoly Capitalism an Illusion?" pp. 41–42.
90. Joseph M. Gillman, *Prosperity in Crisis* (New York: Marzani and Munsell, 1965), p. 152. Lenin put the essential point even more succinctly: "Even if monopolies have now begun to retard progress, it is not an argument in favor of free

competition, which has become impossible after it has given rise to monopoly." See Lenin, *Imperialism,* p. 106.

4. Accumulation and Crisis

1. The interpretation of economic crisis arising out of the synthesis of the underconsumptionist position with the theory of monopoly capitalism is often labeled "overaccumulation theory" in Sweezy's more recent writings. See Harry Magdoff and Paul M. Sweezy, *The Deepening Crisis of U.S. Capitalism* (New York: Monthly Review Press, 1981), p. 179. To avoid possible misinterpretation, it should be stated at the outset that "overaccumulation," in this sense, means an excess of potential surplus product over actual, realized surplus product, rooted in an overcapacity to produce in relation to final demand, and reflected in a level of current investment which fails to absorb the entire investment-seeking surplus. It is therefore consistent with the Keynesian principle, enuciated by Alvin Hansen, that "while savings and investment are always *equal,* they are not always in *equilibrium,*" with intended savings (or the investment-seeking surplus) often outweighing intended investment. See Alvin H. Hansen, *A Guide to Keynes* (New York: McGraw-Hill, 1953), p. 59.
2. Erik Olin Wright, *Class, Crisis, and the State* (London: New Left Books, 1978), p. 179; Anwar Shaikh, "An Introduction to the History of Crisis Theories," in Union for Radical Political Economics, ed., *U.S. Capitalism in Crisis* (New York: Union for Radical Political Economics, 1978), p. 230.
3. The exaggerated character of Wright's criticism of realization crisis theory suggests that he was probably following the common practice among Marxist political economists of simply excluding the work of Kalecki and Steindl from the corpus of Marxist thought (notwithstanding their well-known influence on Baran and Sweezy) on the questionable grounds that they belong primarily to the Keynesian tradition. Here it is appropriate to recall Oskar Lange's remark that "Kalecki's model is often wrongly reckoned with those based on Keynes' theory; in fact it is derived from the Marxist theory of reproduction and accumulation. It first appeared in Kalecki's *Proba teorii Koniunktury* (An Essay on the Theory of the Business Cycles) . . . Warsaw 1933." Oskar Lange, *Political Economy,* vol. I (Oxford: Pergamon Press, 1963), p. 309n. The 1933 date is significant since it is on the basis of this monograph and a few additional essays that Kalecki has often been credited (by such diverse theorists as Joan Robinson, Roy Harrod, Oskar Lange, Lawrence Klein, George Feiwell, Paul Sweezy, and Harry Magdoff) with having "invented" the Keynesian revolution prior to the publication of Keynes's *General Theory.* See Harry Magdoff and Paul M. Sweezy, "Listen, Keynesians!" *Monthly Review* 34, no. 8 (January 1983): 9; John Bellamy Foster and Henryk Szlajfer, Editors' Introduction, in Foster and Szlajfer, eds., *The Faltering Economy: The Problem of Accumulation under Monopoly Capitalism* (New York: Monthly Review Press, 1984), pp. 11–12, 21.
4. David Yaffe, "The Marxian Theory of Crisis, Capital, and the State," *Economy and Society* 2, no. 2 (1973): 212–16.
5. See Rosa Luxemburg, "The Second and Third Volumes," in Franz Mehring, *Karl Marx: The Story of His Life* (London: George Allen & Unwin, 1936), p. 378; Paul M. Sweezy, *The Theory of Capitalist Development* (New York: Monthly Review Press, 1942), pp. 176, 184, 201; Paul Baran, *The Longer View* (New York: Monthly Review Press, 1969), pp. 186–87; Jonathon Penzner, Harry Magdoff, and Paul M. Sweezy, "The Classic Contradiction of Capitalism," *Monthly Review* 33, no. 11 (April 1982): 57–60; Alexander Cockburn, "Can Capitalism be

Saved? A Chat with Sweezy and Magdoff," *The Nation,* 9 June 1984, p. 704; Howard J. Sherman, "Realization Crisis Theory and the Labor Theory of Value," *Science and Society* 57, no. 2 (Summer 1983): 205–6.

6. Joseph Schumpeter considered all underconsumption theories to belong to one of the following three types: (1) the "oversaving type" (Malthus and Hobson), which argues that "stagnation ensues when people save and invest to such an extent as 'to leave no motive to a further increase in production' owing to the incident fall in prices and profits"; (2) the "nonspending type" that "emphasizes disturbances which arise from saving decisions that are *not* offset by decisions to invest"; and (3) the "mass poverty type" that "attributes gluts to the inability of labor, owing to low wages, to 'buy its own product' " (Sismondi and Rodbertus). Marx and Engels concentrated their attacks on the third type, which was obviously fallacious. The first type, according to Schumpeter, is erroneous if it is used to explain cyclical crises as such, rather than stagnation. This type, in the case of Hobson, was also criticized by Keynes for failing to recognize that intended savings that are not invested simply disappear, and that the problem is properly understood as one of underinvestment rather than overinvestment. Still, Keynes, while obviously correct, may have been too harsh in his criticism of Hobson (and most later economists even more so). This point is strongly argued by John Allett, who quotes John Maurice Clark's statement: "Hobson's views differed from present theories, which emphasize underinvestment relative to savings. Hobson concentrated on excessive investment relative to demand. . . .Yet this feature is not to be rejected merely because the present emphasis lies elsewhere. As a step in the process leading to a falling-off of investment it may deserve a place in a more balanced synthesis." In any case, all modern Marxian underconsumption (or realization crisis) theories belong to the "nonspending type" in Schumpeter's typology (reflecting the Keynesian revolution). See Joseph A. Schumpeter, *A History of Economic Analysis* (New York: Oxford University Press, 1954), p. 740n; John Maynard Keynes, *The General Theory of Employment, Interest, and Money,* in *Collected Writings,* vol. VII (London: Macmillan, 1973), pp. 366–70; John Allett, *New Liberalism: The Political Economy of J. A. Hobson* (Toronto: University of Toronto Press, 1981), p. 130. Compare Michael Bleaney, *Underconsumption Theories* (New York: International Publishers, 1976), pp. 11, 14, 115–18, 231, 236–37.
7. Sweezy, *The Theory of Capitalist Development,* p. 180.
8. Quoted in ibid., p. 172.
9. Ibid., pp. 168–69; Penzner, Magdoff, and Sweezy, "The Classic Contradiction of Capitalism," p. 59.
10. Quoted in Sweezy, *The Theory of Capitalist Development,* pp. 168–69n. Maurice Dobb wrote: "J. B. Clark's picture of building 'mills to build more mills for ever' can never be actualized, since in the real world mills are always specialized to a particular current stream of demand connected with consumption in the near future, and not a stream of demand stretching to an indefinite future." Maurice Dobb, *Political Economy and Capitalism* (London: Routledge & Sons, 1937), p. 104.
11. Sweezy, *The Theory of Capitalist Development,* p. 172.
12. Ibid., pp. 180–81. Sweezy did not actually specify, in his argument, that surplus value would rise as a proportion of national income, although this was strongly implied and was a necessary link in the logical chain. Thus it seems wise to follow Steindl's lead in incorporating it as an essential element in any exegesis of Sweezy's theory. See Josef Steindl, *Maturity and Stagnation in American Capitalism* (New York: Monthly Review Press, 1976), pp. 243–44.
13. Sweezy, *The Theory of Capitalist Development,* pp. 182–83, 186–89; Carl Snyder,

"Capital Supply and National Well-Being," *American Economic Review* 31, no. 2 (June 1936): 195–224.

14. Sweezy, *The Theory of Capitalist Development,* p. 180.
15. Ibid., pp. 217–18.
16. Ibid., pp. 218–21.
17. Ibid., pp. 226–31.
18. Ibid., pp. 231–34.
19. Ibid., pp. 198–99, 231.
20. Abba P. Lerner, "Marxism and Economics: Sweezy and Robinson," *Journal of Political Economy* 53, no. 1 (March 1945): 83.
21. There is, however, the difficulty that while it is perfectly reasonable to assume that total income is equal to consumption plus investment in a simple model of the capitalist economy, one must move beyond simple assumptions of this sort in analyzing statistical material. Nevertheless, the relationship that Sweezy specified between investment and consumption was not without considerable backing in the economic literature, since it was equivalent to the original form of the accelerator principle, as developed especially by John Maurice Clark in *Strategic Factors in Business Cycles.* See William E. Stoneman, *A History of the Economic Analysis of the Great Depression in America* (New York: Garland Publishing, 1979), pp. 65–69; John Bellamy Foster, "Understanding the Significance of the Great Depression," *Studies in Political Economy,* no. 11 (Summer 1983): 183–85.
22. Penzner, Magdoff, and Sweezy, "The Classic Contradiction of Capitalism," p. 59.
23. This was indicated by Sweezy himself in *The Theory of Capitalist Development,* p. 187n, as well as in Steindl, *Maturity and Stagnation in American Capitalism,* p. 244. The accelerator principle as such (the idea that income and investment were positively related in such a way that a given change in income would induce a proportionately larger change in investment, both on the upswing and the downswing) later took a back seat in neo-Marxian analysis, since it originally rested on the notion that in order to increase output it was necessary to expand capital stock, and was therefore unrealistic in an economy with considerable excess capacity. In his own theory of monopolistic accumulation (upon which Baran and Sweezy's was to be based), Kalecki substituted the more realistic thesis that "investment is an increasing function of the level of profits and a decreasing function of the stock of capital equipment." Michal Kalecki, *Theory of Economic Dynamics* (New York: Augustus M. Kelley, 1969), p. 102. Still, there was no logical difficulty in Sweezy's own use of the accelerator principle in his proof of a contradiction in the accumulation process, since he began by assuming full capacity utilization. See also note 39.
24. Paul M. Sweezy, *The Present as History* (New York: Monthly Review Press, 1953), p. 353. Sweezy was later to abandon the classic accelerator principle on historical grounds, in his adoption of the Kaleckian theory. See notes 23 above and 39 below.
25. Although Sweezy had been quite critical of the falling rate of profit theory in *The Theory of Capitalist Development,* already arguing that it had to be interpreted as a historically contingent law, he still seemed to believe that it played some role in the twentieth century, second to that of underconsumption tendencies. But his treatment of the rising organic composition theory became increasingly critical as the later development of the underconsumptionist framework, in conjunction with the Kalecki-Steindl theory, made it increasingly apparent that a rising rate of exploitation far outweighed the much weaker tendency toward increasing organic composition in "the present as

history." See Sweezy, *The Theory of Capitalist Development,* pp. 147–48, 285; Paul M. Sweezy, *Four Lectures on Marxism* (New York: Monthly Review Press, 1981), pp. 46–54.

26. Sydney Coontz, *Population Theories and the Economic Interpretation* (London: Routledge & Kegan Paul, 1961), pp. 120–23.
27. Shaikh, "An Introduction to the History of Crisis Theories," p. 229.
28. See especially Bukharin in Rosa Luxemburg, *The Accumulation of Capital: An Anti-Critique*/Nikolai Bukharin, *Imperialism and the Accumulation of Capital* (New York: Monthly Review Press, 1972), pp. 224–37; Michal Kalecki, "The Problem of Effective Demand with Tugan-Baranovski and Rosa Luxemburg," in Foster and Szlajfer, eds., *The Faltering Economy,* pp. 157–58; Sydney Coontz, *Productive Labor and Effective Demand* (London: Routledge & Kegan Paul, 1965).
29. Evsey D. Domar, *Essays in the Theory of Economic Growth* (New York: Oxford University Press, 1957), pp. 109–28.
30. Ibid., pp. 120–21.
31. Ibid., pp. 109–10, 122–28.
32. Sweezy, *The Present as History,* pp. 358–59.
33. Steindl, *Maturity and Stagnation in American Capitalism,* pp. 243–44. Although Steindl raised a few minor objections, they were clearly of a secondary order, relating mainly to exposition.
34. Ibid., pp. 245–46.
35. Ibid. Although underconsumption theory is often associated with rising or stable profits, this only relates to *potential* profits. Steindl's approach bridged the gap between the theory of underconsumption as a proof of the impossibility of ever greater shares of investment in total output and the reality of an economy in which both the rate of accumulation and the realized rate of profit are depressed in relation to their potential.
36. Ibid.
37. See Foster and Szlajfer, Editors' Introduction, in Foster and Szlajfer, eds., *The Faltering Economy,* pp. 11–17.
38. Steindl, *Maturity and Stagnation in American Capitalism,* pp. 245–46.
39. Ibid., pp. xiii–xiv, 9–14, 127–37, 245–46; John Bellamy Foster, "The Limits of U.S. Capitalism: Surplus Capacity and Capacity Surplus," in Foster and Szlajfer, eds., *The Faltering Economy,* pp. 198–213. Sylos-Labini has indicated that "Changes in this ratio ["the expected degree of capacity utilization"] embody the substance of the most recent version of the acceleration principle, the 'capital stock adjustment principle.'" Paolo Sylos-Labini, "The Problem of Effective Demand," in Foster and Szlajfer, eds., *The Faltering Economy,* p. 144.
40. Steindl, *Maturity and Stagnation in American Capitalism,* p. 246.
41. Kalecki, "The Problem of Effective Demand with Rosa Luxemburg and Tugan-Baranovski," p. 157.
42. Steindl, *Maturity and Stagnation in American Capitalism, p. 191.*
43. *Paul M. Sweezy, "Maturity and Stagnation in American Capitalism," Econometrica* 22, no. 4 (October 1954): 532.
44. Paul A. Baran, *The Political Economy of Growth* (New York: Monthly Review Press, 1957), pp. 81, 85.
45. Ibid., pp. xxiv–xxv; John Bellamy Foster, "The Political Economy of Joseph Schumpeter: A Theory of Capitalist Development and Decline," *Studies in Political Economy,* no. 15 (Fall 1984): 30–32.
46. D. M. Nuti summarized Kalecki's concept of "degree of monopoly" as follows: "Kalecki assumed a reverse L-shaped cost curve, prime costs being constant up to full capacity output and marginal costs equal to average prime costs. The degree of monopoly, defined as the excess of price over marginal cost, divided

by price, was hence equal to the share of profits in the output of each firm, and the share of profits in the national income was a weighted average of the degree of monopoly in all firms of the economy." D. M. Nuti, "'Vulgar Economy' in the Theory of Income Distribution," *Science and Society* 35, no. 1 (Spring 1971): 31. Although formulated as the ratio of price minus marginal cost to price, it should be understood that the degree of monopoly is primarily a reflection of the mark-up over unit prime costs. See Keith Cowling, *Monopoly Capitalism* (New York: John Wiley and Sons, 1982), pp. 5–7.

47. Cockburn, "Can Capitalism Survive? A Chat with Sweezy and Magdoff," p. 704.
48. Baran and Sweezy, *Monopoly Capital,* p. 79.
49. Devine defines the "Tugan-Baranovski path" as the situation "where the demand for means of production justifies investment, which then creates more demand for means of production." James Devine, "Underconsumption, Over-Investment, and the Origins of the Great Depression," *Review of Radical Political Economics* 15, no. 2 (Summer 1983): 4.
50. Baran and Sweezy, *Monopoly Capital,* p. 81n.
51. Ibid., p. 81.
52. Ibid., p. 82.
53. See Steindl, *Maturity and Stagnation in American Capitalism,* p. xiv. In the passage cited here, Steindl distinguishes between his own approach and that of Kalecki, suggesting that excess capacity was simply a "passive variable" in Kalecki's theory, while for Steindl it was partly the result of the planning of firms. It seems clear that in this sense Baran and Sweezy's approach was closer to that of Kalecki than Steindl. See Kalecki, *Theory of Economic Dynamics,* pp. 96–99. For a detailed discussion of the relationship between the targeting of prices, profit margins, and profit rates, and control over capacity utilization, in the day-to-day operations of firms, see Neil Chamberlain, *The Firm: Micro-Economic Planning and Action* (New York: McGraw-Hill, 1962), pp. 191–212.
54. See for example, Alvin H. Hansen, "Growth or Stagnation in the American Economy," *Review of Economics and Statistics* 36, no. 4 (November 1945): pp. 411–12. In his own short-run theory, Kalecki referred to the "boundaries set to investment plans" by the "limited market for the firm's products" (the demand side), and "limitation of the capital market" (the supply side), rather than to "investment outlets" as such. This reflected his view that the effect of cyclical overcapacity was partly one of dampened "expectations" and not simply "vanishing investment opportunities." Kalecki, *Theory of Economic Dynamics,* pp. 96–98. Needless to say, the subtle differences in *emphasis* that can be detected in the writings of Kalecki, Steindl, Baran, and Sweezy in this respect were mainly just that: a search for the most appropriate mode of expression. As orthodox Marxists, Baran and Sweezy were understandably reluctant to refer directly to "expectations," even when governed by the utilization of productive capacity. Moreover, by focusing on investment outlets they were able to link up directly with the long-run issues raised by Hansen (discussed in section 5).
55. The assumption of constant variable costs over the relevant range of output was based on classical economics, Kalecki, and empirical studies of capacity utilization. See Michal Kalecki, *Studies in the Theory of Business Cycles* (New York: Augustus M. Kelley, 1966), pp. 53–56, and *Theory of Economic Dynamics,* p. 12n; Steindl, *Maturity and Stagnation in American Capitalism,* pp. 82–83.
56. Aggregate profitability schedules can also be constructed for the entire economy, providing further substantiation for Baran and Sweezy's analysis, as demonstrated for the years 1948–83 in John Bellamy Foster, "Sources of

Instability in the U.S. Political Economy and Empire," paper presented at the Annual Conference of the Canadian Political Science Association, Guelph, Canada, May 1984.

57. Baran and Sweezy, *Monopoly Capital,* p. 88.
58. If there was a weakness in Baran and Sweezy's explanation of the investment cycle it lay in a failure to place enough emphasis (after the manner of Kalecki and Steindl) on excess capacity as a thermostatic device governing investment in the short run—although we have every reason to believe that this was a major factor underpinning their theory. In Sweezy's later writings, and those of Harry Magdoff, this aspect has been made more explicit. See Paul M. Sweezy, *Modern Capitalism* (New York: Monthly Review Press, 1972), p. 8; Harry Magdoff and Paul M. Sweezy, "Supply-Side Theory and Capital Investment," *Monthly Review* 34, no. 11 (April 1983): 1–6; Magdoff and Sweezy, *The Deepening Crisis of U.S. Capitalism,* pp. 24–27, 52, 179, 201–2.
59. The significance of this relationship for the accumulation process was succinctly summed up by James Devine: "The ability of capitalism to fulfill the production conditions allowing expanded reproduction can be measured by the rate of profit at any given capacity utilization rate." Devine, "Underconsumption, Over-Investment, and the Origins of the Great Depression," p. 10.
60. For one of the earliest attempts to connect a theory of monopolistic accumulation with empirical evidence on excess capacity, see Arther R. Burns, *The Decline of Competition: A Study of the Evolution of American Industry* (New York: McGraw-Hill, 1936), pp. 266–72; also Foster, "Understanding the Significance of the Great Depression," pp. 182–83.
61. Michal Kalecki, *Essays in the Theory of Economic Fluctuations* (New York: Russell and Russell, 1939), p. 149.
62. Baran and Sweezy, *Monopoly Capital,* p. 88.
63. Ibid., p. 91.
64. Ibid., pp. 93–94.
65. Ibid., p. 97.
66. Kalecki, *Theory of Economic Dynamics,* p. 159.
67. Ibid., pp. 131, 147; Foster, "The Limits of U.S. Capitalism," p. 208.
68. Kalecki, *Theory of Economic Dynamics,* p. 159.
69. Henryk Szlajfer, "Economic Surplus and Surplus Value under Monopoly Capitalism" and "Waste, Marxian Theory, and Monopoly Capital: Toward a New Synthesis," in Foster and Szlajfer, eds., *The Faltering Economy,* pp. 262–321.
70. Kalecki, *Theory of Economic Dynamics,* pp. 51–52; Szlajfer, "Waste, Marxian Theory, and Monopoly Capital," p. 307.
71. Baran and Sweezy, *Monopoly Capital,* p. 79. Kalecki and Steindl applied the concept of waste in relation to state spending on Department III-type outlets, but using a more complex argument (entering explicitly into the area of state finance) and not encompassing all the forms of waste envisioned by Baran and Sweezy. See, for example, Michal Kalecki, *The Last Phase in the Transformation of Capitalism* (New York: Monthly Review Press, 1972), pp. 89–95.
72. Baran and Sweezy, *Monopoly Capital,* p. 113.
73. Ibid., pp. 112–13; Sweezy, *Modern Capitalism,* pp. 49–50.
74. Baran and Sweezy, *Monopoly Capital,* p. 114.
75. Ibid., pp. 115, 139–41, 379–80; see also Harry Magdoff and Paul M. Sweezy, "Production and Finance," *Monthly Review* 35, no. 1 (May 1983): 1–13.
76. Kalecki always argued in terms of gross investment, for empirical reasons.
77. Steindl, *Maturity and Stagnation in American Capitalism,* pp. 241–42.
78. Compare Erik Olin Wright, *Class, Crisis, and the State,* pp. 142–43; and Jacob

Morris, "Profit Rates and Capital Formation in American Monopoly Capitalism," in Foster and Szlajfer, eds., *The Faltering Economy,* pp. 226–27. Naturally, a formulation of the realization problem in this way only translates into a theory of the accumulation process insofar as we can determine the various components of demand itself (given the rate of exploitation in production), particularly in the case of investment. Thus in the Kaleckian view, to which Baran and Sweezy basically subscribed, "the rate of investment decisions . . . is, as a first approximation, an increasing function of gross saving . . . and of the rate of change in aggregate profits . . . and a decreasing function of the rate of change in the stock of capital equipment." Kalecki, *Theory of Economic Dynamics,* p. 98.

79. Szlajfer, "Economic Surplus and Surplus Value under Monopoly Capitalism," pp. 272–76.
80. Ibid., p. 276.
81. See Michal Kalecki, "The Marxian Equations of Reproduction and Modern Economics," in Foster and Szlajfer, eds., *The Faltering Economy,* pp. 159–66; John Bellamy Foster, "Marxian Economics and the State," in ibid., pp. 276–79.
82. Jacob Morris, "Unemployment and Unproductive Employment," *Science and Society* 22, no. 3 (Summer 1958): 193–206; Justin Blake, "Jacob Morris on Unproductive Employment," *Science and Society* 24, no. 2 (Spring 1960): 169–73; Peter Meiksins, "Productive and Unproductive Labor and Marx's Theory of Class," *Review of Radical Political Economics* 13, no. 3 (Fall 1981): 42.
83. In contrast to the interpretation offered here, Laurence Harris has recently declared that Baran and Sweezy's work was "revisionist in character," and that their extension of the concept of waste to the penetration of the productive apparatus by the sales effort was "irrelevant for Marx's concept of surplus value or productive and unproductive labour." Laurence Harris, "Monopoly Capitalism," in Tom Bottomore, ed., *A Dictionary of Marxist Thought* (Oxford: Blackwell, 1983), pp. 340–41. It is worth reiterating (see note 33 to chapter 2) that Baran and Sweezy's application of the principles of historical specificity and production in general to the problem of waste under monopoly capitalism, was in conformity with Hilferding's designation of productive labor as that labor which is "necessary for the social purpose of production, and thus independent of the determined historical form"; with unproductive labor, then, consisting of "labor which is expended only for the purposes of capitalist circulation, i.e., which originates with the determined historical organization of production, does not create value." As quoted in I. I. Rubin, *Essays on Marx's Theory of Value* (Detroit: Black and Red, 1972), pp. 274–75. Compare also the following statement by Sydney Coontz: "In the Marxian analysis, the terms 'productive' and unproductive labor are treated as historical categories, i.e., the value or the validity of the concepts is determined by the specific problems of the epoch." *Productive Labor and Effective Demand,* p. 67.
84. See also the discussion in chapter 2 above.
85. Szlajfer, "Waste, Marxian Theory, and Monopoly Capital," p. 304.
86. Ibid.; Foster, "Marxian Economics and the State," pp. 338–42.
87. Karl Marx, "Results of the Immediate Process of Production," printed as an appendix in Marx, *Capital,* vol. I (New York: Vintage Books, 1976), pp. 1045–46; Ian Gough, *The Political Economy of the Welfare State* (London: Macmillan, 1979); Foster, "Marxian Economics and the State," pp. 338–42; Jacob Morris, "Reply to Justin Blake," *Science and Society* 24, no. 2 (Spring 1960): 174–75, and "Underconsumption and the General Crisis: Gillman's Theory," *Science and Society* 47, no. 3 (Fall 1983): 323–29.
88. Szlajfer, "Economic Surplus and Surplus Value under Monopoly Capitalism,"

p. 272; Michael Kidron, *Western Capitalism since the War* (Middlesex, England: Penguin Books, 1970), pp. 55–56.

89. Piero Sraffa, *Production of Commodities by Means of Commodities* (Cambridge, England: Cambridge University Press, 1960), pp. 7–8.
90. Szlajfer, "Waste, Marxian Theory, and Monopoly Capital," pp. 299–304.
91. See chapter 2 above. It should be added that the schema that leads from unproductive labor proper to unreproductive labor to socially useless labor should be regarded as successive approximations in the development of the concept of unproductive labor (in the generic sense), moving, respectively, from the viewpoint of individual capital to that of global capital to that of society as a whole (and production in general). A socialist critique of capitalism is only complete insofar as it encompasses all three levels of analysis.
92. See Henryk Szlajfer, "Economic Surplus and Surplus Value: An Attempt at Comparison," *Review of Radical Political Economics* 15, no. 1 (Spring 1983): 125.
93. Szlajfer, "Economic Surplus and Surplus Value under Monopoly Capitalism," p. 282.
94. Szlajfer, "Waste, Marxian Theory, and Monopoly Capital," p. 297.
95. Joan Robinson, *Contributions to Modern Economics* (Oxford: Basil Blackwell, 1978), p. 8.
96. Compare Szlajfer, "Waste, Marxian Theory, and Monopoly Capital," p. 275.
97. Baran, *The Political Economy of Growth,* pp. 120–29; *Business Week,* 3 August 1981, p. 12; Foster, "Marxian Economics and the State," pp. 337–38, 345.
98. Keynes, *The General Theory of Employment, Interest, and Money,* p. 219.
99. Steindl, *Maturity and Stagnation in American Capitalism,* p. xiii; Michal Kalecki, "Some Remarks on Keynes' Theory," *Australian Economic Papers* 21, no. 39 (December 1982): 245, 251–53.
100. Steindl, *Maturity and Stagnation in American Capitalism,* p. 133.
101. Baran and Sweezy, *Monopoly Capital,* p. 222; Foster, "The Political Economy of Joseph Schumpeter."
102. Baran and Sweezy, *Monopoly Capital,* p. 220, 235. During the early 1940s, Walter Isard developed a theory of the "transport-business cycle," in which he showed that the relatively strong growth pattern of the 1920s could be attributed to "autos and construction as the unitary backbone of the system." Walter Isard, "Transport Development and Business Cycles," *Quarterly Journal of Economics* 57, no. 4 (November 1942): 90–112; Foster, "Understanding the Significance of the Great Depression," pp. 187–88.
103. Baran and Sweezy, *Monopoly Capital,* p. 222.
104. Sweezy, *The Present as History,* pp. 341–51.
105. Foster, "Investment and Capitalist Maturity," in Foster and Szlajfer, eds., *The Faltering Economy,* pp. 62–65.
106. According to neo-Marxian analysis, all of the major theories of secular crisis, including the tendential law of falling rate of profit, are historically contingent. This view appears to differ from that of some fundamentalist Marxists, who seem to believe that the falling rate of profit tendency (based on a rising organic composition) is an inherent feature of the capitalist mode of production. On this see Paul M. Sweezy, "Some Problems in the Theory of Capital Accumulation," in Foster and Szlajfer, eds., *The Faltering Economy,* pp. 49–51.
107. Sweezy, *Four Lectures on Marxism,* p. 39; also Coontz, *Productive Labour and Effective Demand,* pp. 82–84.
108. Sweezy, *Four Lectures on Marxism,* p. 39.
109. See Harry Magdoff, "International Economic Distress and the Third World," *Monthly Review* 33, no. 11 (April 1982): 1–5.
110. Kalecki, "The Marxian Equations of Reproduction and Modern Economics,"

p. 164; Harry Magdoff and Paul M. Sweezy, "Listen, Keynesians!" *Monthly Review* 34, no. 8 (January 1983): p. 9.

111. Of course, the neo-Marxist theory of investment had already been elaborated in much greater detail in Kalecki and Steindl. See note 3 above.
112. Wright, *Class, Crisis, and the State,* p. 147.
113. The same objection does not hold for the falling rate of profit theory advanced by Joseph Gillman and Jacob Morris, which is more closely connected to Baran and Sweezy's analysis. See Joseph Gillman, *The Falling Rate of Profit* (New York: Cameron Associates, 1958); Morris, "Profit Rates and Capital Formation in American Monopoly Capitalism."
114. Although the necessity of viewing accumulation in this way is particularly important under conditions of monopoly capitalism, there is a sense in which it applies to economic theory in general. See Harry Magdoff and Paul M. Sweezy, "A New New Deal?" *Monthly Review* 33, no. 9 (February 1982): 2–4.
115. Magdoff and Sweezy, "Listen, Keynesians!" p. 2; Szlajfer, "Economic Surplus and Surplus Value under Monopoly Capitalism," p. 274.

5. The Issue of Excess Capacity

1. Paul A. Baran and Paul M. Sweezy, *Monopoly Capital* (New York: Monthly Review Press, 1966), p. 218. See also An Economic Observer, "Idle Machines," *Monthly Review* 14, no. 2 (June 1962): 84–95.
2. Ibid.
3. Thorstein Veblen, *The Vested Interests and the Common Man* (New York: Augustus M. Kelley, 1964), pp. 78–79.
4. Ibid., pp. 79–81.
5. Ibid., p. 81.
6. References to Veblen appear throughout Baran and Sweezy's work, and their description of monopoly corporations as "waste makers" has a Veblen-like twist to it. See David Horowitz, "The Case of a Neo-Marxist Theory," *International Socialist Review* 28, no. 4 (July–August 1967): 28.
7. There are, of course, many reasons for limiting production to levels below engineering capacity besides profit requirements—for example, the problem of bottlenecks, This, however, only qualifies our conclusion and does not fundamentally alter it. Nowadays the term "capital utilization," as distinct from "capacity utilization," is used to refer to the problem of numbers of shifts, i.e., to a concept of engineering capacity. See N. Phan-Thuy, "Concepts and Measures of Capacity and Capital Utilisation: A Survey," in *Industrial Capacity and Employment Promotion: Case Studies of Sri Lanka, Nigeria, Morocco, and Over-all Survey of Other Developing Countries* (Westmead, England: Gower Publishing Co., 1981).
8. Ron Stanfield, *The Economic Surplus and Neo-Marxism* (Lexington, MA: D.C. Heath and Co., 1973), p. 62.
9. Harold Loeb, Director, *Report of the National Survey of Potential Product Capacity* (New York: New York Housing Authority, 1935).
10. As quoted in Stanfield, *The Economic Surplus and Neo-Marxism,* p. 62.
11. The second and third Loeb definitions are difficult to distinguish and mirror the problem that Szlajfer has discovered in relation to Baran's concepts of potential and planned surpluses (see chapter 2 above); that is, there is considerable conceptual overlap, since both the second and third definitions seem to point beyond the system to some extent. It is therefore helpful to think of the second Loeb definition as connected to potential surplus, as Szlajfer has

reformulated it (reflecting the standpoint of global capital and excluding all aspects of planned surplus), and to conceive of the third definition as one that points toward planned surplus (involving optimal changes in the composition of output). Since the third definition goes far beyond the usual issue of productive capacity, as a concept strictly geared to existing plant and equipment, and is clearly related to the larger problem of "social engineering," it has little direct relevance to the issue of excess capacity per se. Nevertheless, it is important to keep this definition in mind, since it points to the real capacity to produce that would be *available* to a more rationally ordered society. From Veblen's remarks on capacity, it seems obvious that he had in mind a concept of productive potential similar to that of the third Loeb definition—rooted in a notion of planned surplus.

12. Ibid., p. 63.
13. Ibid., p. 62.
14. One of the characteristics of the "economic" as opposed to the more "technical" or "engineering" definitions of productive capacity is that the first is seen as structurally related to the current price structure and the existing social organization of production. The term "economic"—as commonly used in this context—therefore has a built-in conservative bias (often referring to the perspective of individual capital, as opposed to both global capital and society as a whole). While for our present purpose it is impossible to avoid referring to the "economic" in this conventional sense, it should always be kept in mind that in the larger sense of the term—moving to the perspective of the capitalist class as a whole—production at technically rated capacity (or something relatively close to it) is perfectly possible *economically.* Indeed, in times of war production the visible possibilities for capital, and therefore the sphere of the economic (viewed conservatively), dramatically expands.
15. Edwin G. Nourse et al., *America's Capacity to Produce* (Washington, D.C.: The Brookings Institution, 1934), p. 23; Stanfield, *The Economic Surplus and Neo-Marxism,* p. 69.
16. Board of Governors of the Federal Reserve System, *Federal Reserve Measures of Capacity and Capacity Utilization* (Washington, D.C.: Board of Governors of the Federal Reserve System, February 1978), p. 22n.
17. George L. Perry, "Capacity in Manufacturing," *Brookings Papers on Economic Activity,* no. 3 (1973): 706. This is not to say that the McGraw-Hill survey leaves its respondents entirely "in the dark" about the kind of concept of capacity being employed. For example, respondents were encouraged *not* to include plant and equipment that has been "retired" in their estimates. See *Measures of Productive Capacity,* Hearings Before the Subcommittee on Economic Statistics of the Joint Economic Committee, 87th Congress, 2nd Session, May 14, 22, 23, and 24, 1962, p. 19.
18. Lawrence R. Klein and Robert Summers, *The Wharton Index of Capacity Utilization* (Philadelphia, PA: Economics Research Unit, University of Pennsylvania, 1966), p. 2.
19. Josef Steindl, *Maturity and Stagnation in American Capitalism* (New York: Monthly Review Press, 1976), p. 13. Moreover, capacity studies themselves have shown that unit costs are constant over the relevant range of output, in clear contravention of neoclassical theory; see ibid., pp. 6–8, 14. This, of course, does not apply to wartime conditions.
20. John E. Cremeans, "Capacity Utilization Rates—What Do They Mean?" *Business Economics* 13, no. 3 (May 1978): 42.
21. Steindl, *Maturity and Stagnation in American Capitalism,* p. 13.
22. Daniel Creamer, *Capital Expansion and Capacity in Postwar Manufacturing* (New

York: National Industrial Conference Board, 1961), p. 19.
23. Baran and Sweezy, *Monopoly Capital,* p. 246n.
24. Donald Streever, "Capacity Utilization and Business Investment," *University of Illinois Bulletin 52,* no. 55 (March 1960); cited in Stanfield, *The Economic Surplus and Neo-Marxism,* p. 65.
25. Baran and Sweezy, *Monopoly Capital,* pp. 237, 242; V. Lewis Bassie, *Economic Forecasting* (New York: McGraw-Hill, 1958), pp. 681–91.
26. Their argument was anticipated in An Economic Observer, "Idle Machines."
27. Stanfield, *The Economic Surplus and Neo-Marxism,* p. 65; *The Economic Report of the President, 1984,* p. 271.
28. Cremeans, "Capacity Utilization Rates," p. 41.
29. Perry, "Capacity in Manufacturing," p. 704.
30. Ibid.
31. For a useful study of this problem see James F. Ragan, "Measuring Capacity Utilization in Manufacturing," *Federal Reserve Bank of New York Quarterly Review* 1 (Winter 1976): 13–20.
32. Baran and Sweezy, *Monopoly Capital,* p. 246n.
33. Perry, "Capacity in Manufacturing," p. 731.
34. Stanfield, *The Economic Surplus and Neo-Marxism,* p. 64.
35. Cremeans, "Capacity Utilization Rates," p. 45; Ragan "Measuring Capacity Utilization," p. 17.
36. Ragan, "Measuring Capacity Utilization," p. 14.
37. Ibid.
38. Perry, "Capacity in Manufacturing," p. 709.
39. Ibid.
40. See Ragan, "Measuring Capacity Utilization," p. 15 (chart).
41. Perry, "Capacity in Manufacturing," p. 707.
42. Ibid.
43. Ragan, "Measuring Capacity Utilization," p. 16.
44. Stanfield, *The Economic Surplus and Neo-Marxism,* pp. 69–79.
45. Nourse et al., *America's Capacity to Produce,* p. 415.
46. The presumed minimum unemployment rate of 4 percent reflects the Keynesian notion of "full employment output," defined in terms of some "threshold unemployment rate." Any reduction in unemployment beyond this threshold is supposed to produce a sharp acceleration of inflation. In the 1960s the acceptable level of unemployment, in this sense, was usually considered to be 4 percent—although unemployment had actually dropped as low as 2.9 percent in 1953, during the Korean war. In the early 1980s the threshold was officially designated as somewhere "between 6 and 7 percent." See *The Economic Report of the President, 1983,* p. 41. Hence, it should be apparent that calculations of productive potential in terms of "full employment output" are, as a rule, far more conservative in their initial assumptions than those measures that focus on idle capacity.
47. See Stanfield, *The Economic Surplus and Neo-Marxism,* pp. 78–79.
48. Thus Kolko uses the correspondence between five capacity utilization indexes to bolster a point about the significance of the 1974–75 downturn. See Gabriel Kolko, *Main Currents in Modern American History* (New York: Harper and Row, 1976), p. 339. On the recent proliferation of such indexes, see Board of Governors of the Federal Reserve System, *Federal Reserve Measures of Capacity and Capacity Utilization,* p. 1.
49. See Baran and Sweezy, *Monopoly Capital,* pp. 73–74.
50. Perry, "Capacity in Manufacturing," p. 703.

51. *Business Week,* 3 August 1981, p. 12.
52. *Economic Report of the President, 1983,* pp. 199, 213.
53. The Bureau of Economic Analysis, the Federal Reserve Board, and the Wharton School have all published breakdowns on capacity utilization by industrial groupings for certain years. For the FRB data, see Board of Governors of the Federal Reserve System, *Federal Reserve Measures of Capacity and Capacity Utilization,* pp. 33–40. It should be understood that a 20 percent gap in utilization does not mean that the designated unemployment rate must also be close to 20 percent to provide a large enough labor force to fill the production gap. First, unemployment figures are notoriously conservative in that they do not count the underemployed or those who have failed to look for jobs during the four weeks previous to the government survey, i.e., "discouraged" job seekers. See Bertram Gross and Stanely Moss, "Real Unemployment Is Much Higher Than They Say," in David Mermelstein, ed., *The Economic Crisis Reader* (New York: Vintage Books, 1976); Paul M. Sweezy and Harry Magdoff, *The Dynamics of U.S. Capitalism* (New York: Monthly Review Press, 1972), pp. 43–53; and Richard Du Boff, "Unemployment in the United States: An Historical Survey," *Monthly Review* 29, no. 6 (November 1977): 11–18. Second, unemployment figures obviously do not incorporate those who are unproductively (or unreproductively) employed. Third, since underutilization means lower rates of productivity than would otherwise pertain, the hiring of additional workers may have a more than proportionate effect on output. From a Marxian standpoint, it can be said that the sum of unemployed, underemployed, and misemployed workers is always far in excess of the labor necessary to operate existing plant and equipment (full capacity utilization). Thus certain social liberal economists distinguish between Keynesian unemployment (unemployment associated with less than full capacity operation) and "Marxian unemployment" (the amount of unemployment that would remain even after productive capacity is fully utilized). See Adrian Wood, *A Theory of Profits* (Cambridge, England: Cambridge University Press, 1975), pp. 124–28; John Bellamy Foster, "The Limits of U.S. Capitalism: Surplus Capacity and Capacity Surplus," in John Bellamy Foster and Henryk Szlajfer, eds., *The Faltering Economy: The Problem of Accumulation under Monopoly Capitalism* (New York: Monthly Review Press, 1984), p. 211.
54. Baran and Sweezy, *Monopoly Capital,* pp. 237, 242; Du Boff, "Unemployment in the United States," pp. 11–18.
55. Paul A. Baran, *The Political Economy of Growth* (New York: Monthly Review Press, 1957), p. 40.
56. Harry Magdoff and Paul M. Sweezy, *The End of Prosperity* (New York: Monthly Review Press, 1977), p. 97.
57. Stanfield, *The Economic Surplus and Neo-Marxism,* p. 65. Bassie's corresponding estimate for 1944 is 137 percent; see Bassie, *Economic Forecasting,* p. 688.
58. *Economic Report of the President, 1984,* p. 271.
59. Stanfield, *The Economic Surplus and Neo-Marxism,* p. 66.
60. *Economic Report of the President, 1984,* p. 271. In 1982 the rate of capacity utilization dropped to 71.1 percent.
61. Depending on whether one is using the official unemployment figure (8.5 percent) or a more accurate estimate of real unemployment (11 percent). See Du Boff, "Unemployment in the United States," p. 17.
62. Paul M. Sweezy, "Marxian Value Theory and Crises," in Foster and Szlajfer, eds., *The Faltering Economy,* p. 245.
63. Ibid., p. 248.

64. Bureau of the Census, *U.S. Statistical Abstract,* p. 794; *Survey of Current Business,* December 1979, p. 18; Bureau of Economic Analysis, *Handbook of Cyclical Indicators,* May 1977, p. 149.
65. Lewis Robb, "Industrial Capacity and Its Utilization," *Science and Society* 17 (Fall 1953): 318–25.
66. Ibid.; Stanfield, *The Economic Surplus and Neo-Marxism,* p. 65.
67. Baran and Sweezy, *Monopoly Capital,* pp. 242–43.
68. Robb, "Industrial Capacity and Its Utilization," p. 320; see also Stanfield, *The Economic Surplus and Neo-Marxism,* p. 100.
69. Ibid.
70. Cremeans, "Capacity Utilization Rates," p. 42.
71. Ibid.
72. See John Kendrick, "Productivity Trends and Prospects," in U.S. Congress, Joint Economic Committee, *U.S. Economic Growth from 1976 to 1986,* Volume I (Washington, D.C.: U.S. Government Printing Office, 1976), p. 9. The statistics purporting to show a slowdown in the rate of productivity growth are questionable for a large number of reasons, not least of all because there was no drop in the rate of growth of manufacturing productivity prior to the onset of the secular decline in the level of capacity utilization. To the extent that this statistical trend has any meaning at all, then, it can be traced to changes in the level and composition of production rather than the other way around. Hence, according to this explanation, the reduction in the rate of expansion of measured productivity can be attributed to increases in unemployment and misemployment; these in turn reflect the fact that the productive potential of the U.S. economy (in the context of an endemic realization crisis) is too high rather than too low. See Harry Magdoff, "A Statistical Fiction," *The Nation,* 10–17 July 1982, pp. 47–48; Harry Magdoff and Paul M. Sweezy, *The Deepening Crisis of U.S. Capitalism* (New York: Monthly Review Press, 1981), pp. 115–26, 196–97; John Bellamy Foster, "Investment and Capitalist Maturity," in Foster and Szlajfer, eds., *The Faltering Economy,* pp. 68–70.

6. The State Economy

1. James O'Connor, *The Fiscal Crisis of the State* (New York: St. Martin's Press, 1973), p. 9.
2. Hugh Mosley, "Is There a Fiscal Crisis of the State?" *Monthly Review* 30, no. 1 (May 1978): 36.
3. Ibid., pp. 43–44.
4. Ibid., p. 207.
5. Joseph A. Schumpeter, "The Crisis of the Tax State," *International Economic Papers,* no. 4 (1954): 20.
6. Ibid., pp. 22–23.
7. David Ricardo, *On the Principles of Political Economy and Taxation,* in *The Works and Correspondence of David Ricardo,* vol. I (Cambridge: Cambridge University Press, 1951), p. 153.
8. Paolo Sylos-Labini, "The *General Theory:* Critical Reflections Suggested by Some Important Problems of Our Time," in Fausto Vicarelli, ed., *Keynes's Relevance Today* (Philadelphia: University of Pennsylvania Press, 1985), p. 139.
9. Paul A. Baran and Paul M. Sweezy, *Monopoly Capital* (New York: Monthly Review Press, 1966), p. 143.
10. Ibid, p. 149.
11. Ibid., p. 150.

12. Keynes treated consumption primarily in terms of a psychological "propensity to consume," and thus did not generally conceive the distinction between consumption and saving in class terms. Kalecki, in contrast, always adopted the assumption that workers consumed their entire income (i.e., that saving by workers was nonexistent). This allowed him to highlight the real class basis of the demand problem.
13. Michal Kalecki, *Selected Essays on the Dynamics of the Capitalist Economy* (Cambridge: Cambridge University Press, 1971), pp. 35–42; see also Albert Szymanski, *Stagnation: The Normal State of Monopoly Capitalism* (London: Zed Press, forthcoming).
14. Kalecki, *Selected Essays on the Dynamics of the Capitalist Economy,* p. 38.
15. The subscript *c* refers to capital whether used in relation to capitalist consumption (C_c) or taxation of capital (T_c).
16. Ibid., p. 41.
17. O'Connor, *The Fiscal Crisis of the State,* p. 208.
18. Kalecki, *Selected Essays on the Dynamics of the Capitalist Economy,* p. 42.
19. Michal Kalecki, *The Last Phase in the Transformation of Capitalism* (New York: Monthly Review Press, 1972), p. 92.
20. Josef Steindl, *Maturity and Stagnation in American Capitalism* (New York: Monthly Review Press, 1976), p. ix.
21. Michal Kalecki, "The Problem of Effective Demand with Rosa Luxemburg and Tugan-Baranovski," in John Bellamy Foster and Henryk Szlajfer, eds., *The Faltering Economy: The Problem of the Accumulation under Monopoly Capitalism* (New York: Monthly Review Press, 1984), pp. 156–57; also Joan Robinson, Introduction to Rosa Luxemburg, *The Accumulation of Capital* (New York: Monthly Review Press, 1951), p. 27.
22. Michael Bleaney, *Underconsumption Theories* (New York: International Publishers, 1976), pp. 232–33.
23. Ibid.
24. To be sure, such a situation would be likely to generate a strong tendency for workers to increase their wage demands in order to maintain their real after-tax purchasing power.
25. Paul A. Baran, *The Political Economy of Growth* (New York: Monthly Review Press, 1957), p. 125.
26. Ibid., pp. 126–27.
27. Compare Bob Russell, "The Politics of Labour-Force Reproduction," *Studies in Political Economy,* no. 14 (Summer 1984): 47–50.
28. Leo Huberman and Paul M. Sweezy, "The Kennedy-Johnson Boom," *Monthly Review* 16, no. 10 (February 1965): 579–80.
29. Ibid., p. 581.
30. Ibid., p. 582.
31. The significance of taxes that cut into workers' consumption for the realization problem was recognized by Sweezy, at the level of general principle, as early as 1942; see Paul M. Sweezy, *The Theory of Capitalist Development* (New York: Monthly Review Press, 1942), p. 233.
32. Dudley Jackson, H. A. Turner, and Frank Wilkinson, *Do Trade Unions Cause Inflation?* (Cambridge: Cambridge University Press, 1975), pp. 79–81.
33. Josef Steindl, "Stagnation Theory and Stagnation Policy," in Foster and Szlajfer, eds., *The Faltering Economy,* pp. 179–97.
34. Ibid., p. 190.
35. Ibid., pp. 194–96.
36. Craig Medlen, "Corporate Taxes and the Federal Deficit," *Monthly Review* 36, no. 6 (November 1984): 13–14.

37. Ibid., p. 24.
38. *Business Week,* 16 September 1985, p. 79.
39. Joseph A. Pechman, *Federal Tax Policy* (Washington, D.C.: The Brookings Institution, 1983), p. 136.
40. Craig Medlen, "The Corporate Income Tax," *Monthly Review* 36, no. 11 (April 1985): 52–53.
41. Medlen points out that elimination of much of the accelerated depreciation and investment tax provisions of the corporate income tax structure (changes *contemplated* in the Reagan administration's current tax reform package) would make the corporate income tax into more of a "pure" percentage tax, with no production elements mixed in; this would therefore strengthen the force of his argument. See ibid., pp. 55–56.
42. Ibid., p. 54.
43. Ibid., pp. 54–55.
44. Harry Magdoff and Paul M. Sweezy, "The Need for Tax Reform," *Monthly Review* 36, no. 6 (November 1984): 4.
45. Gabriel Kolko, *Maincurrents in Modern American History* (New York: Pantheon, 1984), p. 405.
46. Robert Kuttner, *The Economic Illusion* (Boston: Houghton Mifflin, 1984), p. 189; also Vincente Navarro, "The Road Ahead," *Monthly Review* 37, no. 3 (July–August 1985): 37–42.
47. Kuttner, *The Economic Illusion,* p. 223.
48. Sylos-Labini, "The *General Theory,*" p. 142.
49. Baran and Sweezy, *Monopoly Capital,* pp. 151–77; see also the discussions in chapters 2 and 4 above.
50. Baran and Sweezy, *Monopoly Capital,* pp. 151–52.
51. Ibid.
52. Ibid.
53. Ibid., p. 153.
54. Ibid. In a later estimate of the effect of defense spending on unemployment, Magdoff and Sweezy were to raise this figure to as much as 25 percent; see John Bellamy Foster, "Marxian Economics and the State," in Foster and Szlajfer, eds., *The Faltering Economy,* pp. 338–39.
55. Baran and Sweezy, *Monopoly Capital,* pp. 154–55.
56. Sweezy, *The Theory of Capitalist Development,* pp. 240–44. Ralph Miliband presented the "instrumentalist" view in the following way: "In the Marxist scheme, the 'ruling class' of capitalist society is that class which owns and controls the means of production and which is able, by virtue of the economic power thus conferred upon it, to use the state as its instrument for the domination of society." Ralph Miliband, *The State in Capitalist Society* (London: Quartet Books, 1973), p. 23.
57. David A. Gold, Clarence Y. H. Lo, and Erik Olin Wright, "Recent Developments in Marxist Theories of the Capitalist State," Part I, *Monthly Review* 27, no. 5 (October 1976); 39.
58. Sweezy, *The Theory of Capitalist Development,* p. 348.
59. On the necessity of distinguishing between theories of growth on the basis of determinant historical (and institutional) characteristics, see Michal Kalecki, "Theories of Growth in Different Social Systems," *Monthly Review* 23, no. 5 (October 1971): 72–79.
60. Sweezy, *The Theory of Capitalist Development,* p. 349.
61. Ibid., pp. 250–51; Baran and Sweezy, *Monopoly Capital,* p. 155.
62. Karl Marx, *The Class Struggles in France: 1848–1850* (New York: International

Publishers, 1934), pp. 69–70, as quoted in Baran and Sweezy, *Monopoly Capital,* p. 155n.

63. Sweezy, *The Theory of Capitalist Development,* p. 351.
64. Ibid., p. 330.
65. Ibid., p. 249.
66. Paul A. Baran, *The Longer View* (New York: Monthly Review Press, 1969), pp. 135–38; Joseph A. Schumpeter, *Capitalism, Socialism, and Democracy* (New York: Harper & Row, 1950), p. 419.
67. Baran, *The Longer View,* pp. 135–36.
68. Ibid., p. 137.
69. Ibid.
70. Ibid., pp. 137–38.
71. Baran and Sweezy, *Monopoly Capital,* p. 155.
72. Ibid., p. 157.
73. Ibid., p. 156.
74. John Bellamy Foster, "Understanding the Significance of the Great Depression," *Studies in Political Economy,* no. 11 (Summer 1983): 191.
75. Baran and Sweezy, *Monopoly Capital,* p. 161.
76. Ibid., pp. 165–68.
77. Ibid., p. 171.
78. Ibid., pp. 305–35.
79. Ibid., p. 174.
80. See Paul M. Sweezy, "Cars and Cities," *Monthly Review* 24, no. 11 (April 1973): 1–18; Henryk Szlajfer, "Waste, Marxian Theory, and Monopoly Capital," in Foster and Szlajfer, eds., *The Faltering Economy,* p. 313.
81. Harry Magdoff and Paul M. Sweezy, *The End of Prosperity* (New York: Monthly Review Press, 1977), pp. 72–73.
82. Gabriel Kolko, *The Triumph of Conservatism: A Reinterpretation of American History* (New York: The Free Press, 1963), p. 3.
83. Ibid., p. 178.
84. Paul M. Sweezy, "Investment Banking Revisited," *Monthly Review* 33, no. 10 (March 1982): 2–3. The concurrence between the ideas of Kolko and Sweezy in this area can be traced primarily to the influence that Veblen's analysis of the turn-of-the-century transition exercised on the thinking of both.
85. Kolko, *Maincurrents in Modern American History,* p. 339. Looking back at the beginnings of "political capitalism" in the early decades of the century, Kolko has written: "The economy had its own problems, dictated by technological innovation, underconsumption, crises, and competition. But these difficulties were increasingly controlled by political means to the extent that the consideration of economic problems outside their political context is meaningless. The 'laws of capitalist development' were not self-contained imperatives in the technological, economic, or political sphere, but an inseparable unification of all three elements." Kolko, *The Triumph of Conservatism,* pp. 301–2.
86. The argument made here is presented in greater detail in John Bellamy Foster, "Sources of Instability in the U.S. Political Economy and Empire," *Science and Society* 49, no. 2 (Summer 1985): 167–93, from which some of the above passages have been taken.
87. "Editorial Perspectives," *Science and Society* 49, no. 2 (Summer 1985).
88. Kolko, *Maincurrents in Modern American History,* p. 318.
89. *Survey of Current Business* (April 1984), p. 15.
90. Robert L. Heilbroner, *The Making of Economic Society* (Englewood Cliffs, NJ: Prentice-Hall, 1980), p. 288.

91. James M. Cypher, "The Basic Economics of Rearming America," *Monthly Review* 33, no. 6 (November 1981): 12; Howard J. Sherman, *Stagflation* (New York: Harper & Row, 1983), p. 148.
92. Thorstein Veblen, *The Theory of Business Enterprise* (Clifton, NJ: Augustus M. Kelley, 1904), p. 393.
93. Quoted in Baran and Sweezy, *Monopoly Capital*, p. 212.
94. Ibid., pp. 213–17.
95. Quoted in Paul M. Sweezy, "Competition and Monopoly," in Foster and Szlajfer, eds., *The Faltering Economy*, pp. 38–39.
96. Ibid., p. 39.
97. Harry Magdoff and Paul M. Sweezy, "The Responsibility of the Left," *Monthly Review* 34, no. 7 (December 1982): 5–6; see also Kim Moody, "Going Public: In Search of an Economy That Works," *The Progressive* 47, no. 7 (July 1983): 18–21.
98. Prudence Posner Pace, "On the Responsibility of the Left," *Monthly Review* 36, no. 1 (May 1984): 53n. The designation "anticorporatist" may be slightly confusing since, in political theory terms, the position of these thinkers would be described as "societal corporatism." Pace's own point, of course, is that the argument is directed against certain corporate policies rather than against the system itself. At an economic level, the wage squeeze on profits theory of such "anticorporatist" theorists as Bowles, Gordon, and Weisskopf falls under the rubric of what Howard Sherman has called "supply-side Marxism." For critiques of this perspective see John Bellamy Foster, "Marxian Economics and the State," in Foster and Szlajfer, eds., *The Faltering Economy*, pp. 325–49; and Howard J. Sherman and Gary Evans, *Macro-Economics: Keynesian, Monetarist, and Marxist Views* (New York: Harper & Row, 1984), pp. 270–79.
99. Ibid., p. 50.
100. Quoted in Magdoff and Sweezy, "The Responsibility of the Left," p. 3.

7. Imperialism and the Political Economy of Growth

1. John Weeks, "The Differences Between Materialist Theory and Dependency Theory and Why They Matter," in Ronald H. Chilcote, ed., *Dependency and Marxism* (Boulder, CO: Westview Press, 1982), p. 122.
2. John Weeks and Elizabeth Dore, "International Exchange and the Causes of Backwardness," *Latin American Perspectives* 6, no. 2 (Spring 1979): 64.
3. Ibid., p. 66; see also Elizabeth Dore, "Dependency Theory," in Tom Bottomore, ed., *A Dictionary of Marxist Thought* (Oxford: Basil Blackwell, 1983), pp. 115–16.
4. In criticizing Baran, Weeks and Dore focus much of their argument on a single passage in *The Political Economy of Growth* in which Baran stated that if the advanced capitalist countries had proffered "genuine cooperation and assistance rather than . . . oppression and exploitation" to the underdeveloped countries, the position of the latter would have been incomparably better. As a partial example, Baran compared the development of technology in the United States by British settlers to the opium trade that Britain imposed on China. For Weeks and Dore this is the "logical *reducto absurdum* [sic] of the surplus-extraction thesis" because "if capitalism is characterized by general laws, then these must be manifest in all cases, in the United States or China. . . ." Without going into Weeks and Dore's understanding of "general laws," it should be sufficient to note that Baran based his argument in these pages on the distinction between (a) *white settler colonies*, where the native

population ("the exploits of Davy Crockett notwithstanding") had been relatively sparse, and (b) the kind of colonialism that was characteristic in the periphery. See Paul A. Baran, *The Political Economy of Growth* (New York: Monthly Review Press, 1957), pp. 140–42, 162; Weeks and Dore, "International Exchange and the Causes of Backwardness," pp. 65–67.

5. Richard R. Fagen, "Theories of Development: The Question of Class," *Monthly Review* 35, no. 4 (September 1983): 16.
6. Samir Amin, *The Law of Value and Historical Materialism* (New York: Monthly Review Press, 1978), p. 57.
7. Quoted in Paul M. Sweezy, "Obstacles to Economic Development,"in C. H. Feinstein, ed., *Socialism, Capitalism, and Economic Growth: Essays Presented to Maurice Dobb* (Cambridge: Cambridge University Press, 1967), p. 191; Henryk Szlajfer, "Economic Surplus and Surplus Value under Monopoly Capitalism," in Foster and Szlajfer, eds., *The Faltering Economy: The Problem of Accumulation under Monopoly Capitalism* (New York: Monthly Review Press, 1984), pp. 264, 289.
8. Rudolfo Stavenhagen, *Social Classes in Agrarian Societies* (Garden City, NY: Doubleday, 1975), p. 11.
9. Baran, *The Political Economy of Growth,* p. 164.
10. Ibid., pp. 136, 142.
11. Ibid., p. 144.
12. Irving M. Zeitlin, *Capitalism and Imperialism: An Introduction to Neo-Marxian Concepts* (Chicago: Markham, 1972), p. 15.
13. Baran, *The Political Economy of Growth,* p. 148. Although it has long been an article of faith among European Marxists that Marx himself believed that India and other underdeveloped countries would follow the West along the road to economic development (and that imperialism should therefore be understood as essentially progressive), more recent scholarship has made it clear that his views shifted during his later years, in line with notions of dependency and nonlinear development. Thus Baran was able to cite Marx when describing the "roots of backwardness" in India. See Sunti Kumar Ghosh, "Marx on India," *Monthly Review* 35, no. 8 (January 1984): 39–53; Teodor Shanin, ed., *Late Marx and the Russian Road: Marx and the "Peripheries of Capitalism"* (New York: Monthly Review Press, 1983).
14. Baran, *The Political Economy of Growth,* p. 158.
15. Ibid.
16. Ibid., pp. 159–60.
17. Ibid., p. 161.
18. Ibid., p. 227.
19. Ibid.,
20. Alice H. Amsden, "An International Comparison of the Rate of Surplus Value in Manufacturing Industry," *Cambridge Journal of Economics* 5, no. 3 (September 1981): 233.
21. Baran, *The Political Economy of Growth,* p. 234.
22. Ibid., p. 236.
23. Ibid., p. 237n.
24. Ibid., pp. 237, 242.
25. Ibid., pp. 247–48.
26. G. E. M. de Ste. Croix, *The Class Struggle in the Ancient Greek World* (London: Duckworth, 1981), p. 43.
27. Quoted in ibid., p. 52.
28. Ibid.
29. Ibid., p. 44.

30. Baran, *The Political Economy of Growth,* pp. 164–65.
31. Ibid., p. 166.
32. Ibid., pp. 168–69.
33. Ibid.,, pp. 170–71.
34. Ibid., p. 173.
35. Ibid., p. 174.
36. Ibid.
37. Ibid., p. 175; Samir Amin, *Unequal Development* (New York: Monthly Review Press, 1976), pp. 233–39.
38. Baran, *The Political Economy of Growth,* p. 177.
39. Ibid., p. 184.
40. Ibid., p. 193.
41. Ibid., pp. 194–95.
42. Ibid., p. 195.
43. Ibid., p. 219.
44. Ibid., p. 221.
45. The location of many of these imperial client states is itself interesting. As Clive Thomas has written, "Coincidentally(!) . . . all of the small underdeveloped economies attempting to construct a socialist system are geographically juxtaposed to one or other of these outstanding 'high growth' economies. Thus we have North and South Korea, Tanzania and Zambia and Kenya, and Cuba and Puerto Rico and Jamaica, all exhibiting marked contrasts within a limited geographical range." Clive Y. Thomas, *Dependence and Transformation: The Economics of the Transition to Socialism* (New York: Monthly Review Press, 1974), p. 83.
46. Baran, *The Political Economy of Growth,* pp. 221–22.
47. In contrast, Samir Amin has argued that the Japanese road is now closed. See the discussion of his ideas below.
48. Ibid., p. 225.
49. Ibid., p. 226.
50. Ibid., p. 174.
51. Peter Evans, *Dependent Development: The Alliance of Multinational, State, and Local Capital in Brazil* (Princeton, NJ: Princeton University Press, 1979). The term "dependent development" can, of course, also be understood in the much wider sense of growth within the parameters of dependency.
52. Baran, *The Political Economy of Growth,* p. 197.
53. See Walter Rodney, *How Europe Underdeveloped Africa* (Washington, D.C.: Howard University Press, 1972); Colin Leys, *Underdevelopment in Kenya* (Berkeley: University of California Press, 1975); L. S. Stavrianos, *Global Rift: The Third World Comes of Age* (New York: William Morrow, 1981).
54. Andre Gunder Frank, *Capitalism and Underdevelopment in Latin America* (New York: Monthly Review Press, 1969), pp. 6–7.
55. Ibid., p. 8.
56. Ibid., p. 11.
57. See Andre Gunder Frank, *Lumpenbourgeoisie and Lumpendevelopment* (New York: Monthly Review Press, 1972).
58. For a more extended version of this argument see John Bellamy Foster, "The Political Economy of Joseph Schumpeter: A Theory of Capitalist Development and Decline," *Studies in Political Economy,* no. 15 (Fall 1984): 24–27.
59. Quoted in Paul M. Sweezy, Four Lectures on Marxism (New York: Monthly Review Press, 1981), p. 75.
60. Ibid., p. 76.
61. Ibid.

62. Ibid., p. 77.
63. Samir Amin, "Self-Reliance and the New International Economic Order," *Monthly Review* 29, no. 3 (July–August 1977): 3.
64. Ibid., pp. 4–5.
65. Samir Amin, *Imperialism and Unequal Development* (New York: Monthly Review Press, 1977), pp. 229–33. Amin's references to the "falling rate of profit" are a possible source of confusion since he employs the idea in a very distinctive way. Although he clearly bases his analysis on Marx's famous discussion, Amin's approach to the question gives primacy to historical factors rather than to the "tendential law" in abstraction. Hence his emphasis on the falling rate of profit in the nineteenth-century context seems to center on increasing raw material prices. Ibid, p. 226. For a systematic explanation of Marx's original theory in these terms see Michael Lebowitz, "The General and Specific in Marx's Theory of Crisis," *Studies in Political Economy,* no. 7 (Winter 1982): 5–25. Where monopoly capitalism is concerned, Amin sees the problem of a "falling rate of profit" in terms of the dilemma of surplus absorption, as manifested in the work of Roy Harrod and Baran and Sweezy; see Samir Amin, *Unequal Development* (New York: Monthly Review Press, 1976), pp. 100–2, 175–82. The fact that the "tendency of the surplus to rise" is quite consistent with a falling profits tendency systematically related to Marx's original law (but not with rising organic composition as its primary cause) has already been pointed out in chapter 4 above. On the relationship between Harrod's theory and that of Steindl, see Josef Steindl, "Stagnation Theory and Stagnation Policy," in Foster and Szlajfer, eds., *The Faltering Economy,* pp. 179–88.
66. Amin, "Self-Reliance and the New International Economic Order," p. 6.
67. Amin, *Imperialism and Unequal Development* (New York: Monthly Review Press, 1977), p. 218.
68. Sweezy, *Four Lectures on Marxism,* p. 79; compare Bill Warren, "Imperialism and Capitalist Industrialization," *New Left Review,* no. 81 (September–October 1973): 3–44.
69. Amin, "Self-Reliance and the New International Economic Order," p. 6.
70. Ibid., p. 7.
71. Ibid., p. 8. Also Amin, "Crisis, Nationalism, and Socialism," in Samir Amin, Giovanni Arrighi, Andre Gunder Frank, and Immanuel Wallerstein, *Dynamics of the Global Crisis* (New York: Monthly Review Press, 1982), pp. 172–74; Amin, *Imperialism and Unequal Development,* pp. 229–35; Sweezy, *Four Lectures on Marxism,* p. 77. Amin seems to place great emphasis on the national bourgeoisie and relatively little on the problem of the petty bourgeoisie, although he does recognize the importance of the latter; see Amin, *Unequal Development,* p. 349. On the role of the latter in both colonial and postcolonial contexts see John S. Saul, *The State and Revolution in Eastern Africa* (New York: Monthly Review Press, 1979), pp. 167–99; and Clive Y. Thomas, *The Rise of the Authoritarian State in Peripheral Societies* (New York: Monthly Review Press, 1984).
72. Amin, "Self-Reliance and the New International Economic Order," pp. 10–11.
73. Amin, "Crisis, Nationalism, and Socialism," p. 192.
74. Ibid., p. 168.
75. See Amin, *Unequal Development,* p. 180.
76. Paul A. Baran and Paul M. Sweezy, *Monopoly Capital* (New York: Monthly Review Press, 1966), pp. 107–8.
77. Ibid., p. 105.
78. Albert J. Szymanski, *The Logic of Imperialism* (New York: Praeger, 1981), pp. 101–6; for Szymanski's views on advanced capitalism see his book, *Stagnation: The Normal State of Monopoly Capitalism* (London: Zed Press, forthcoming).

79. Szymanski, *The Logic of Imperialism,* p. 301.
80. Ibid., p. 306.
81. Szymanski was able to make a better case with respect to the net flow between the United States and third world states. Thus his figures for 1976–78 showed a private inflow to the United States of $12.1 billion dollars from underdeveloped countries, compared to a private outflow of $17.3 billion; see Table 9.1 in ibid., p. 264. However, as Szymanski's table shows, this apparent "reversal" of the historical trend during the years 1973–78 was entirely due to a vast upsurge in U.S. bank loans to third world states, which brought on the international debt crisis of the early 1980s, with its dampening effect on further loan transfers from center to periphery. Obviously, what was true for net capital flows between the third world and the United States was also true (though in a less dramatic way) for net capital flows between the third world and all of the OECD states. Equally obvious is the fact that the entire process occurred almost simultaneously with the emergence of double-digit interest rates, and the underdeveloped countries are now being forced to pay for their loans at interest rates far in excess of their economic growth rates. To be sure, the debt crisis has two sides, with the third world debt exposure of the nine largest U.S. banks equaling 341 percent of the banks' capital in 1982. Harry Magdoff and Paul M. Sweezy, "The Two Faces of Third World Debt," *Monthly Review* 35, no. 8 (January 1984): 8. But so far the real hardships have been felt only in the periphery. Thus, for example, the imposition of draconian terms of conditionality by the IMF with respect to the Dominican Republic led to food riots in April 1984, resulting in the death of 55 people and the injury of 200 others at the hands of the forces of order. See *New York Times,* 4 May 1984.
82. Harry Magdoff, *The Age of Imperialism: The Economics of U.S. Foreign Policy* (New York: Monthly Review Press, 1969), p. 153.
83. John C. Pool and Stephen C. Stamos, "The Uneasy Calm: Third World Debt—The Case of Mexico," *Monthly Review* 36, no. 10 (March 1985): 9.
84. Magdoff, *The Age of Imperialism,* p. 154.
85. Magdoff and Sweezy, "The Two Faces of Third World Debt," pp. 2–3.
86. Ibid., p. 3.
87. Pool and Stamos, "The Uneasy Calm," p. 9.
88. Ibid., pp. 10–19.
89. Szymanski, *The Logic of Imperialism,* p. 76.
90. See ibid., p. 37; compare Harry Magdoff, *Imperialism: From the Colonial Age to the Present* (New York: Monthly Review Press, 1978), pp. 40–41, 267–68, 294–98.
91. "As Oskar Lange wrote some forty years ago: 'The pursuit of surplus monopoly profits suffices to explain completely the imperialist nature of present-day capitalism. Consequently, special theories of imperialism which resort to artificial constructions, such as Rosa Luxemburg's theory, are quite unnecessary.'" Paul M. Sweezy, *Modern Capitalism* (New York: Monthly Review Press, 1972), p. 47.
92. Magdoff, *Imperialism,* p. 238; Szymanski, *The Logic of Imperialism,* pp. 78–79.
93. Magdoff, *Imperialism,* pp. 260–61.
94. Weeks and Dore, "International Exchange and the Causes of Backwardness," p. 66; the reference to Marx is actually to be found in Karl Marx, *Capital,* vol. II (New York: International Publishers, 1967), p. 34.
95. Marx, *Capital,* vol. III (New York: International Publishers, 1967), pp. 791–92; de Ste. Croix, *The Class Struggle in the Ancient Greek World,* p. 51.
96. Samir Amin, *Accumulation on a World Scale* (New York: Monthly Review Press, 1974), p. 590.
97. Sweezy, *Four Lectures on Marxism,* p. 75.

8. Some Notes on Socialist Construction and Postrevolutionary Society

1. From Paul A. Baran, *The Political Economy of Growth* (New York: Monthly Review Press, 1957), pp. 261–95.
2. Paul M. Sweezy, *Post-Revolutionary Society* (New York: Monthly Review Press, 1980), p. 85.
3. Baran, *The Political Economy of Growth,* p. 267.
4. Ibid., pp. 266–68.
5. Mieczyslaw Kabaj, "Utilization of Industrial Capacity, Shift Work, and Employment Promotion in Developing Countries," in N. Phan-Thuy, Roger R. Betancourt, Gordon C. Winston, and Mieczyslaw Kabaj, *Industrial Capacity and Employment Promotion* (Westmead, England: Gower Publishing, 1981), pp. 255–58.
6. Baran, *The Political Economy of Growth,* p. 285n.
7. Maurice Dobb, *Capitalism, Development, and Planning* (New York: International Publishers, 1967), pp. 109–10.
8. Ibid., p. 111n.
9. Baran, *The Political Economy of Growth,* pp. 284–85; see also Evsey Domar, *Essays in the Theory of Economic Growth* (New York: Oxford University Press, 1957), pp. 223–58; Andrew Zimbalist and Howard Sherman, *Comparing Economic Systems* (Orlando, FL: Academic Press, 1984), pp. 178–82.
10. Baran, *The Political Economy of Growth,* p. 287.
11. Harry Magdoff, "China: Contrasts with the U.S.S.R.," *Monthly Review* 27, no. 3 (July–August 1975): 20.
12. Ibid., p. 19.
13. Ibid., p. 23.
14. Victor D. Lippit, *Land Reform and Economic Development in China* (White Plains, NY: International Arts and Sciences Press, 1974), pp. 3–4.
15. Ibid., p. ix.
16. Ibid., p. 11.
17. Ibid., p. 12.
18. See chapter 2, and Henryk Szlajfer, "Economic Surplus and Surplus Value under Monopoly Capitalism," in John Bellamy Foster and Henryk Szlajfer, eds., *The Faltering Economy: The Problem of Accumulation under Monopoly Capitalism* (New York: Monthly Review Press, 1984), pp. 264–69.
19. Lippit, *Land Reform and Economic Development in China,* p. 3.
20. Ibid., p. 8.
21. Ibid., p. 124.
22. Ibid., pp. 123–24.
23. Ibid., p. 142.
24. See Mao Tsetung, *A Critique of Soviet Economics* (New York: Monthly Review Press, 1977).
25. See John G. Gurley, *China's Economy and the Maoist Strategy* (New York: Monthly Review Press, 1976), pp. 127–39, 238–41.
26. Leo Huberman and Paul M. Sweezy, *Socialism in Cuba* (New York: Monthly Review Press, 1969), p. 74.
27. Clive Y. Thomas, *Dependence and Transformation: The Economics of the Transition to Socialism* (New York: Monthly Review Press, 1974), pp. 123–27.
28. Ibid., p. 20.
29. Ibid., pp. 130–33.
30. Ibid., p. 163.
31. Ibid., p. 152.

32. Ibid., pp. 190–91.
33. Ibid., pp. 195–96.
34. Ibid., p. 198.
35. Magdoff, "China: Contrasts with the U.S.S.R.," pp. 25–26.
36. Paul M. Sweezy, *Four Lectures on Marxism* (New York: Monthly Review Press, 1981), p. 79.
37. Thomas, *Dependence and Transformation,* pp. 124–25.
38. Baran, *The Political Economy of Growth,* pp. xiv, xvi; as quoted in Thomas, *Dependence and Transformation,* p. 267.
39. See John Kenneth Galbraith, *The Affluent Society* (New York: Houghton Mifflin, 1984), pp. 121–28.
40. Quoted in Thomas, *Dependence and Transformation,* p. 269.
41. Ibid., p. 252.
42. Ibid., pp. 242–48.
43. Ibid., p. 114.
44. Ibid., p. 115.
45. Clive Y. Thomas, *The Rise of the Authoritarian State in Peripheral Societies* (New York: Monthly Review Press, 1984), pp. xiii–xiv.
46. Ibid., pp. 83–86.
47. Ibid., p. 129.
48. This seems to be a strong implication of Thomas's analysis, although he does not sufficiently distinguish between postrevolutionary societies of this type and postcolonial formations; see ibid., pp. 134–35.
49. Paul M. Sweezy, "On Socialism," *Monthly Review* 35, no. 5 (October 1983): 37.
50. Ibid. See also John E. Elliott, "Contending Perspectives on the Nature of Soviet Economic Society," *International Journal of Social Economics* 11, no. 5 (1984): 41–42. As an example of this general view see Albert J. Szymanski, *Is the Red Flag Flying? The Political Economy of the Soviet Union Today* (London: Zed Press, 1979).
51. Sweezy, "On Socialism," p. 38; Elliott, "Contending Perspectives on the Nature of Soviet Economic Policy," pp. 47–49.
52. Sweezy, "On Socialism," p. 38; Charles Bettelheim, *Class Struggles in the U.S.S.R.,* volumes I and II (New York: Monthly Review Press, 1976–78).
53. See Sweezy, *Post-Revolutionary Society.*
54. Harry Braverman, *Labor and Monopoly Capital: The Degradation of Work in the Twentieth Century* (New York: Monthly Review Press, 1974), p. 15n.
55. On the *nachal'niki* class of top bosses see Moshe Lewin, "Society and the Stalinist State in the Period of the Five Year Plans," *Social History,* no. 2 (May 1976): 172–73; Sweezy, *Post-Revolutionary Society,* pp. 144–45.
56. See Charles Bettelheim, "The Specificity of Soviet Capitalism," *Monthly Review* 37, no. 4 (September 1985): 43–56.
57. Paul M. Sweezy, "After Capitalism—What?" *Monthly Review* 37, no. 3 (July–August 1985): 105.
58. Ibid., p. 101.
59. Paul M. Sweezy, Rejoinder to Charles Bettelheim, "The Specificity of Soviet Capitalism," *Monthly Review* 37, no. 4 (September 1985): 58.
60. Sweezy, "After Capitalism—What?" p. 108.
61. Sweezy, *Post-Revolutionary Society,* p. 147.
62. The virtual elimination of the industrial reserve army as a structural feature of the economy in these societies can be referred to as the "partial decommoditization of labor power."
63. Zimbalist and Sherman, *Comparing Economic Systems,* pp. 24–25.
64. On this see Fred Halliday, *The Making of the Second Cold War* (London: New Left Books, 1983).

65. Sweezy, "After Capitalism—What?" pp. 109–10.
66. Karl Marx, *Capital,* vol. I (New York: International Publishers, 1967), p. 217; G. E. M. de Ste. Croix, *The Class Struggle in the Ancient Greek World* (London: Duckworth, 1981), p. 51.
67. Two notes: (1) The observation that labor power is "relatively uncoerced" has to do with the fact that the threat of unemployment—undoubtedly the main coercive mechanism enforcing discipline in the labor process under capitalism—is absent. In this sense (though only in this sense) we can say that labor power is "partially decommoditized." (2) The fact that each act of appropriation is a separate act and has no logically continuous character expresses the reality that the domination of exchange value over use value is considerably weakened in Soviet-type societies, where accumulation as a *self-propelling* process is nonexistent.
68. Harry Magdoff, "Are There Economic Laws of Socialism?" *Monthly Review* 37, no. 3 (July–August 1983): 117.
69. The principle of payment according to work is entirely compatible with certain kinds of income inequality, although it is a progressive stance vis-à-vis capitalist principles of income distribution.
70. Paul A. Baran, "Economic Philosophy," *American Economic Review* 53, no. 3 (June 1963): 455–58, as quoted in John O'Neil, "Introduction: Marxism and the Sociological Imagination," in Paul A. Baran, *The Longer View* (New York: Monthly Review Press, 1969), p. xxvi.
71. See Baran, *The Longer View,* pp. 363–73.
72. Ibid., pp. 32–40.
73. Michael Bleaney, *Underconsumption Theories* (New York: International Publishers, 1976), p. 235.
74. Paul A. Baran and Paul M. Sweezy, *Monopoly Capital* (New York: Monthly Review Press, 1966), pp. 336–38.
75. Baran, *The Political Economy of Growth,* p. 120.
76. Ibid., p. 120n.
77. Henryk Szlajfer, "Waste, Marxian Theory, and Monopoly Capital: Toward a New Synthesis," in Foster and Szlajfer, eds., *The Faltering Economy,* pp. 313–14.
78. Karl Marx, *Theories of Surplus Value* (Moscow: Progress Publishers, 1963), p. 175; quoted in Baran, *The Political Economy of Growth,* p. 305.
79. Paul M. Sweezy, *The Present as History* (New York: Monthly Review Press, 1953), p. 220.
80. Baran and Sweezy, *Monopoly Capital,* p. 364.
81. Paul M. Sweezy, "Marxism and Revolution 100 Years After Marx," *Monthly Review* 34, no. 10 (March 1983): 6.
82. Ibid., p. 6n.
83. See Teodor Shanin, ed., *Late Marx and the Russian Road: Marx and the "Peripheries of Capitalism"* (New York: Monthly Review Press, 1983).
84. Samir Amin, *Imperialism and Unequal Development* (New York: Monthly Review Press, 1977), pp. 9–10.
85. Sweezy, *Post-Revolutionary Society,* pp. 133.
86. L. S. Stavrianos,*Global Rift: The Third World Comes of Age* (New York: William Morrow, 1981), p. 814.

Index